Practical Prayers for Catholics

A collection of new and traditional prayers

Ann Fitch

Full Stop Press
Phoenix, AZ

Cover design by Amy Fitch

Published by Full Stop Press, Phoenix, AZ
www.FullStopPress.com

For additional prayers and to purchase books by Ann Fitch, please visit:

www.PracticalPrayers.com

Library of Congress Control Number: 2016920209

ISBN-13: 978-0-692-80751-4

ISBN: 0-692-80751-9

DEDICATION

This book is dedicated to the Most Holy Trinity.

May the Father, Son and Holy Spirit be glorified and adored, loved and praised through the use of this book.

Contents

Prayers For Specific Needs **37**

Prayers to Patron Saints 205

Prayers Before and After Communion 231

Prayers Before the Blessed Sacrament ... 241

Litanies..267

Ann Fitch

INTRODUCTION

Years ago, in response to the scripture, ***"pray without ceasing"*** (1 Thessalonians 5:17) I began praying more throughout my day. As I prayed I realized I really didn't know what I was doing. Like many, I spent most of my time praying written prayers and repeating memorized prayers from childhood. While all of these prayers were helpful, I longed for more.

As my prayer life began to develop I grew more interested in the saints and what they had to say about prayer. St. Cyprian of Carthage said, *"Jesus prayed continually: how much more ought we."* And, St, John Vianney said, *"The more we pray, the more we wish to pray."* How true I found these statements to be. The more I prayed, the more I wanted to pray. I longed to pray all throughout my day but didn't know how to do that. I felt like I had no idea how to pray continuously. It just seemed so hard. But over time I came to realize that prayer is as simple and natural as breathing. It is a conversation with God, a sharing of your deepest, most intimate thoughts, feelings and desires with God Who loves you and a quiet listening to God speaking in the depths of your heart and soul. Prayer is having a heart to heart with God.

Prayer can be spontaneous and constant. You can talk to God anywhere, anytime, anyplace because He is all knowing, all powerful, all present, and all loving. He's always there, always listening, always available. He loves us and wants to communicate with us. He wants to share His love with us and bless us.

In the Old Testament God said, ***"When you call to me, and come and pray to me, I will listen to you."*** (Jeremiah 29:12) That's a

1

promise you can count on, believe in, and trust in. God's help is just a prayer away, a breath away.

I don't believe that there is a right or wrong way to pray. Prayer can be read, memorized, meditative, or contemplative. It can be praise, a song, adoration or thanksgiving. It can be surrender, a question, a sigh, or a simple, "I love You." As the Catholic Catechism states, "Prayer is the loving interaction of God's children with the Father, Son, and Holy Spirit." (CCC § 2525)

I do know that prayer nourishes you and opens you up to receive the blessings God wishes to bestow upon you. As St. Padre Pio said, *"Prayer is the oxygen of the soul."* Prayer is the very thing that gives life to the soul. The more you pray the closer you come to God. The more time you spend nurturing your relationship with God through prayer the deeper and more intimate that relationship becomes. And isn't that the ultimate goal of prayer – intimacy with God?

As Catholics we have a rich tradition of prayer. We have consecrations, novenas, litanies, rosaries, chaplets, prayers to patron saints, even Gregorian chant. In this book I have included many prayers written by the saints, commonly known Catholic prayers, and many new prayers that I hope you will find helpful and useful to your prayer life. This book is meant to be practical – a book you can turn to that has prayers for most of life's challenges and problems that uplift, inspire, strengthen and fortify you as you pray them. My prayer is that you will be encouraged in finding prayers that are suitable for your needs and those of your loved ones, that God will touch your heart and mind and bring healing and hope, and that your life will be richly blessed with answers to prayer.

"Do not worry about anything, but in everything by prayer and supplication with thanksgiving let your requests be made known to God. And the peace of God, which surpasses all understanding, will guard your hearts and your minds in Christ Jesus." (Philippians 4:6-7)

CATHOLIC PRAYERS

There are many traditional Catholic prayers that are perfect for praying every day. There are prayers of adoration, consecration, submission, petition, and thanksgiving. Many are written by the saints. I have included them in this section. This is by no means a complete compilation of Catholic prayers but merely a taste of what is richly available to us as Catholics. I hope the prayers included are a blessing to you and your loved ones and enrich your prayer life.

"The Lord is near to all who call upon him." (Psalm 145:18)

Purification Prayer
(St. Mary Magdalen Pazzi)

This prayer is prayed first, before other prayers, as it is meant to purify all prayers offered. I included it because it is beautiful and a truly blessed way to begin prayer time.

Almighty Father, I place the Precious Blood of Jesus before my lips before I pray, that my prayers may be purified before they ascend to Your divine altar. Amen.

Angels, Archangels

Prayer to Your Guardian Angel

Angel of God, my guardian dear, to whom God's love commits me here, ever this day be at my side, to light and guard, to rule and guide. Amen.

Guardian Angel Prayer

Guardian Angel from Heaven so bright, watching beside me to lead me aright, fold thy wings round me, and guard me with love, softly sing songs to me of Heaven above.   Amen.

Prayer to Your Guardian Angel
(St. Padre Pio)

Angel of God, my guardian to whom the goodness of the Heavenly Father entrusts me, enlighten, protect, and guide me, now and forever.   Amen.

Prayer to St. Michael the Archangel

St. Michael the Archangel, defend us in battle. Be our defense against the wickedness and snares of the Devil. May God rebuke him, we humbly pray, and do thou, O Prince of the Heavenly Hosts, by the power of God, thrust into Hell Satan, and all the evil spirits, who prowl about the world seeking the ruin of souls.   Amen.

A Prayer to the Archangels

Heavenly King, You have given us archangels to assist us during our pilgrimage on Earth. You gave us St. Michael as our protector; I ask him to come to my aid, fight for all my loved ones, and protect us from danger. You gave us St. Gabriel as a messenger of the Good News; I ask him to help me clearly hear Your voice and to teach me the truth. You gave us St. Raphael as the healing angel; I ask him to take my need for healing and that of everyone I know, lift it up to Your throne of grace and deliver back to us the gift of recovery. Help us, O Lord, to realize more fully the reality of the archangels and their desire to help us. O holy archangels, pray for us.   Amen.

Blessed Virgin Mary

Offering to Mary

Mary, I offer you all that I am, all that I have, all that I hope to be. Place me within your Immaculate Heart and teach me how to honor and glorify God in all I do.   Amen.

Offering to the Blessed Mother
(Fr. Zucchi)

My Queen, my Mother, I give myself entirely to you, and to show my devotion to you, I consecrate to you this day, my eyes, my ears, my mouth, my heart, my whole being without reserve. Wherefore good Mother as I am your own, keep me, guard me, as your property and possession.   Amen.

Prayer of Dedication to Mary
(St. Thomas Aquinas)

Virgin full of goodness, Mother of Mercy, I entrust to you my body and my soul, my thoughts and my actions, my life and my death. My Queen, come to my aid and deliver me from the snares of the devil. Obtain for me the grace of loving my Lord Jesus Christ, your Son, with a true and perfect love, and after Him, O Mary, of loving you with all my heart and above all things.   Amen.

Prayer to Mary
(St. Aloysius Gonzaga)

O holy Mary, my Mistress, into your blessed trust and special keeping, into the bosom of your tender mercy, this day, every day of my life and at the hour of my death, I commend my soul and body; to you I entrust all my hopes and consolations, all my trials and miseries, my life and the end of my life, that through your most holy intercession and your merits, all my actions may be ordered and disposed according to your will and that of your divine Son.   Amen.

Prayer for the Spirit of Mary
(St. Louis de Montfort)

My powerful Queen, you are mine through your mercy, and I am all yours. Take away from me all that may displease God and cultivate in me all that is pleasing to Him.

May the light of your faith dispel the darkness of my mind, your deep humility take the place of my pride, your continual sight of God fill my memory with His presence. May the fire of the charity of your heart inflame the lukewarmness of my own heart. May your virtues take the place of my sins. May your merits be the enrichment and make up for all that is wanting in me before God.

My beloved Mother, grant that I may have no other spirit but your spirit, to know Jesus Christ and His Divine Will and to praise and glorify the Lord, that I may love God with burning love like yours. Amen.

Consecration to the Immaculate Heart of Mary

I offer you, my holy Mother Mary, all my thoughts, all my actions, all my prayers and acts of charity, all my faith and good works, all the sacrifices that I make today.

Grant me the grace to do everything in my life with a pure intention and a desire to please God. I consecrate myself to your Immaculate Heart, and I pray, through the merits of your intercession, that I may adore the Divine Heart of Jesus, and through His mercy, obtain the grace of conversion and the remission of my sins.

O Mary, my Blessed Mother, watch over me and protect me from all sin and from all evil I encounter this day.   Amen.

Daily Renewal of Consecration to the Immaculate Heart of Mary

Queen of the Most Holy Rosary, I renew my consecration to you and to your Immaculate Heart. Please accept me, my dear Mother, and use me as you wish to accomplish your designs upon the world. I am all yours, my Mother, my Queen, and all that I have is yours. Amen.

Dearest Mother
(Ann Fitch)

Dearest Mother, as you magnified your Son with your life,
  may I magnify Him with mine.

Dearest Mother, as you did the will of the Father with your life,
  may I do His will in mine.

Dearest Mother, as you allowed the Holy Spirit to guide your life,
  may I allow Him to guide mine.

Dearest Mother, help me to love God as You love Him.   Amen.

Prayer to Our Lady of Grace
(Ann Fitch)

Our Lady of Grace, I turn to you who are Queen of Heaven and mediatrix of all grace. I have full confidence that through you God will bestow upon me every grace I need to faithfully live my life consecrated to Him. O heavenly treasurer of grace, thank you for the many graces you have already obtained for me.

I humbly beseech you, with all of my heart, to carry this cause (*mention request*) to the Holy Trinity and ask that it be granted only if it is Their holy will for me. O most gracious advocate, pour out your grace into my heart and help me to serve God with all my being. Amen.

Salutation to the Blessed Virgin Mary
(St. John Eudes)

Hail Mary, Daughter of God the Father.
Hail Mary, Mother of God the Son.
Hail Mary, Spouse of the Holy Ghost.
Hail Mary, Temple of the Most Blessed Trinity.

Hail Mary, Immaculate lily of the resplendent and ever peaceful
Trinity.

Hail Mary, Celestial Rose of the ineffable love of God.

Hail Mary, Virgin pure and humble of whom the King of Heaven
willed to be born and with your milk to be nourished.

Hail Mary, Virgin of Virgins, Hail Mary, Queen of martyrs, whose soul
was pierced with a sword of sorrow.

Hail Mary, lady most blessed! Unto whom all power in Heaven and
Earth is given.

Hail Mary, queen of my heart, my Mother, my life, my sweetness and
my hope.

Hail Mary, mother most amiable.

Hail Mary, mother most admirable.

Hail Mary, mother of Divine Love.

Hail Mary, Immaculate, conceived without sin.

Hail Mary, full of grace, the Lord is with You.

Hail Mary, blessed are You among women.

Hail Mary, blessed is the fruit of Your womb, Jesus.

Blessed be your spouse, St. Joseph.

Blessed be your father, St. Joachim.

Blessed be your mother, St. Anne.

Blessed be your guardian, St. John

Blessed be your angel, St. Gabriel.

Glory be to God the Father, Who chose you.

Glory be to God the Son, Who loved you.

Glory be to God the Holy Ghost, Who espoused you.

Blessed be forever all those who bless and who love you. Holy Mary,
Mother of God! Pray for us and bless us now and at death, in the
Name of Jesus, your Divine Son!   Amen.

Common Catholic Prayers

Our Father

Our Father, Who art in Heaven, hallowed be Thy name. Thy kingdom come, Thy will be done on Earth as it is in Heaven. Give us this day our daily bread. And forgive us our trespasses, as we forgive those who trespass against us. And lead us not into temptation, but deliver us from evil. Amen.

Glory Be

Glory be to the Father, and to the Son, and to the Holy Spirit. As it was in the beginning, is now, and ever shall be, world without end. Amen.

Hail, Mary

Hail, Mary, full of grace, the Lord is with thee. Blessed are thou among women and blessed is the fruit of thy womb, Jesus. Holy Mary, Mother of God, pray for us sinners now, and at the hour of our death. Amen.

Memorare
(St. Bernard)

Remember, O most gracious Virgin Mary, that never was it known that anyone who fled to your protection, implored your help or sought your intercession was left unaided. Inspired by this confidence, I fly to you, O Virgin of Virgins, my Mother. To you I come, before you I stand sinful and sorrowful. O Mother of the Word Incarnate, do not ignore my petitions but in your mercy hear and answer me. Amen.

Hail, Holy Queen

Hail, Holy Queen, Mother of Mercy, our life, our sweetness, and our hope. To thee do we cry, poor banished children of Eve. To thee

9

do we send up our sighs mourning and weeping in this valley of tears. Turn then, most gracious advocate, thine eyes of mercy toward us, and after this our exile show us the blessed fruit of thy womb, Jesus. O clement, O loving, O sweet Virgin Mary. Pray for us, O Holy Mother of God that we may be made worthy of the promises of Christ. Amen.

The Angelus

Verse.   The Angel of the Lord declared unto Mary.

Response. And she conceived of the Holy Spirit.

      Pray one **Hail Mary**.

V. Behold the handmaid of the Lord.

R. Be it done unto me according to thy word.

      Pray one **Hail Mary**.

V. And the Word was made Flesh.

R. And dwelt among us.

      Pray one **Hail Mary**.

V. Pray for us, O holy Mother of God.

R. That we may be made worthy of the promises of Christ.

Let us pray:

Pour forth, we beseech You, O Lord, Your grace into our hearts, that we to whom the Incarnation of Christ Your Son was made known by the message of an angel, may by His passion and cross be brought to the glory of His resurrection. Through the same Christ Our Lord. Amen.

Apostles' Creed

I believe in God, the Father almighty, Creator of Heaven and Earth, and in Jesus Christ, His only Son, our Lord, who was conceived by the Holy Spirit, and born of the Virgin Mary, suffered under Pontius Pilate, was crucified, died and was buried. He descended into Hell; on the third day He rose again from the dead. He ascended into Heaven, and is seated at the right hand of God the Father Almighty; from there He will come to judge the living and the dead. I believe in the Holy Spirit, the holy Catholic Church, the communion of saints, the forgiveness of sins, the resurrection of the body, and life everlasting. Amen.

Nicene Creed

I believe in one God, the Father Almighty, maker of Heaven and Earth, of all things visible and invisible.

I believe in one Lord, Jesus Christ, the only Begotten Son of God, born of the Father before all ages. God from God, light from light, true God from true God, begotten, not made, consubstantial with the Father. Through Him all things were made. For us men and for our salvation, He came down from Heaven, and by the Holy Spirit, was incarnate of the Virgin Mary and became man. For our sake, He was crucified under Pontius Pilate. He suffered death and was buried and rose again on the third day in accordance with the Scriptures. He ascended into Heaven and is seated at the right hand of the Father. He will come again in glory to judge the living and the dead and His kingdom will have no end.

I believe in the Holy Spirit, the Lord, the Giver of Life, Who proceeds from the Father and the Son, Who with the Father and the Son is adored and glorified, Who has spoken through the prophets.

I believe in one, Holy, Catholic, and apostolic Church. I confess one baptism for the forgiveness of sins and I look forward to the resurrection of the dead and the life of the world to come.   Amen.

Peace Prayer
(St. Francis of Assisi)

Lord, make me an instrument of your peace:
  where there is hatred, let me sow love;

where there is injury, pardon;

where there is doubt, faith;

where there is despair, hope;

where there is darkness, light;

where there is sadness, joy.

O divine Master, grant that I may not so much seek:

to be consoled as to console,

to be understood as to understand,

to be loved as to love.

For it is in giving that we receive,

it is in pardoning that we are pardoned,

and it is in dying that we are born to eternal life.   Amen.

The Divine Praises
(Luigi Felici & Pope Pius VII)

Blessed be God.

Blessed be His Holy Name.

Blessed be Jesus Christ, true God and true man.

Blessed be the Name of Jesus.

Blessed be His Most Sacred Heart.

Blessed be His Most Precious Blood.

Blessed be Jesus in the Most Holy Sacrament of the Altar.

Blessed be the Holy Spirit, the Paraclete.

Blessed be the great Mother of God, Mary most holy.

Blessed be her holy and Immaculate Conception.

Blessed be her glorious Assumption.

Blessed be the name of Mary, Virgin and Mother.

Blessed be St. Joseph, her most chaste spouse.

Blessed be God in His angels and in His saints.

Anima Christi

(St. Ignatius Loyola)

Soul of Christ, sanctify me.

Body of Christ, save me.

Blood of Christ, inebriate me.

Water from the side of Christ, wash me.

Passion of Christ, strengthen me.

O good Jesus, hear me.

Within Your wounds, hide me.

Never let me be separated from You.

From the malignant enemy, defend me.

At the hour of death, call me; and bid me come to You.

That with Your saints I may praise You forever and ever.   Amen.

Act of Faith, Hope, and Love

O my God, I believe that You are one God in three divine Persons: the Father, the Son and the Holy Spirit. I believe that Jesus became man, died on the cross for my sins, rose from the dead, ascended into Heaven, and that He shall come again to judge the living and the dead. I believe that You sent Your Spirit to enlighten mankind and lead Your holy Church in love and truth.

O my God, I hope, through Your infinite love and mercy, to obtain pardon for my sins, and with the help of Your grace, to have everlasting life in union with You, the Blessed Virgin, Mary, and all the angels and saints.

O my God, I love You above all things, with my whole heart, mind and soul, because You are all-good and worthy of all my love. For love of You, I love my neighbor as myself and I forgive all who have hurt me, and humbly ask pardon of all whom I have harmed in any way.

O my God, keep me ever close to You and grant that I may always walk in Your love and grace, doing that which is Your holy will for Your greater honor and glory.   Amen.

13

Act of Contrition

O my God, I am heartily sorry for having offended You, and I detest all my sins because I dread the loss of Heaven and the pains of Hell; but most of all because they offend You, my God, Who are all good and deserving of all my love. I firmly resolve, with the help of Your grace, to confess my sins, to do penance and amend my life. Amen.

An Act of Sorrow

Forgive me my sins, O Lord, forgive me my sins; the sins of my youth, the sins of my age, the sins of my soul, the sins of my body; my idle sins, my serious voluntary sins, the sins I know, the sins I have concealed so long, and which are now hidden from my memory. I am truly sorry for every sin, mortal and venial, for all the sins of my childhood up to the present hour. I know my sins have wounded Your tender Heart, O my Savior, let me be freed from the bonds of evil through Your most bitter Passion. O my Jesus, forget and forgive what I have been. Amen.

Grace Before Meals

Bless us O Lord and these Your gifts which we are about to receive through Christ our Lord. Amen. May the souls of the faithfully departed through the mercy of God rest in peace. Amen.

Dedication and Submission to God

Ignatian Offering
(St. Ignatius Loyola)

My God, I offer You my prayers, works, joys and sufferings of this day in union with the holy sacrifice of the Mass throughout the world. I offer them for all the intentions of Your Son's Sacred Heart, for the salvation of souls, reparation for sin, and the reunion of Christians.

14

Prayer of Abandonment
(Bl. Charles de Foucauld)

Father, I abandon myself into Your hands; do with me what You will. Whatever You may do, I thank You: I am ready for all, I accept all. Let only Your will be done in me, and in all Your creatures - I wish no more than this, O Lord.

Into Your hands I commend my soul; I offer it to You with all the love of my heart, for I love You Lord, and so need to give myself, to surrender myself into Your hands, without reserve, and with boundless confidence, for You are my Father.   Amen.

Prayer of Submission
(St. Edmund)

Into Your hands, O Lord, and into the hands of Your holy angels, I commit and entrust this day my soul, my relations, my benefactors, my friends and enemies, and all Your Catholic people. Keep us, O Lord, through the day, by the merits and intercession of the Blessed Virgin Mary and of all Your Saints, from all vicious and unruly desires, from all sins and temptations of the devil, and from sudden and unprovided death and the pains of Hell. Illuminate my heart with the grace of Your Holy Spirit; grant that I may ever be obedient to Your commandments; suffer me not to be separated from You, O God, Who lives and reigns with God the Father and the same Holy Spirit for ever and ever.   Amen.

Prayer of Resignation

O my God, I accept from Your hands whatever You wish to send me; health or sickness, joy or sorrow, comfort or suffering. I know that You, my infinitely loving Father, will allow nothing that is not for Your glory and for my good. I accept all things in obedience to Your Divine Will. Do with me what You wish in this short life, O Father of infinite goodness, but bring me safely by Your mercy and protection to the happiness of Your home in Heaven.   Amen.

Take, Lord, Receive
(St. Ignatius Loyola)

Take O Lord, and receive all my liberty, my memory, my understanding, and my entire will, all that I have and possess. You have given all to me. To You, O Lord, I return it. All is Yours, dispose of it wholly according to Your will. Give me Your love and Your grace, for this is sufficient for me.   Amen.

A Spirit to Know You
(St. Benedict)

Gracious and Holy Father, please give me:

intellect to understand You,

reason to discern You,

diligence to seek You,

wisdom to find You,

a spirit to know You,

a heart to meditate upon You,

ears to hear You,

eyes to see You,

a tongue to proclaim You,

a way of life pleasing to You,

patience to wait for You

and perseverance to look for You.

Grant me:

a perfect end,

Your holy presence,

a blessed resurrection,

and life everlasting.   Amen.

Grant Us Grace

(St. Anselm)

O Lord our God, grant us grace to desire You with our whole heart, that so desiring, we may seek and find You; and so finding You we may love You; and loving You we may hate those sins from which You have redeemed us; for the sake of Jesus Christ.   Amen.

Let Me Know You

(St. Augustine)

I beg of You, my God, let me know You and love You so that I may be happy in You. And though I cannot do this fully in this life, yet let me improve from day to day till I may do so to the full. Let me know You more and more in this life, that I may know You perfectly in Heaven. Let me know You more and more here, so that I may love you perfectly there, so that my joy may be great in itself here, and complete in Heaven with You.

O truthful God, let me receive the happiness of Heaven which You promise so that my joy may be full. In the meantime, let my mind think of it, let my tongue talk of it, let my heart long for it, let my mouth speak of it, let my soul hunger after it, let my flesh thirst after it, let my whole being desire it, until such time as I may enter through death into the joy of my Lord, there to continue forever, world without end.   Amen.

Grant Me, O Lord

(St. Thomas Aquinas)

Grant me, O Lord my God, a mind to know You, a heart to seek You, wisdom to find You, conduct pleasing to You, faithful perseverance in waiting for You, and a hope of finally embracing You. Amen.

May You Always Be

Dear God, may You always be my hope, my trust, my riches, my delight, my joy and gladness, my rest and quiet, my food, my refreshment, my refuge and help, my wisdom, portion and possession, my treasure in which my mind and heart shall be rooted forever, fixed, firm and immovable.   Amen

Prayer of Submission to the Will of God
(St. Marie Eugenie Milleret)

Yes, my God, I assent to, I accept, I love Your will because You will it; it fills me with delight. I cling to You, my God; You are my only desire and my soul's hope. I want all You want Lord, how You want it, when You want it, by whom You want it and because You want it. Amen.

Prayer to Know God's Will
(St. Ignatius Loyola)

May it please the supreme and divine Goodness to give us all abundant grace ever to know His most holy will and perfectly to fulfill it.   Amen.

Prayer of Submission to the Will of God
(Fr. Jean-Pierre de Caussade)

My God, I desire with all my heart to do Your holy will, I submit in all things and absolutely to Your good pleasure for time and eternity; and I wish to do this, Oh my God, for two reasons; first: because You are my Sovereign Lord and it is but just that Your will should be accomplished; secondly: because I am convinced by faith, and by experience that Your will is in all things as good and beneficient as it is just and adorable, while my own desires are always blind and corrupt; blind, because I know not what I ought to desire or to avoid; corrupt, because I nearly always long for what would do me harm. Therefore, from henceforth, I renounce my own will to follow Yours in all things;

dispose of me, Oh my God, according to Your good will and pleasure. Amen.

Prayer of Trust in God's Will

(Ann Fitch)

Heavenly Father, I know that You have a plan for my life. I know that You have guided me thus far and that You will continue to guide me and lead me according to Your will for me. Allow me to clearly see Your will for my life. Allow me to work with You so that Your will is accomplished in my life in a way that brings honor and glory to You and happiness and peace to me.

When I am unsure about what You would have me do, grant me patience and fortitude so that I will persevere in faith. When I struggle in knowing which way to go, I ask You to pour out Your Spirit upon me so that I walk in wisdom, knowledge, peace, joy, courage, strength, and love. Help me to trust totally in Your timing because it is always perfect.

Thank You for blessing me and keeping me in Your ways. I trust You and believe that You will always lead me closer to You and keep me in Your love. Amen.

Offering to the Father

Eternal Father, I offer You all the wounds of Your dearly beloved Son, Jesus Christ; the pains and agonies of His Sacred Heart; and, His Most Precious Blood which gushed out from all His wounds for the reparation of my sins and those of the whole world. Amen.

Holy Spirit

Act of Consecration to the Holy Ghost

On my knees before the great multitude of heavenly witnesses, I offer myself soul and body to You, eternal Spirit of God. I adore the brightness of Your purity, the unerring keenness of Your justice, and the might of Your love. You are the strength and light of my soul. In You I live and move and am. I desire never to grieve You by unfaithfulness to grace, and I pray with all my heart to be kept from the smallest sin against You. Mercifully guard my every thought and grant that I may always watch for Your light and listen to Your voice and follow Your gracious inspirations.

I cling to You and give myself to You and ask You by Your compassion to watch over me in my weakness. Holding the pierced feet of Jesus and looking at His five wounds and trusting in His Precious Blood and adoring His opened side and stricken heart, I implore You adorable Spirit, helper of my infirmity, to keep me in Your grace that I may never sin against You. Give me grace O Holy Ghost, Spirit of the Father and the Son, to say to You always and everywhere, "Speak Lord, for Your servant is listening." Amen.

Prayer for Enlightenment

O Holy Ghost, divine Spirit of light and love, I consecrate to You my understanding, my heart and my will, my whole being for time and for eternity. May my understanding be always obedient to Your heavenly inspirations and the teachings of the holy Catholic Church, of which You are the infallible guide; may my heart be ever inflamed with love of God and of my neighbor; may my will be ever conformed to the divine will, and may my whole life be a faithful following of the life and virtues of Our Lord and Savior Jesus Christ, to Whom with the Father and You be honor and glory forever. Amen.

Daily Prayer to the Holy Spirit

O Holy Spirit, I humbly implore You, be with me always so that in all things, I may act under the influence of Your holy inspiration. Amen.

Prayer to the Holy Spirit
(St. Augustine)

Breathe in me, O Holy Spirit, that all my thoughts may be holy. Act in me, O Holy Spirit, that all my work may be holy. Fill my heart, O Holy Spirit, that I may love only that which is holy. Strengthen me, O Holy Spirit, ever to defend what is holy. Guard me always, O Holy Spirit, that I may ever remain holy.   Amen.

Prayer to the Holy Spirit
(Cardinal Mercier)

O Holy Spirit, beloved of my soul, I adore You. Enlighten me, guide me, strengthen me, console me. Tell me what I should do; give me Your orders. I promise to submit myself to all that You desire of me and to accept all that You permit to happen to me. Let me only know Your will.   Amen.

Prayer to the Holy Spirit

Come, Holy Spirit, fill my heart with Your holy gifts. Let my weakness be penetrated with Your strength this very day that I may fulfill all the duties of my state conscientiously, that I may do what is right and just. Let my charity be such as to offend no one, and hurt no one's feelings; so generous as to pardon sincerely any wrong done to me. Assist me, O Holy Spirit, in all my trials of life, enlighten me in my ignorance, advise me in my doubts, strengthen me in my weakness, help me in all my needs, protect me in temptations and console me in afflictions. Graciously hear me, O Holy Spirit, and pour Your light into my heart, my soul, and my mind. Assist me to live a holy life and to grow in goodness and grace.   Amen.

Prayer for the Seven Gifts of the Holy Spirit

God grant me:

the spirit of wisdom that I may despise the perishable things of this world and aspire only after the things that are eternal;

the spirit of understanding to enlighten my mind with the light of Your divine truth;

the spirit of counsel that I may ever choose the surest way of pleasing You and gaining Heaven;

the spirit of fortitude that I may bear my cross with You and that I may overcome with courage all the obstacles that oppose my salvation;

the spirit of knowledge that I may know You and myself;

the spirit of piety that I may find the service of You sweet and amiable;

and, the spirit of fear that I may be filled with a loving reverence towards You and may dread in any way to displease You.   Amen.

Jesus

Consecration to the Sacred Heart
(Ann Fitch)

Sacred Heart of Jesus I consecrate to You, my mind, my words, my body, my heart, and my soul in order that Your will be done through me this day.   Amen.

Act of Consecration to the Sacred Heart of Jesus

O Sacred Heart of Jesus, filled with infinite love, broken by my ingratitude, pierced by my sins, yet loving me still – accept the consecration that I make to You of all that I am and all that I have. Take every faculty of my soul and body. Draw me, day by day, nearer and nearer to Your Sacred Heart, and there, as I can bear the lesson, teach me Your blessed ways.   Amen.

Prayer to the Sacred Heart of Jesus

O most Sacred Heart of Jesus, fountain of every blessing, I adore You, I love You, and with true sorrow for my sins, I offer You this poor heart of mine. Make me humble, patient, pure and wholly obedient to Your will. Grant, good Jesus, that I may live in You and for You. Protect me in the midst of danger, comfort me in my afflictions, give me health of body, assistance in my temporal needs, Your blessing on all that I do, and the grace of a holy death. Amen.

Hail, Heart of Jesus

(St. Margaret Mary Alacoque)

Hail, Heart of Jesus, save me!

Hail, Heart of my Creator, perfect me!

Hail, Heart of my Savior, deliver me!

Hail, Heart of my Judge, grant me pardon!

Hail, Heart of my Father, govern me!

Hail, Heart of my Spouse, grant me love!

Hail, Heart of my Master, teach me!

Hail, Heart of my King, be my crown!

Hail, Heart of my Benefactor, enrich me!

Hail, Heart of my Shepherd, guard me!

Hail, Heart of my Friend, comfort me!

Hail, Heart of my Brother, stay with me!

Hail, Heart of the Child Jesus, draw me to Yourself!

Hail, Heart of Jesus dying on the Cross, redeem me!

Hail, Heart of Jesus in all your states, give Yourself to me!

Hail, Heart of incomparable goodness, have mercy on me!

Hail, Heart of splendor, shine within me!

Hail, most loving Heart, inflame me!

Hail, most merciful Heart, work within me!

Hail, most humble Heart, dwell within me!

Hail, most patient Heart, support me!

Hail, most faithful Heart, be my reward!

Hail, most admirable and most worthy Heart, bless me!   Amen.

Prayer of Trust in the Sacred Heart

In all my temptations, I place my trust in You, O Sacred Heart of Jesus.

In all my weaknesses, I place my trust in You, O Sacred Heart of Jesus.

In all my difficulties, I place my trust in You, O Sacred Heart of Jesus.

In all my trials, I place my trust in You, O Sacred Heart of Jesus.

In all my sorrows, I place my trust in You, O Sacred Heart of Jesus.

In all my work, I place my trust in You, O Sacred Heart of Jesus.

In every failure, I place my trust in You, O Sacred Heart of Jesus.

In every discouragement, I place my trust in You, O Sacred Heart of Jesus.

In life and in death, I place my trust in You, O Sacred Heart of Jesus.

In time and in eternity, I place my trust in You, O Sacred Heart of Jesus.

Prayer to the Precious Blood
(St. Catherine of Siena)

Precious Blood, ocean of Divine Mercy, flow upon us!

Precious Blood, most pure offering, procure us every grace!

Precious Blood, hope and refuge of sinners, atone for us!

Precious Blood, delight of the holy souls, draw us!   Amen.

Petition Through the Precious Blood

Eternal Father, I offer You the Precious Blood of Jesus Christ, the merits, love, and sufferings of His Sacred Heart, the tears and sorrows of our Immaculate Mother, as the price of the favor I wish to obtain (*mention request*), if it is for Your glory and my salvation.   Amen.

Prayer Before a Crucifix

Look down upon me, good and gentle Jesus, while before Your face I humbly kneel and, with burning soul, pray and beseech You to fix deep in my heart lively sentiments of faith, hope and charity; true contrition for my sins, and a firm purpose of amendment. While I contemplate, with great love and tender pity, Your five most precious wounds, pondering over them within me and calling to mind the words which David, Your prophet, said of You, my Jesus: *"They have pierced my hands and my feet, they have numbered all my bones."* Amen.

Act of Petition
(St. Peter Julian Eymard)

My dear Jesus, abide in my heart. Never leave it. Remove from it whatever displeases You and place in it whatever pleases You. Amen.

Act of Love and Desire
(St. Peter Julian Eymard)

My dear Jesus, I love You with all my heart and above all things, I long to be one with You. Amen.

Prayer for Trust in Jesus
(St. Ignatius Loyola)

O Christ Jesus, when all is darkness and we feel our weakness and helplessness, give us the sense of Your presence, Your love, and Your strength. Help us to have perfect trust in Your protecting love and strengthening power, so that nothing may frighten or worry us, for, living close to You, we shall see Your hand, Your purpose, Your will through all things. Amen.

Bless Me

Lord Jesus, bless my memory, that it may ever recollect You.
Bless my understanding, that it may ever think of You.

Bless my will, that it may never seek or desire that which displeases
  You.
Bless my body and all its actions.
Bless my heart with all its affections.
Bless me now and at the hour of my death. Amen.

Prayer to the Divine Child Jesus

Divine Child Jesus,
In my difficulties, help me.
From enemies of my soul, save me.
In my errors, enlighten me.
In my doubts and pains, comfort me.
In my solitude, be with me.
In my diseases, invigorate me.
When others despise me, encourage me.
In temptations, defend me.
In difficult hours, strengthen me.
With Your Sacred Heart, love me.
And, into Your arms, when I die, receive me.   Amen

Prayer of Confidence in the Divine Child Jesus
(Ann Fitch)

O Divine Child Jesus, humble and merciful, I place all my needs in
Your Divine Hands (*mention needs*). I have entrusted all my problems
to You. Grant me Your peace and comfort my heart. O Holy Child
Jesus, You are my Savior and my King. I place all my trust in You. O
Divine Child, in Your infinite love bless me.   Amen.

Prayer to the Holy Face of Jesus
(Fr. Emery Pethro)

Holy Face of Jesus, be my joy.
Holy Face of Jesus, be my strength.

Holy Face of Jesus, be my health.

Holy Face of Jesus, be my courage.

Holy Face of Jesus, be my wisdom.

Holy Face of Jesus, image of the Father, provide for me.

Holy Face of Jesus, mirror of Your priestly Heart, be my zeal.

Holy Face of Jesus, gift of the Spirit, show me Your love.

Holy Face of Jesus, saddened by sorrow, grant my requests through Your merits.   Amen.

Shine Through Me
(St. John Neumann)

Dear Jesus, help me to spread Your Fragrance everywhere I go. Penetrate and possess my whole being so utterly that all my life may only be a radiance of Yours. Shine through me and be so in me, that every soul I come in contact with may feel Your presence in my soul: let them look up and see no longer me - but only You.   Amen.

Prayer for Generosity
(St. Ignatius Loyola)

Eternal Word, only begotten Son of God, teach me true generosity. Teach me to serve You as you deserve, to give without counting the cost, to fight heedless of wounds, to labor without seeking rest, to sacrifice myself without thought of any reward save the knowledge that I have done Your will.   Amen.

Grant Me, O Lord
(David Bennett)

O Lord,

Grant me Your strength, so I will have courage in every situation;

Grant me Your love, so I may love others as You love me;

Grant me Your wisdom, so I will show others the path to success;

Grant me Your mercy, so I will forgive those who have hurt me;

Grant me Your peace, so I will find the best in everybody;

Grant me Your hope, so I will never give up;

Grant me Your joy, so I will be thankful for all my blessings;

And grant me Your grace, so You will always be at my side.   Amen.

Help Me, Lord
(Ann Fitch)

Help me, Lord, to have a heart that is merciful, so that I feel empathy, compassion, and love for those You put in my life.

Help me, Lord, to have eyes that are merciful, so that I do not judge others or myself, but instead see Your presence within.

Help me, Lord, to have hands that are merciful, so that I allow You to touch and bless others through me.

Help me, Lord, to have feet that are merciful, so that I may always run towards those in need and assist them in any way I can.

Help me, Lord, to have ears that are merciful, so that I hear the needs of others and do my best to attend to them in Your love.

Help me, Lord, to have a tongue that is merciful, so that I only speak words of wisdom, kindness, love, and understanding.

Help me, Lord, to be merciful towards all and bless me with Your mercy.   Amen.

"Jesus Help Me!"
(Fr. John Hardon, S.J.)

In every need, let me come to You with humble trust, saying: "Jesus help me!"

In times of doubt, perplexity or temptation, "Jesus help me!"

In hours of illness, loneliness, weariness, and trial, "Jesus help me!"

When my plans fail and I am disappointed or troubled, "Jesus help me!"

When others fail me, and Your grace alone can assist me, "Jesus help me!"

When I throw myself on Your tender love, as brother and Savior,
"Jesus help me!"

When my heart is cast down and I see no good come from my efforts,
"Jesus help me!"

When I feel impatient and my cross irritates me, "Jesus help me!"

When my sins overwhelm me, "Jesus help me!"

Always, always, in spite of my weakness and shortcomings, "Jesus
help me!"   Amen.

Prayer of Submission to the Will of God
(St. Gianna Beretta Molla)

Jesus, I promise You to submit myself to all that You permit to
befall me, make me only know Your will. My most sweet Jesus,
infinitely merciful God, most tender Father of souls, and in a particular
way of the most weak, most miserable, most infirm which You carry
with special tenderness between Your divine arms, I come to You to
ask You, through the love and merits of Your Sacred Heart, the grace
to comprehend and to do always Your holy will, the grace to confide
in You, the grace to rest securely through time and eternity in Your
loving divine arms.   Amen.

Morning and Evening Prayers

Morning Offering

O Jesus, through the Immaculate Heart of Mary, I offer You my
prayers, works, joys, and sufferings of this day in union with the Holy
Sacrifice of the Mass throughout the world. I offer them for all the
intentions of Your Sacred Heart: the salvation of souls, reparation for
sins, the reunion of all Christians. I offer them for the intentions of
our bishops, and of all the apostles of prayer, and in particular for
those recommended by our Holy Father for this month.   Amen.

A Morning Prayer
(St. Therese of Lisieux)

O my God! I offer You all my actions of this day for the intentions and for the glory of the Sacred Heart of Jesus. I desire to sanctify every beat of my heart, my every thought, my simplest works, by uniting them to Its infinite merits; and I wish to make reparation for my sins by casting them into the furnace of Its merciful love. O my God! I ask of You for myself and for those whom I hold dear, the grace to fulfill perfectly Your holy will, to accept for love of You the joys and sorrows of this passing life, so that we may one day be united together in Heaven for all eternity. Amen.

Daily Offering
(St. Frances de Sales)

My God, I give You this day. I offer You, now, all of the good that I shall do and I promise to accept, for love of You, all of the difficulty that I shall meet. Help me to conduct myself during this day in a manner pleasing to You. Amen.

Prayer for Strength and Wisdom

Lord, give me strength and wisdom to live this day as I ought. Give me strength to overcome every temptation which may come to me, to do well every task which is assigned to me, and to shoulder every responsibility which is laid upon my shoulders. Give me wisdom to know when to speak and when to keep silent, to know when to act and when to refrain from action, and to know when to speak my mind and when to hold my peace. So bring me to the end of this day in goodness, in happiness, and in peace. Amen.

Evening Prayer to the Sacred Heart

Sacred Heart of Jesus, I thank You for all You have done for me, in me, and through me today. Sacred Heart of Jesus, pierced by my sins, in Your mercy and love, forgive me. Sacred Heart of Jesus, worthy of all praise, I offer You my heart and soul and ask my angel to sing Your praises as I sleep. Sacred Heart of Jesus, watch over me this night and bless me with Your peace. Amen.

Evening Prayer to the Heart of Jesus
(St. Maria Soledad Torres Acosta)

O most loving Heart of Jesus, I commend to You this night my loving heart and soul that they may rest peacefully in You. Since I cannot praise You while I sleep, may my guardian angel replace me that all my heart's beats may be so many acts of praise and thanksgiving offered to Your loving Heart and that of Your eternal Father. Amen.

Evening Prayer
(St. Macarius)

O eternal God and Ruler of all creation, You have allowed me to reach this hour. Forgive the sins I have committed this day by word, deed or thought. Purify me, O Lord, from every spiritual and physical stain. Grant that I may rise from this sleep to glorify You by my deeds throughout my entire lifetime, and that I be victorious over every spiritual and physical enemy. Deliver me, O Lord, from all vain thoughts and from evil desires, for Yours is the kingdom, and the power, and the glory, Father, Son, and Holy Spirit, now and forever. Amen.

Evening Prayer to the Son of God
(St. Anthiocus)

O Only-Begotten Word of the Father, Jesus Christ, Who alone are perfect: according to the greatness of Your mercy, do not abandon me, Your servant, but ever rest in my heart. O Sweet Jesus, Good Shepherd of Your flock, deliver me from the attacks of the enemy. Do not allow me to become the prey of Satan's evil intent, even though I have within me the seed of eternal damnation.

Instead, O Lord Jesus Christ, adorable God, holy King, while I sleep, protect me by Your Holy spirit, through Whom You sanctified Your Apostles. Enlighten my mind by the light of the holy gospel, my soul by the love of Your cross, my heart by the purity of Your teaching. Protect my body by Your sacred passion, my senses by Your humility, and awaken me in due time for Your glorification. For You, above all, are adorable, together with Your eternal Father, and the Holy Spirit, now and ever, and forever. Amen.

Prayer Before Going to Sleep
(St. Alphonsus Liguori)

Jesus Christ, my God, I adore You and I thank You for the many favors You have bestowed on me this day. I offer You my sleep and all the moments of this night, and I pray that You preserve me from sin. Therefore, I place myself in Your most sacred side, and under the mantle of our Blessed Lady, my Mother. May the holy angels assist me and keep me in peace, and may Your blessing be upon me. Amen.

Purgatory

Prayer to Jesus of Mercy for the Souls in Purgatory
(St. Alphonsus Liguori)

Jesus of Mercy, through the bloody sweat, which You did suffer in the Garden of Gethsemane, have mercy on the souls in Purgatory and bring them to everlasting peace in Heaven.

Jesus of Mercy, through the pains, which You did suffer during Your most cruel scourging, have mercy on the souls in Purgatory and bring them to everlasting peace in Heaven.

Jesus of Mercy, through the pains, which You did suffer in Your most painful crowning with thorns, have mercy on the souls in Purgatory and bring them to everlasting peace in Heaven.

Jesus of Mercy, through the pains, which You did suffer in carrying Your cross to Calvary, have mercy on the souls in Purgatory and bring them to everlasting peace in Heaven.

Jesus of Mercy, through the pains, which You did suffer during Your most cruel crucifixion, have mercy on the souls in Purgatory and bring them to everlasting peace in Heaven.

Jesus of Mercy, through the pains, which You did suffer in Your most bitter agony on the cross, have mercy on the souls in Purgatory and bring them to everlasting peace in Heaven.

Jesus of Mercy, through the immense pain, which You did suffer in breathing forth Your Blessed Soul, have mercy on the souls in Purgatory and bring them to everlasting peace in Heaven.   Amen.

A Prayer for the Souls in Purgatory
(St. Gertrude)

Eternal Father, I offer You the most Precious Blood of Your Divine Son, Jesus, in union with the Masses said throughout the world today, for all the holy souls in Purgatory.   Amen.

Prayer for the Souls in Purgatory

O God of love and mercy, in Your infinite goodness, grant we beseech You, that through the merits of Your Son's death and resurrection, that the souls of our friends, enemies, family members, and acquaintances, especially those for whom we now pray (*mention them here*), be brought out of the crucible of purification in Purgatory and into the joy of Heaven which they earnestly desire. Welcome them into the fullness of Your light and peace. May they with reverence and joy behold Your glorious face and with the angels and saints sing hymns of praise and thanksgiving to You for all eternity. Amen.

A Prayer for the Souls in Purgatory

Most merciful Father, we commend our departed ones into Your hands. We are filled with the sure hope that our departed ones will rise again on the last day with all those who have died in Christ. We thank You for all the good things You have given during our departed loved one's earthly life. O Father, in Your great mercy, accept our prayer that the gates of paradise may be opened for Your servants. In our turn, may we, too, be comforted in the hope of the resurrection until we greet Christ in the glory of Heaven and are united with You and our departed loved ones. Amen.

A Prayer for the Holy Souls in Purgatory

O Lord, Who are ever merciful and bounteous with Your gifts, look down upon the suffering souls in Purgatory. Remember not their offenses and negligences, but be mindful of Your loving mercy, which is from all eternity. Cleanse them of their sins and fulfill their ardent desires that they might be made worthy to behold You face to face in Your glory. May they soon be united with You and hear those blessed words which will call them to their heavenly home: *"Come, blessed of My Father, take possession of the kingdom prepared for you from the foundation of the world."* Amen.

Trinity

Prayer to the Blessed Trinity

I believe in You, I hope in You, I adore You, O blessed Trinity, one God. Have mercy on me now and at the hour of my death, and save me. Amen.

Trinity Prayer

Love of Jesus fill us. Holy Spirit guide us. Will of the Father be done. Amen.

Prayer to the Holy Trinity

Glory be to the Father, Who by His almighty power and love created me, making me in the image and likeness of God. Glory be to the Son, Who by His Precious Blood delivered me from Hell, and opened for me the gates of Heaven. Glory be to the Holy Spirit, Who has sanctified me in the sacrament of Baptism, and continues to sanctify me by the graces I receive daily from His bounty. Glory be to the Three adorable Persons of the Holy Trinity, now and forever. Amen.

Act of Faith in the Holy Trinity

O my God, I firmly believe that You are one God in three Divine Persons, the Father, the Son, and the Holy Spirit.   Amen.

Act of Praise of the Holy Trinity

I praise You, Father all-powerful. I praise You, Divine Son, our Lord and Savior. I praise You, Spirit of Love and Consolation. One God, three Persons, Triune Unity, be near me in the temple of my soul. Draw me to share in Your life and love. In Your kindness grant to me and to my family the riches of Your mercy, and a share in Your blessing, that we may come to the glory of Your Kingdom and rejoice in loving You for all eternity.   Amen.

To the Trinity Dwelling in the Soul

O Most Holy Trinity, I adore You Who are dwelling by Your grace within my soul.

O Most Holy Trinity, Who are dwelling by Your grace within my soul, make me love You more and more.

O Most Holy Trinity, Who are dwelling by Your grace within my soul, sanctify me more and more.

Abide with me, O Lord; be my true joy.   Amen.

In Praise of the Trinity

With our whole heart and voice we glorify You, we praise You, we bless You, God the Father unbegotten, the only-begotten Son, the Holy Ghost, the Paraclete, the holy and undivided Trinity. For You are great, and do wonderful things: You alone are God. To You be praise, to You glory, to You thanksgiving forever and ever, O blessed Trinity! Amen.

O Sanctissima

O most Holy Trinity, I adore You Who dwell by Your grace in my soul. Sanctify me more and more, make me love You more and more, abide with me evermore and be my true joy. Amen.

PRAYERS FOR SPECIFIC NEEDS

Jesus said, *"pray always and not to lose heart."* (Luke 18:1). I firmly believe that we should present our every need to God and ask that He answer us according to His will for our lives. We have countless needs that we can invite God into. In our everyday lives we encounter people who ask us to pray for them and their intentions and often we search for the right words to pray at that moment or a prayer to pray for them and find there is nothing that is suitable.

The prayers in this section are meant to help you find the words you need when you are asked to pray for others as well as prayers to pray for yourself and your loved ones. Any prayer I have written can be made suitable for others by changing the pronouns. As I mentioned in the introduction – there is no right or wrong way to pray. Simply open your heart, invite God in, and make yourself available to Him and He will bless you profoundly.

"And we have this confidence in him, that if we ask anything according to his will, he hears us." (1 John 5:14)

Addiction

Prayer for an Addict
(Ann Fitch)

Dear Lord, I come before You seeking healing and freedom for (*name person*) who is addicted. I trust in You. My hope is in You. I believe You can do anything. Break the chains of addiction that have held him/her bound and set him/her free to live a life of health, happiness, and hope. Give (*name person*) clarity of thought and peace of mind. Look with compassion upon him/her and in Your infinite mercy fill his/her life with people who will hold him accountable for his actions and help him/her stay away from that which held him/her bound. Thank You, Lord for Your love for (*name person*) and for blessing him/her with Your healing and love. Amen.

Addict's Prayer
(Ann Fitch)

Lord, I no longer wish to be held captive by addiction and I ask You to bless me with freedom and healing from it. I am ready to make a change, to choose health, happiness, and hope. I know that in You I can have clarity of thought and peace of mind and that only You can restore me to fullness of health and give me victory over this addiction that has held me bound. I truly want to live a life that is free and whole, a life that is from moment to moment dedicated to health in mind, body, and soul. I take responsibility for my health and responsibility for all I say, think, and do.

Let my every thought, word, and action be a reflection of Your power, love, and presence in my life. May my attitude be positive and may I truly love myself as You love me, unconditionally. I choose to surround myself with people who are helpful, understanding, and who want the very best for me – freedom and peace. I surrender myself to You, Lord, and I trust You to lead me to a full, healthy, happy, sane life. I believe I can be free and know that in You I can do anything for nothing is impossible for You.   Amen.

Prayer for an Alcoholic
(Ann Fitch)

Gracious and ever loving God (*name person*) is an alcoholic and his/her drinking has caused such turmoil and damage. I pray that (*name person*) can admit he/she is an alcoholic and find the will to change his/her ways and stop drinking forever. (*Name person*) has not only abused alcohol but also those closest to him/her. The damage that's been done to his/her relationships is extensive and they cannot be repaired until he/she stops drinking altogether.

Help (*name person*) break free from this debilitating addiction and find healing and peace. Bless his/her heart and mind and pour out Your Spirit upon (*name person*) and give him/her the courage and strength to live his/her life free from alcohol. If (*name person*) must hit rock bottom before he/she turns away from alcohol please let that happen so that he/she can begin walking the road to healing and recovery. In Your infinite mercy forgive (*name person*) for all the wrongs he/she has committed and bless him/her with the ability to forgive himself/herself.

Send strong men and women into his/her life who will hold (*name person*) accountable for all his/her actions and help him/her stay clean and sober. Guide (*name person*) to treatment, therapy, and meetings that will help him/her overcome his/her addiction and live a happy, healthy life.

Thank You for loving (*name person*) and for never giving up on him/her. Thank You for being with (*name person*) at his/her darkest moments and for the graces You have bestowed upon him/her. May (*name person*) soon find complete freedom from alcohol in You and through You.   Amen.

Prayer for a Drug Addict
(Ann Fitch)

O Lord, I turn to You desperately seeking Your blessing upon (*name person*) who is addicted to drugs. Acquiring and doing drugs has taken over his/her life and he/she is out of control. (*Name person*) has left all semblance of normalcy and is fixated on his/her next high. My heart breaks for (*name person*). He/she has hurt so many people and done so many destructive things. I am so worried about (*name person*) and I pray that You will show him/her how desperate his/her life has become before he/she overdoses.

I know You love (*name person*) even more than I do and that You want his/her freedom and happiness. I ask You to fill (*name person*) with an overwhelming desire to stop doing drugs altogether and pray that You will give him/her the grace and strength to find freedom and peace away from drugs. I beg of You to intervene in his/her life and provide him/her with a way to healing, health and wholeness.

Please, Lord, help (*name person*) be open to entering treatment so that he/she can get clean and stay clean. Surround (*name person*) with good, wholesome, God fearing people who are a positive influence on him/her and will hold him/her accountable for his/her actions and support him/her as he/she works to be free from the influence of drugs.

Restore (*name person*) to full health in mind, body, heart and soul. Thank You, Lord for blessing (*name person*) today and for loving him/her without condition.   Amen.

Prayer for a Gambling Addict
(Ann Fitch)

Heavenly Father, (*name person*) is addicted to gambling and his/her life is spiraling out of control. (*Name person*) gambles away every penny he/she earns or borrows. He/she is so caught up in his/her addiction that he/she truly believes he/she will win big on the next bet. Please Father, open his/her eyes to see how this horrendous addiction has damaged his/her relationships. It has caused animosity, distrust, and discord. (*Name person*) has lost not only money but loved ones, friends, and the respect and trust of others.

I beg You, Father, to give (*name person*) the grace and strength to break free of this destructive addiction. Help (*name person*) take back control of his/her life and find liberation from his/her compulsion to gamble. Place supportive and encouraging people in his/her life who will challenge him/her and hold him/her accountable for his/her actions. If (*name person*) needs to get treatment to overcome this terrible addiction open the door to where he/she can receive help and make it possible for him/her to afford treatment and therapy.

I know that with You, Father, (*name person*) can find healing, freedom, and health. I believe that You can and will work miracles of grace in his/her life. Thank You, Father, for all You are doing in and for (*name person*). Amen.

Prayer for a Pornography Addict
(Ann Fitch)

Lord, I believe that nothing is impossible for You. I come to You today asking You to pour out Your Spirit upon (*name person*) who is addicted to pornography and give him/her the grace and strength to turn away from this addiction and desire purity of heart and mind. I place his/her addiction to pornography at the foot of the cross and ask You to free him/her from its terrible and destructive grip.

Bless (*name person*) profoundly and let Your Precious Blood flow down upon him/her and cleanse him/her from this habitual sin. Bless (*name person*) with an overwhelming desire to remain pure in thought and action. In Your infinite goodness take any sexually explicit images that are in his/her mind and replace them with holy images that will lead him/her closer to You and to a grace filled, happy, healthy life. Bring what has been kept in secret out into Your light and bring freedom and healing to (*name person*).

Help (*name person*) to keep his/her eyes upon You and help (*name person*) steer clear of any magazines, websites, phone apps, videos or movies that contain sexually explicit material. Send someone into his/her life who will confidentially help him/her be accountable for his/her actions and help him/her stay free from any influence of pornography.

Thank You for blessing (*name person*). I believe that You are calling him/her out of darkness and that You are filling him/her with the courage, grace, and strength to find freedom from this destructive addiction. Amen.

Prayer for a Shopping Addict
(Ann Fitch)

O God, provider of all things, I come to You seeking Your blessing and healing upon (*name person*) who is addicted to shopping. (*Name person*) shops constantly and buys things that he/she doesn't need and honestly cannot afford. His/her spending is out of control and unless he/she stops this cycle of spending he/she will be in a grave place financially.

I ask You to fill (*name person*) with the will to stop shopping on TV, online, in catalogues, and in stores. Give him/her the will to say no to the urge to spend and the strength to stand firm against the compulsion to shop. When (*name person*) is weak and the temptation to shop arises, bless (*name person*) with a firm resolve to not succumb to the temptation but rather fill him/her with the desire to turn to You in prayer and embrace the grace and strength he/she needs to overcome that inclination to spend.

Lord, I ask that (*name person*) feel fulfilled by You and Your love for him/her and no longer by shopping. Help (*name person*) to have complete freedom and grant him/her the inner strength to no longer be held captive by this addiction. Amen.

Prayer for Someone to Quit Smoking
(Ann Fitch)

Lord, I turn to You today seeking Your strength and grace for (*name person*) who wants to quit smoking. Smoking has taken over his/her life. Breaking free from this addiction will be difficult for him/her but I believe that with You (*name person*) can conquer smoking and find freedom. Lord, eliminate his/her desire to smoke. Help (*name person*) to be master over his/her body and liberate him/her from the grips of this addiction.

When the temptation to smoke arises give (*name person*) the fortitude to not succumb to the temptation. Lead (*name person*) to aids and coping skills that will help him/her in his/her fight to stop smoking. Empower (*name person*) and surround him/her with loving, supportive, and understanding family and friends who will help him/her find liberation from smoking. Thank You, Lord, for strengthening (*name person*) and giving him/her the courage, grace, and will to live his/her life free from smoking. Amen.

Advent, Christmas & Lent

Blessing of an Advent Wreath
(Ann Fitch)

Heavenly Father, as we prepare to enter into the season of Advent we ask You to bless this wreath. Each week, as we light the candles of this wreath, may we reflect on the light of Your Son coming into the world dispelling the darkness that envelops us and illuminating our hearts and souls with the light of faith. As Advent progresses, may this wreath help us to rejoice in hope and prepare for the birth of Your blessed Son. When all the candles are burning, may the fire of Divine Love enflame us and fill us with peace. Amen.

Prayer for the Christmas Season
(Ann Fitch)

Lord, Jesus Christ, during this Christmas season may Your light shine forth from our eyes, Your love be manifest in all that we say and do, and may we work tirelessly to bring Your hope and peace to all we encounter. Amen.

Blessing of a Crèche
(Ann Fitch)

Lord of all, from the beginning of time You have blessed mankind with Your love. In time, You sent Your Son and our Savior to be born of the Virgin Mary. Into our lives He brings light, hope, peace, joy, forgiveness, mercy, and love.

May all who look upon this crèche be blessed with every gift and grace. May it be a reminder of Your Son coming into the world bringing to all the light of faith and the hope of everlasting life. May this crèche help us to remember Your love for us and inspire us to be generous with our time, talents, treasure and love. By gazing upon this crèche may we become more aware of Your loving kindness and desire to share that with everyone we encounter. Amen.

Christmas Tree Blessing
(Ann Fitch)

Heavenly Father, creator of trees, bless with Your abundant grace this our Christmas tree as a symbol of joy. May its evergreen branches be a sign of Your never-fading promises. May its colorful lights and ornaments call us to decorate with love our home and world. May the gifts that surround this tree be symbols of the gifts Christ received from the Magi. And may Your peace and joy come and nest in its branches and in our hearts. Amen.

A Christmas Prayer
(Ann Fitch)

Heavenly Father, on Christmas may we join the Alleluia chorus of the angels and experience the gladness and awe of the shepherds who first encountered Jesus, Your Loving Son. With His birth You opened the door for all to encounter You Who are love Itself. With every gift given may true kindness be experienced and may every greeting be one of hope and cheer.

Bless us all with merry and joyful hearts as we celebrate Christ's coming into the world. On Christmas morning may we all rise to celebrate and exclaim Your greatness. Throughout the day may we set aside all differences and be people of forgiveness and acceptance. And, as evening falls, may we rejoice with grateful hearts that are filled with grace and peace. Amen.

Christmas Prayer
(Ann Fitch)

Heavenly Father, through the gift of the Holy Spirit You have infused everlasting light in my heart, leading me to Your Son and my Savior. Grant that I would eagerly follow where the star of Your holy will leads me.

May I joyfully bring my gifts and talents to Your Infant Son for His honor and glory just as the Wise Men brought gifts to Him. Inspire me more and more with the light of Your holy Word. May I shine brightly with Your love and grace and sing Your praises each day. I know You have called me out of darkness to walk in the light of Your love and to be a witness to the power and majesty of Jesus Christ, my Lord and Redeemer. I ask that I be able to faithfully do all this in His holy Name. Amen.

Christmas Prayer for Someone Whose Loved One Died
(Ann Fitch)

Heavenly Father, on this most holy Christmas day, I turn to You Who are all-loving and all-knowing and entrust (*name person*) to You. Help him/her to open his/her heart and soul to You. As he/she mourns the loss of his/her loved one(s) I ask You to hold (*name person*) in Your arms.

You know his/her heart is broken and I know that only You can put the shattered pieces back together in a way that honors and glorifies You. The pain (*name person*) is experiencing makes it hard for him/her to share the joy of Your Son's coming with others. Take his/her brokenness and use it for the souls in most need of Your mercy. Transform it into a gift of blessing.

As (*name person*) encounters family and friends, help him/her to accept their words of encouragement and comfort with gratitude and poise. Give (*name person*) the strength to smile and graciously share himself/herself with them. I thank You for pouring Your Spirit out upon (*name person*) and for blessing him/her with all that he/she needs on this Christmas day. Amen.

Christmas Prayer Of One Who Is Grieving
(Ann Fitch)

Heavenly Father, on this most holy Christmas day, I turn to You Who are all-loving and all-knowing and entrust myself to You. I open my heart and soul to You and ask You to hold me in Your arms and comfort me as I mourn the loss of my loved one(s).

You know my heart is broken and I know that only You can put the shattered pieces back together in a way that honors and glorifies You. The pain I am experiencing makes it hard for me to share the joy of Your Son's coming with others. I offer my brokenness to You for the souls in most need of Your mercy. Transform it into a gift of blessing.

As I encounter family and friends, help me to accept their words of encouragement and comfort with gratitude and poise. Give me the strength to smile and graciously share myself with them. I thank You for pouring Your Spirit out upon me and for blessing me with all that I need on this Christmas day. Amen.

Lenten Prayer
(Ann Fitch)

Heavenly Father, during this most holy season of Lent I ask You to pour out Your blessings upon me and draw me into a deeper, more intimate relationship with You, Your Son and my Savior, Jesus Christ and the Holy Spirit. Inspire me to strive for holiness and walk in grace and virtue. Help me to follow Your commandments, fast, give alms, and pray more each day.

Through Your Word, teach me and strengthen my faith in You and in Your holy Church. Through the Sacrament of Penance bless me with Your infinite mercy and cleanse me of my sins. Strengthen me and fortify me so that I can turn away from sinful habits and walk more fully in Your light and love. Through the reception of Holy Communion each week may I be transformed into a truer reflection of Your love and find the grace to follow You faithfully, doing Your will at all times. Amen.

Prayer When Deciding How to Fast
(Ann Fitch)

O God, I know You are calling me to fast. Instill within my heart and mind how You would have me fast. Be it from food or drink, a pleasurable activity or a bad habit may I know Your will for me and have the grace and strength to faithfully fulfill that fast with joy. Amen.

Prayer When Fasting
(Ann Fitch)

Lord, as I fast may I be drawn closer to You in Your Triune form. May my attitude be positive and may I have a cheerful, joyful demeanor. Encourage me, sustain me, and strengthen me. Bless me with the grace to offer You every temptation to break my fast for the souls in most need of Your love and mercy. Renew and refresh my spirit and fill me with peace in knowing that I am opening myself up more fully to You and Your grace.

As I deny my flesh with fasting and turn to You in prayer may I experience Your love and mercy, be aware of Your presence within me, hear Your voice speaking to me in the quiet of my heart and soul, and be blessed in every way.   Amen.

Assault & Abuse

Prayer for Those Who Have Been Abused
(Ann Fitch)

O Lord, God of Heaven and Earth, You see and know all. Bless the hearts, minds, bodies and souls of those who have suffered the pain of abuse. Bless them and fill them with Your healing love. In Your infinite mercy fill them to overflowing with the gifts of Your Spirit. Touch their brokenness and restore them to health. Renew their hope in the goodness of humanity by sending kind and gentle souls into their lives to be bearers of comfort and support. Empower them with courage and strength and help them to trust themselves and others once again. May they find peace of mind in forgiving and be blessed with every grace they need to live full and happy lives. Amen.

Prayer for Healing After Abuse
(Ann Fitch)

Lord, You know the abuse I have suffered and I come before You seeking healing and peace. Take away my hurt, anger, depression, sleeplessness, inability to trust, feelings of being trapped, alone, hopeless and helpless and bless me with healing of my emotions, my mind, and my body. I give You all that I am and all that is within me and ask You to let Your healing light and love permeate every fiber of my being bringing restoration and renewal.

Take away my self-doubt and poor self-esteem and fill me with trust in myself. Bless me with self-acceptance, where I am, as I am. Help me to love myself without condition, the way You love me. Pour out Your Spirit upon me and bless me with confidence, strength, courage, dignity, hope, and joy. Rid my heart of fear and fill me with Your peace. Bless me with the ability to trust others and believe that they truly want what is best for me, what will make me happy, healthy and whole and that I am worthy of that type of love, friendship and care. Help me to nurture and cherish myself. Let me see my beauty, my uniqueness, my gifts, my talents, and my true value as a beloved child of Yours.

Bless me with the ability to forgive and let go of my hurt, anguish and pain so that I can move forward with my life and have peace of mind. Thank You, Lord, for Your gentle, compassionate, and all-encompassing love. Thank You for blessing me, healing me, and filling me with Your hope and peace. Amen.

Prayer for Someone Who has Been Assaulted
(Ann Fitch)

Lord we ask You to comfort and console (*name person*) who was assaulted. In Your infinite love take him/her into Your arms and fill him/her with Your love. (*Name person*) needs to feel the safety of Your embrace. Take from (*name person*) any feelings of unworthiness, impurity, or loss of dignity and replace those with a

49

new sense of self-acceptance, self-love, and self-worth. We ask You to take away any fear or anxiety (*name person*) has as a result of this incident. Surround (*name person*) with loved ones who will tend to his/her needs with gentleness, understanding and wisdom. Heal his/her brokenness and bless (*name person*) with Your peace.   Amen.

Prayer for Healing After Rape
(Ann Fitch)

O tender and ever-loving God, I am broken and hurting. At times my pain is too much to bear. Please be my strength and my hope. I feel dirty, ashamed, embarrassed, humiliated and violated. I know I did nothing to encourage my rapist, but I still feel as if I should have been able to do more to stop him/her. Sometimes I feel emotionally numb and at other times I am overwhelmed by depression, confusion or anger.

Inside I feel like I have brought shame upon my family and myself. I know in my heart of hearts that's not true but I cannot help thinking that way. I want to move forward with my life and I humbly ask You to heal me emotionally and psychologically. Touch my mind and help me to think clearly and have a proper perspective of myself and what was brutally done to me. Pour out Your Spirit upon me and bless me with a new sense of self-respect, self-acceptance, and self-love. Help me to have healthy, trusting relationships with others and bless me with a healthy sense of my own purity and sexuality.

O compassionate and gracious Lord, when nights are long and I cannot sleep please be with me blessing me with peace and tranquility. When I have flashbacks or memories of what happened flood my mind, pour Your healing light into those moments and heal my fear and shame and allow me to see myself as You see me, cherished, beloved, and beautiful. O gentle and loving God, touch my heart and mind with Your healing and bless me with courage, strength, and serenity.

Please take away my anger and bless me with a content and happy heart. I give You all that is broken within me and ask You to transform it into wholeness and fill me completely with Your reassuring love. Thank You for always being with me, for restoring my mind and heart with Your healing Spirit, and for caring so deeply and tenderly for me.   Amen.

Celebrating Sacraments

Prayer for a Child Being Baptized
(Ann Fitch)

Heavenly Father, we thank You for the gift of this child (*name child*). We ask that You fill him/her with the Holy Spirit that he/she may be born again in Spirit and truth. Cleanse (*name child*) from all sin and in Your infinite mercy fill (*name child*) with every gift and grace. You have called (*name child*) by name and we trust that You will be with him/her loving, caring, guiding, and protecting him/her every day of his/her life. May Your light always shine upon (*name child*) and may he/she walk through life trusting in Your love and goodness. May (*name child*) serve You faithfully and grow in kindness, gentleness, faith, wisdom, knowledge, compassion, understanding, and love. Through Baptism may (*name child*) inherit eternal life and one day enjoy the peace of Your heavenly kingdom. We ask all this through Jesus Christ our Lord who lives and reigns with You forever and ever.   Amen.

Prayer for an Adult Being Baptized
(Ann Fitch)

Heavenly Father, today (*name person*) comes to You for Baptism. We ask that You fill him/her with the Holy Spirit that he/she may be born again in Spirit and truth. Cleanse (*name person*) from all sin and in Your infinite mercy fill (*name person*) with every gift and grace. You have called (*name person*) by name and we trust that You are with him/her loving, caring, guiding, and protecting him/her every day of his/her life. May Your light always shine through (*name person*) drawing others to Your love and may he/she walk through life always trusting in Your love and goodness. May (*name person*) serve You faithfully and grow in kindness, gentleness, faith, wisdom, knowledge, compassion, understanding, and love. Through Baptism may (*name person*) inherit eternal life and one day praise and glorify You in Your heavenly kingdom. We ask all this through Jesus Christ, our Lord, Who lives and reigns with You and the Holy Spirit, one God, forever and ever.   Amen.

Prayer for Someone Being Initiated Into the Church
(Ann Fitch)

Heavenly Father, today (*name person*) comes to You to be initiated into Your Church. We ask that You fill him/her with the Holy Spirit that he/she may be born again in Spirit and truth. Cleanse (*name person*) from all sin and in Your infinite mercy fill (*name person*) with every gift and grace. You have called (*name person*) by name and we trust that You are with him/her loving, caring, guiding, and protecting him/her every day of his/her life. May Your light always shine through (*name person*) drawing others to Your love and may he/she walk through life always trusting in Your love and goodness. Each time he/she receives You in Holy Communion allow Your Body to become one with his/hers and Your Precious Blood to course through his/her veins bringing healing and grace. May (*name person*) serve You and Your holy Church faithfully and grow in kindness, gentleness, faith, wisdom, knowledge, compassion, love, joy, and understanding. Through reception of the Sacraments of Initiation may (*name person*) inherit eternal life and one day praise and glorify You in Your heavenly kingdom. We ask all this through Jesus Christ, our Lord, Who lives and reigns with You and the Holy Spirit, one God, forever and ever.   Amen.

Prayer for Someone Making Their First Communion
(Ann Fitch)

Lord, Jesus Christ, as (*name person*) receives You in Holy Eucharist for the first time sanctify him/her and fill him/her to overflowing with Your love and mercy. Let (*name person*) feel the fire of Your love coursing through him/her, fortifying and strengthening him/her. As Your Body and Precious Blood comingle with his/her body and blood may You become so intertwined that when people look at (*name person*) they see the light of Your love in his/her eyes. May (*name person*) believe with his/her entire being that You are truly present in the Consecrated Host and Cup of Salvation and may he/she always desire, with great love, to receive You in Holy Communion. Lord, may Your Eucharistic presence keep (*name person*) from sin, fill him/her with virtue and grace, and draw him/her into a more intimate relationship with You. May this First Communion have a deep and lasting impact on (*name person*) and as he/she communes with You sacramentally may he/she experience Your unconditional love and grow to love You more completely. Amen.

Prayer for Someone Being Confirmed
(Ann Fitch)

Come Holy Spirit and enkindle in (*name person*) the fire of divine love. Permeate his/her being and fill him/her with every gift and grace. As (*name person*) takes responsibility for his/her relationship with You, the Father, and Jesus Christ the Son, may he/she cultivate his/her love for You and be faithful and true to Your holy Church. By Your infilling may (*name person*) grow in love, joy, peace, patience, kindness, gentleness, faithfulness, wisdom and self-control. Empower (*name person*) with the ability to spread Your love through his/her words and actions. Guide, illuminate and sanctify (*name person*) and forever seal him/her as Your own. May (*name person*) grow in holiness, generosity of heart, and obedience to You and Your will for him/her and may he/she praise, honor and glorify You all the days of his/her life. Amen.

Prayer for Someone Making a First Confession
(Ann Fitch)

Heavenly Father, we ask You to bless (*name person*) who is making his/her First Confession. Be with him/her as he/she enters the confessional. Remove any fears (*name person*) has and replace them with complete trust in Your love and with Your peace that surpasses all understanding. Give (*name person*) the grace to humbly confess the sins he/she has committed and with a contrite heart accept and do his/her penance. May this First Confession be a means of great grace for (*name person*) and may he/she continue to faithfully go to Confession on a regular basis.   Amen.

Prayer Before Going to Confession
(Ann Fitch)

Lord, I ask You to bless me with courage and peace as I contemplate going to Confession. Thank You for drawing me to Yourself in this beautiful sacrament and for instilling in me trust in Your infinite goodness. As I come to You in the Sacrament of Reconciliation open my heart and mind to recall my serious sins. May I be humble, contrite, and calm as I confess those to the priest who patiently and lovingly sits in Your place. As I am absolved of my sins may Your merciful love fill my heart. May I experience true joy in having confessed all to You and exit the confessional happy and serene with a firm resolve to not commit any serious sins in the future.   Amen.

Prayer When Preparing for Confession
(Ann Fitch)

Lord I come before You in humility and honesty. I want to make a good confession and receive Your healing love through the Sacrament of Penance. Open my heart and mind to recall every sin I have committed since my last confession. Show me any patterns of sin that I need to confess and illuminate my mind so that I am clear and concise when I am making my confession. No sin is too small to mention or too great for Your forgiveness. I know this and thank You for Your infinite love and mercy. Touch the heart and mind of the priest who will hear my confession and give him the words of wisdom I need to hear, words that will touch my heart and soul and strengthen me as I go forth from the Sacrament of Reconciliation to live my life. May he be Your presence for me and be a means of grace and blessing. Amen.

Dating & Engagement

Prayer to be Chaste and Pure
(Ann Fitch)

Lord there are so many things that tempt me to have impure thoughts, say impure things or to engage in impure actions. I ask for the grace and strength to not succumb to the temptations but to be strong and pure because of my love for You and my desire to be faithful to Your laws.

I choose to be chaste and pure because I love You and wish to remain in Your grace. Keep my eyes shielded from impure images. Keep my thoughts chaste and pure. Keep my ears from impure words, language, and music. When I am tempted to be impure in any way grant me the grace to immediately turn to You in prayer and give You all that tempts me so that I might be fortified and strengthened by focusing on You, Your purity, Your love for me, and Your desire for me to be happy, healthy and whole in You.

As I keep my eyes, my heart and my thoughts on You bless me with Your peace, Your joy, Your strength and above all a pure, clean heart, mind, body and soul. Amen.

Prayer Before a Date
(Ann Fitch)

Lord, I am preparing to go on a date. I ask You to be with me guiding my words, thoughts and actions. Help me to be considerate and inviting. Allow my sense of humor and personality to shine forth in a way that is attractive and interesting. Bless the time we are going to share with each other. May we enjoy one another's company and get to know each other better. Keep us free from temptations and fill our time with joy and laughter. Amen.

Prayer When Dating
(Ann Fitch)

O Loving God, we come before You asking Your blessing upon our relationship. As we spend time together may we grow in our love for You and in our care for one another. Order our thoughts and help us to remain chaste in thought and in action. May we be a blessing for one another and take delight in each other. Help us to be kind, gentle, compassionate, and respectful. When we are together may we laugh and enjoy each other's company and do that which honors You. Amen.

Prayer When Ending a Relationship
(Ann Fitch)

Lord, I turn to You because I need to end a relationship and my heart is hurting. I know I will miss (*name person*) being a part of my life, but I believe You have called me to end our relationship because it is not healthy. Lord, keep my heart from becoming bitter towards (*name person*) and give me the grace to not discuss the ending of our relationship with others in a way that reflects poorly on him/her. Please help me to be strong, wise, compassionate and understanding. Help me to forgive (*name person*) any wrongs. I truly wish (*name person*) happiness in life. Please pour out Your Spirit upon both of us and help us to move on in a way that brings life, restoration, and blessing into our lives. Thank You, Lord. Amen.

Prayer for During a Breakup
(Ann Fitch)

Lord, I ask You to place me within the confines of Your Sacred Heart. I ask that there You bless me with healing for my broken heart. I ask You to fill me with acceptance and forgiveness. Help me to be merciful and kind as I face this breakup. Do not let anger or resentment fill my heart and mind. Instead, grant me Your understanding and wisdom. Help me to move on trusting in Your love with peace and joy in my heart. In time, Lord, open my heart to love again in a way that brings life, wholeness and happiness to me and to the one You bless me with. Thank You, Lord, for keeping me safe within Your Heart and for Your gentle and healing love. Amen.

Prayer for Another During a Breakup
(Ann Fitch)

Lord, I ask You to bless (*name person*) with Your love and understanding. Take away any hurt or anger he/she has and replace that with acceptance and compassion. You alone know why this breakup occurred and only You can bring peace to (*name person*). May this last relationship be a means of personal growth for him/her. May he/she become more aware of what brings him/her true happiness and learn how to be patient and accepting of his/her own faults and insecurities as well as those of others. Help (*name person*) move on with his/her life and in Your time send that perfect someone into his/her life who can bring wholeness and happiness to him/her. You know what is best for (*name person*). I ask that You keep him/her safe within Your Heart and that You bless him/her with Your merciful love. Amen.

Prayer in Preparation for Meeting Your Spouse
(Ann Fitch)

Lord, as I await meeting my future spouse I ask for the ability to be wise and understanding, humble and kind, patient and compassionate, honest and sincere, selfless and giving, accepting and encouraging, respectful, considerate and caring with all those You place in my life. I ask for the ability to laugh at myself, for a good sense of humor, and for the ability to fearlessly embrace life and all its challenges. I pray to be at peace with myself and that I exhibit the peace and joy of the Holy Spirit.

Lord, as I prepare to meet my future spouse I choose to be fully committed to a deep personal relationship with You so that at the right time I can enter into a deeply personal relationship with him/her. I pray that when we meet I will be willing to provide for, protect, nurture and cherish him/her and mature enough, ready, and capable of building our future together. Thank You, Lord, for preparing our hearts, minds and souls for one another and for blessing us as we wait to meet. Amen.

Prayer for an Engaged Couple
(Ann Fitch)

O loving and eternal God we give You thanks for (*name woman*) and (*name man*) who have found one another and have chosen to join their lives together in holy matrimony. We ask You to bless them profoundly as they prepare to become husband and wife. In Your infinite love and mercy fill (*name woman*) and (*name man*) with every gift and grace they need to grow in their love for one another, be wise in making decisions about their wedding and future, and respectful and cooperative as they begin the process of joining their lives together.

During their engagement strengthen them as individuals and as a couple. Bless them with patience and understanding. When they upset one another help them to admit any wrongdoing and forgive immediately. May their love for one another be selfless, unconditional, and life giving. May (*name woman*) and (*name man*) nurture and cherish one another and place the needs of the other before themselves. We ask You to be with (*name woman*) and (*name man*), guiding them through the engagement process. May they depend on You and find true happiness and joy in one another. Amen.

Engagement Prayer
(Ann Fitch)

Heavenly Father, we come before You grateful that we have found one another and ask You to bless us as we prepare for married life. May our love for one another be giving, sacrificial and constantly growing. Help us to be kind, considerate, caring, patient and compassionate with one another as we adjust to joining our lives together in marriage and plan our wedding. As we address our differences and create a set of values that unify us as a couple help us to grow in trust for one another.

Lord Jesus, help us to share our inner thoughts, dreams, fears, feelings and needs with one another. Help us to truly listen to each other and embrace each other's deepest wants and desires. As we discuss our professional goals, finances and budget, religious beliefs, and plans for a family may we become more cohesive as a couple and grow in appreciation for one another. Help us to accept each other's faults, weaknesses and flaws and do whatever we can to help one another become happier and more fulfilled.

O Holy Spirit, fill us with every gift and grace we need to successfully join our lives together. Strengthen us not only as individuals, but as a couple. When we upset, anger or frustrate one another may we humbly admit wrongdoing, express genuine sorrow, and seek to forgive one another immediately. Help us to place each other's needs before our own. Bless us with the desire to nurture, protect and cherish one another and fill our days with joy, peace, laughter, and above all love.   Amen.

Death & Dying

Watch, O Lord
(St. Augustine)

Watch, O Lord, with those who wake, or watch or weep tonight, and give Your angels charge over those who sleep. Tend Your sick ones, O Lord Jesus Christ; rest Your weary ones; bless Your dying ones; soothe Your suffering ones; pity Your afflicted ones; shield Your joyous ones; and all for Your love's sake. Amen.

Prayer for a Happy Death
(Cardinal Newman)

O my Lord and Savior, support me in my last hour by the strong arms of Your sacraments, and the fragrance of Your consolations. Let Your absolving words be said over me, and the holy oil sign and seal me; and let Your own Body be my food, and Your Precious Blood my sprinkling; and let Your Mother Mary come to me, and my angel whisper peace to me, and Your glorious saints and my own dear patrons smile on me, that in and through them all I may die as I desire to live, in Your Church, in Your faith, in Your love, and in Your loving presence. Amen.

For a Peaceful Parting
(St. Bonaventure)

Holy Virgin, I beg of you, when my soul shall depart from my body, be pleased to meet and receive it. Mary, do not refuse me then the grace of being sustained by your sweet presence. Be for me the ladder and the way to Heaven, and finally assure me of pardon and eternal rest. Amen.

Prayer for Strength When a Loved One is Dying
(Ann Fitch)

O gracious and ever loving God, I am helpless as I watch my loved one slip away. His/her health is failing and I ask for the grace and strength to be patient, loving, kind, gentle, understanding, and nurturing. Help me to be strong for (*name person*). Keep him/her safe within Your loving arms. Please do not let (*name person*) suffer needlessly but use all of his/her suffering for the souls in most need of Your mercy.

Lord, help me to know when he/she needs comfort. Help me to know when he/she needs a listening ear. Help me to know when (*name person*) needs medicine to alleviate his/her pain. And please Lord, help me to let go and trust that (*name person*) is in Your tender care. You know the day and the hour when You will call him/her home. May I be courageous on that day and at the hour of his/her death may I have the strength to rejoice for the gift of his/her life, and with all the angels and saints, pray that You carry (*name person*) peacefully home to be with You forever in Heaven. Amen.

Aspirations for the Dying

To be said in the presence of a dying person.

O God, be gracious to me.

O God, have mercy on me.

O God, forgive me my sins.

O God the Father, have mercy on me.

O Jesus, be gracious to me.

O Holy Spirit, strengthen me.

O God the Father, do not reject me.

O Jesus, do not abandon me.

O God the Holy Spirit, do not forsake me.

O my God, into Your hands I commend my spirit.

O Jesus, Son of David, have mercy on me.

O Jesus, Son of Mary, have mercy on me.

O Jesus, I believe in You.

O Jesus I hope in You.

O Jesus, I love You.

O Jesus, I place all my trust in You.

O Jesus, in Your Sacred Wounds I hide myself.

O Jesus, I enclose myself in Your Sacred Heart.

Holy Mary, Mother of God, assist me.

Holy Mary, protect me from evil spirits.

Holy Mary, turn your eyes of mercy upon me.

O Mary, Mother of mercy, obtain grace for me from your dear Son.

Come to my aid, O Mary, in the moment of my death.

O Mary, enclose me in your virginal Heart.

O Mary, commend me to your Son, present me to your Son, reconcile
  me with your Son.

St. Joseph, obtain for me grace and mercy.

St. Joseph, assist me in my struggle against the enemy of my
  salvation.

St. Joseph, remember me, and obtain mercy for me.

O holy guardian angel, do not abandon me, but combat for me and
  preserve me from the evil one.

My dear patron saints, pray for me.

Jesus, Jesus, Jesus, into Your hands I commend my spirit.

May Mary, the angels, and all the saints come to meet you as you
go forth from this life. May Christ Who was crucified for you bring
you freedom and peace. May Christ, the Son of God, Who died for
you take you into His kingdom. May Christ, the Good Shepherd,
shepherd you home. May Christ forgive your sins and keep you

among His beloved. May you see your Redeemer face to face and enjoy the sight of God forever in Heaven.   Amen.

Prayer After a Sudden Death
(Ann Fitch)

O gracious and ever-loving God, we turn to You today in shock over the sudden death of (*name person*). He/she was so very loved and we are in pain and reeling from the reality that he/she has passed from this life into the next. It is hard to comprehend that we will never see, hear, speak to, embrace or laugh with him/her ever again. We are devastated by this loss and our hearts are shattered. We look to You for comfort and strength. Hold us in Your arms and fill us with the courage we need to face today and the weeks and months to come.

Allow Your peace which surpasses all understanding dwell in our hearts and minds and be a solace for us as we grieve. We know that You love (*name person*) even more than we do. We pray that You have called him/her into the light of Your presence and that You have forgiven his/her sins. We hope that You have blessed (*name person*) with the gift of everlasting joy in Your heavenly kingdom. May his/her soul rest in Your peace and forever sing of Your glory.   Amen.

Prayer for a Loved One Who has Died
(Ann Fitch)

Heavenly Father, we humbly ask You to receive the soul of (*name person*) into the joy of eternal union with You. He/she faithfully served You during his/her life and died in the hope of salvation. May he/she experience the fullness of Your love and forever praise You with the angels and saints. We ask this through Christ our Lord. Amen.

Prayer for Loved Ones After a Death
(Ann Fitch)

Almighty and eternal God, we ask You to be with the loved ones of (*name person*), Your servant, who has fallen asleep in the hope of the resurrection. In Your boundless compassion, Lord, comfort all who mourn his/her death. Renew their hope in the promise of eternal life. Encourage them and heal their brokenness. Fill the void in their hearts with loving memories of (*name person*) and in time turn their sorrow to joy. Grant them strength for the days ahead. May their loved ones and friends fortify and reassure them as they grieve and bring them the consolation of Your love. We ask all this in accordance with Your holy will. Amen.

Prayer After the Death of an Infant
(Ann Fitch)

Heavenly Father, hear our prayer. Our precious child has died before he/she had a chance to live his/her life. Our child's death has left us feeling empty, confused, and brokenhearted. He/she was loved immeasurably and his/her death has been devastating to us. Father, embrace us and pour out Your Spirit upon us. Take away our pain and brokenness. Bring us closer together, fill us with every grace we need to heal, and help us to be sensitive to one another's needs as we grieve.

Lord Jesus, bless us. Be with us in our sorrow, help us to always remember our precious child and the time we had with him/her, and in Your time bless us with a healthy child to love, care for, and nurture. Forgive us for any anger we may have had towards You. Comfort us and fill us with peace in the hope that our beloved child is with You, forever interceding for us with the angels and the saints. On significant days pertaining to this lost and cherished baby, bless us with courage and strength and help us trust in Your love to carry us through. Thank You, Lord. Amen.

Prayer for Others After the Death of an Infant
(Ann Fitch)

Heavenly Father, hear my prayer for (*mother*) and (*father*). Their precious child has died before he/she had a chance to live his/her life. Their child's death has left them feeling empty, confused, and brokenhearted. He/she was loved immeasurably and his/her death has been devastating to them. Father, embrace them and pour out Your Spirit upon them. Take away their pain and brokenness. Bring them closer together, fill them with every grace they need to heal, and help them to be sensitive to one another's needs as they grieve.

Lord Jesus, bless (*mother*) and (*father*). Be with them in their sorrow, help them to always remember this precious child and the time they had with him/her, and in Your time bless them with a healthy child to love, care for, and nurture. Comfort them and fill them with peace in the hope that their beloved child is with You, forever interceding for them with the angels and the saints. On significant days pertaining to this lost and cherished baby, bless (*mother*) and (*father*) with courage and strength and help them trust in Your love to carry them through. Thank You, Lord. Amen.

Prayer When Grieving
(Ann Fitch)

Lord, I know that You said, "*Blessed are those who mourn,*" (Matthew 5:4) but I cannot see past my sorrow and pain to the blessing. My heart is broken and torn apart by grief. I want to see Your blessing in this moment, but I am blinded by my brokenness. Open my eyes, remove the darkness that seems to have enveloped me, and replace it with Your resplendent light. I need You. I need Your comfort and Your love. Embrace me as I am and hold me close. I do not see an end to my heartbreak, but I know You will take my pain and use it to bless others who are in need of Your grace. I give You all that I am experiencing and ask You to bless me with the courage and strength to persevere. In Your infinite goodness, guide me to a place of peace and tranquility.   Amen.

Prayer When Grieving the Loss of a Child
(Ann Fitch)

Heavenly Father, my child has died and I am angry, hurt, broken, and unable to understand why my precious child is gone. There are moments when my pain is so gut wrenching I cannot breathe. Sometimes I feel so overwhelmed that I want to scream out in my agony. In this lifetime I will never again see my child's face or hear his/her voice or laughter. The child I loved with every fiber of my being is no longer here and I am struggling to live my life and move forward loving, being available to, and taking care of my family. The despair I feel makes me wonder if I will ever smile, laugh, or feel joy again.

I know in my heart and in my mind that You are near me, so I turn to You for consolation and comfort. Strengthen me and give me the grace I need to survive this loss. Help me to graciously accept the love and comfort of others. As I struggle to continue on without my beloved child I ask that You take (*name child*) into Your loving arms. I miss (*name child*) so much that my heart aches. I pray that (*name child*) is at peace with You enjoying forever the beauty of Heaven with the angels and saints. May Your comfort and grace carry me through the days, weeks, and years to come.

Thank You, Lord, for the time I had with (*name child*) for all the joy and beauty (*name child*) brought to my life. I will miss (*name child*) every day for the rest of my life. But I believe that one day we will be reunited and on that day all of Heaven will share our joy. Thank You for being with me, blessing me, calming me and helping me move through my grief so that I can live my life with purpose and meaning. Please continue to carry me and bring me to a place of healing, acceptance and peace.   Amen.

Prayer When Grieving the Loss of a Spouse

(Ann Fitch)

Heavenly Father, I know You are with me but I do not feel Your presence and Your love because of my brokenness. My heart feels as if it has shattered into a million pieces. I cannot put into words the depth of my pain. The tears come and it feels as if they'll never stop. Sadness overwhelms me. I ask You to use my pain and suffering to bless the souls who are most need of Your love and mercy. Please send loving friends and family to wipe away my tears, hold me close, listen to me, comfort, console and grieve with me.

Father, I need Your love and comfort. Take me in Your arms and hold me as I grieve the loss of my beloved spouse, (*name spouse*). I feel so lost and alone. He/she was my best friend, my confidant, my lover, my soul mate. And now I am alone facing each day with a broken heart missing (*name spouse*). I miss (*name spouse*) more than anyone could possibly understand. It is hard to realize I will never see (*name spouse*) again. I will never again see his/her smile and I will no longer hear his/her voice or laughter. I will never be able to reach out and touch (*name spouse*) and hold his/her hand or embrace him/her. (*Name spouse*) is gone forever.

Father, I beg You to pour out Your Spirit upon me and fill me with courage, strength, patience, wisdom, gentleness, hope, and peace. In the days, weeks, and months to come I will lean on You, Father, knowing You will provide me with every gift and grace I need to go through the grieving process in a way that is dignified and brings honor and glory to You. I trust You will carry me to a place of healing, hope, and peace. I pray that (*name spouse*) is enjoying the beauty and peace of Heaven and praising You among the angels and the saints. I hope one day to join (*name spouse*) in Your heavenly kingdom and forever rest in Your love praising and glorifying You. Amen.

Prayer When Grieving the Loss of a Mother
(Ann Fitch)

Lord, I turn to You today and ask You to comfort me with Your love. Hold me close and place me within the confines of Your Sacred Heart. You know the aching sadness I am feeling at my mother's death. She was always there to support, guide, and care for me. She taught me through her example how to love and be loved and the importance of caring for and respecting myself and others. She instilled in me a deep faith and trust in You. I feel such loss and have a huge hole in my heart.

I know You understand my grief and that I can draw strength from You Who are all powerful. This day, this hour, this minute I will lean on You and embrace Your grace. I trust that You will carry me through this time of mourning and bring me to a place of healing, hope, and peace. There are bound to be times when sadness will overwhelm me. I offer those times to You as a gift of love and ask that You use them for the souls in most need of Your mercy. When they come, wipe away my tears, and pour out Your Spirit upon me filling me with the courage and strength I need to get through the day.

I know that one day soon I will feel joy again and be able to laugh at the memories of my mother. I pray that she is rejoicing with the angels and saints in Your heavenly kingdom. I pray You have blessed her with eternal peace and joy. One day I hope to be reunited with her and spend eternity praising You for Your infinite love and mercy. Amen.

Prayer When Grieving the Loss of a Father
(Ann Fitch)

Lord, I turn to you today and ask You to comfort me with Your love. Take me into Your arms and hold me close. You know the sadness I am feeling at the loss of my father. I miss him terribly. I know You understand my grief and that I can draw strength from You

Who are all powerful. This day, this hour, this minute I will lean on You and embrace Your grace.

I trust that You will carry me through this time of mourning and bring me to a place of healing, hope, and peace. There are bound to be times when sadness will overwhelm me. I offer those times to You as a gift of love and ask that You use them for the souls in most need of Your mercy. When they come, wipe away my tears, and pour out Your Spirit upon me filling me with the courage and strength I need to get through the day. I know that one day soon I will feel joy again and be able to smile at my memories of my father. I pray that he is rejoicing with You in Your heavenly kingdom and that he is at peace. I hope one day to join him there and forever rest in Your love. When that day comes may the angels and saints join us in praising You for Your infinite and merciful love.   Amen.

Prayer on Significant Days After a Loved One has Died
(Ann Fitch)

Ever loving and gracious God, I turn to You for strength and comfort as I live this day without my loved one, (*name person*). I will always love (*name person*) and I will never get over his/her death but I am learning to live with it. Today as I miss and remember (*name person*) I ask for the grace and strength to get through the day focused on You, Your love for me, and Your love for (*name person*). My love for (*name person*) is but a tiny fraction of Yours and I know You understand how broken my heart is that I must live this day without him/her.

Please let those closest to me reach out and share their love for (*name person*) with me today. What a comfort it would be to openly express how much I truly feel his/her absence. Lord, I thank You for helping me pick up the pieces of my life and begin living it without (*name person*). Thank You for all the healing Your love has brought to me and for allowing my pain to become less raw over time. Keep me close to Your Heart. Bless me and fill me with the grace and strength I need to continue moving forward, growing in hope, happiness, and peace remembering (*name person*) and all the joy (*name person*) brought to my life and the innumerable ways he/she was a blessing to me.   Amen.

Prayer for Those Who Have Committed Suicide
(Ann Fitch)

Dear Lord, we come before You and ask Your blessing and compassion upon the soul of (*name person*). Forgive him/her for taking his/her life. You are our hope and we trust in the fullness of Your love and mercy. In Your goodness have mercy on (*name person*) and grant that he/she may rest in the fullness of Your love and be at peace with You forever and ever.   Amen.

Prayer When a Loved One Commits Suicide
(Ann Fitch)

O Lord, giver of life, bless (*name person*). Grant him/her Your forgiveness and peace, and bring him/her into the fullness of Your love. We thank You for the time we were able to love him/her and await the joy of being reunited in Your love. Tenderly hold us in Your arms and comfort us as we grieve the loss of (*name person*). When sadness overwhelms us wipe away our tears and grant us rest for our weary souls.

Help us to walk gracefully through the grieving process and humbly offer You all our anguish for the benefit of the souls in most need of Your mercy. Strengthen us and bestow upon us the courage we need to face the questions why. Ease the guilt that burdens us, heal our broken hearts, and fill us with renewed hope in You. And, in time, replace our sorrow with precious memories of (*name person*). Amen.

Employment & Finances

Prayer When Creating and Submitting a Resume
(Ann Fitch)

Lord, I come before You asking You to help me choose a format for my resume. May it be professional in appearance and unique in style. As I format it, help me choose the right words to describe my talents, my education, my work experience and myself. May I convey who I am and my credentials in such a way that the companies to whom I will submit my resume will be interested in interviewing me for a possible position within their company. As I submit my resume, open the doors to where You would have me be employed and close the doors to where You would not. I trust that You are leading and blessing me as I create and submit my resume. Thank You for inspiring my words, guiding my actions, and helping me with this task. Amen.

Prayer for Employment
(Ann Fitch)

Heavenly Father, I turn to You for assistance as I look for employment. Open the doors where You desire for me to find employment and close the doors where You do not. I desire to use the gifts and talents You have given me in my workplace and in so doing bring honor and glory to You. Thank You for caring for me and always providing for me.

O Holy Spirit, bless me with wisdom, knowledge, and clarity. Guide my thoughts and words as I write my resume, choose which companies to submit it to, and go through the interview process. Thank You for strengthening me and blessing me with the peace that comes from walking with You each day.

Lord Jesus, I trust You to direct me to the job that is best for me and that will bring me happiness. I know that You will supply all my needs and open the door that allows me financial stability and security. I choose not be anxious. Instead, I will walk in the confidence that You are directing my steps. Thank You for Your love and guidance.   Amen.

Prayer Before an Interview
(Ann Fitch)

Ever present and loving God, source of every grace and blessing, I turn to You before I enter this interview. I give you all my fears, nervousness, and insecurities. I ask You to be with me filling me with confidence and peace. Help me to be calm and composed. Pour out Your Spirit upon me and direct my words and actions. I trust that You will give me the wisdom, clarity, and knowledge I need to answer questions concisely and with intelligence. Bless my interviewer(s). May he/she/they be forthright, kind, and understanding. If it is Your will for me, allow this interview to lead to gainful employment. Amen.

Prayer After an Interview
(Ann Fitch)

Lord, Thank You for being with me as I interviewed. Thank You for blessing me with Your peace. Thank You for pouring out Your Spirit upon me and helping me wisely choose my words so that I confidently conveyed who I am, my education, my aspirations and goals, and my experience and talents. I ask that You continue to work in the hearts and minds of those who interviewed me. May they review my resume, follow up with my references, and find a place within their company where they believe I can be an asset to them. As I await a response, help me to be patient and remain calm.   Bless me with contentment and fill me with hope.   Amen.

Prayer When Hiring
(Ann Fitch)

Lord I am in need of a new employee and I turn to You seeking Your assistance in finding just the right person for the position. I am looking for someone who is personable, dependable, responsible, trustworthy, hardworking, honest, positive, organized and who communicates well. The person I am looking for should have a strong work ethic and all the skills and knowledge needed to do the job well. As resumes come in, lead me to the candidates You would have me interview. As I interview, pour out Your Spirit upon me and bless me with the wisdom I need to choose the person who will best fill the position. Thank You for assisting me and for guiding my decision making. Amen.

Prayer After the Loss of a Job
(Ann Fitch)

Heavenly Father, I turn to You seeking Your guidance in handling the loss of my job. I feel as if I have failed and my self-esteem is low. I turn to You asking for a new sense of self-worth in You and for a deeper trust in Your Divine Will for my life. Help me to believe that my value is not in my monetary worth but in being Your child, wholly and completely loved by You. I know that as my Father You want what is best for me, what will bring me the greatest joy and fulfillment. Help me to be patient as You lay the foundation for my future. Even though I cannot see a way to that future I trust that You have already laid it out for me.

Lord Jesus Christ, I ask You to open my mind and to show me areas in my life where I need to be more like You - humble, kind, generous, loving, confident, and self-assured. I ask You to direct me to those people You wish to be a part of my life who will help me trust more fully in You, who will be a positive influence on me, and who will lead me closer to You. As I focus on being more like You I ask that You direct me to any way I can increase my job skills and make myself more marketable in the workplace. Place upon my heart that which You desire for me and fill me with the desire to do Your will in my life. I know that with You I can accomplish anything because nothing is impossible for You. I believe that You have a future full of hope for me and I trust in Your unending goodness.

O Holy Spirit pour out Your graces upon me. Fill me with wisdom, knowledge, and understanding. Help me to see this loss as an opportunity to grow and become a stronger more loving person in You. Take away any anxiety and fear I am experiencing. Fill me with peace, calm, and tranquility. Help me to honestly evaluate my situation and be wise with the gifts, talents, and monies I have. I ask for the ability to hear Your voice directing me. I pray that You lead me to the job opportunities You want me to pursue. Anoint my words and actions when I am being interviewed and bless me with patience as I await word afterwards. Remove any self-doubt I may experience and bless me with complete trust that You have a perfect position awaiting me.

Thank You, God, for opening my eyes, my heart, and my mind to Your Divine Providence. Thank You for leading me and guiding me to where You desire me to be. Thank You for blessing me with every gift and grace I need at this time. I am so grateful for Your compassion, understanding, comfort, and above all, love. Amen.

Prayer for Another After a Job Loss
(Ann Fitch)

Gracious and ever-loving God, (*name person*) has lost his/her job and is feeling as if he/she has failed. He/she is struggling with self-worth and needs to be reassured by You that his/her true value is as Your child, completely and wholly loved by You not in his/her monetary value. I know that You want what is best for (*name person*) and that You have a purpose and a plan for his/her life. Open his/her eyes, mind, and heart to Your desires for him/her. Fill (*name person*) with complete trust in You as You lay the foundation for his/her future. Remove any fears and anxieties he/she is experiencing and replace those with peace, calm and tranquility. Fill (*name person*) with wisdom, knowledge, and understanding.

May he/she hear Your voice speaking to him/her, leading and guiding him/her. Anoint his/her words as he/she prepares his/her resume and as he/she interviews for positions. Bless him/her with peace as he/she awaits word afterwards and help him/her believe that nothing is impossible with You. I know that You have a future full of hope for (*name person*) and that You will open all the doors needed for him/her to live that future. Thank You for blessing (*name person*) with every gift and grace he/she needs at this time and above all thank You for being compassionate, comforting, and loving towards him/her. Amen.

Prayer of Surrender of Finances
(Ann Fitch)

Lord I surrender my financial needs and affairs to You and Your Divine Providence. Help me to trust that You will provide for me in every way. Bless me with freedom from needless worry, stress or anxiety. I have faith in You and know that You will take complete care of me. I am ever so grateful for all that You have provided for me. Help me to manage what You have blessed me with wisely and to be a good steward of all You have given me in Your love. Let me not spend frivolously or waste money on unnecessary things. I ask for the ability to budget carefully and save what I can so that I can manage my expenses, meet my debts, and be solvent at the end of each month. Thank You, Lord for always providing, for always supplying, for always meeting my needs, and for always blessing me abundantly. Amen.

Prayer to Our Lady When in Financial Need
(Ann Fitch)

Dearest Mother, with a humble heart I approach you and with child-like confidence in your ability to influence your Son's Heart I ask you to assist me with my fiscal responsibilities. Due to circumstances beyond my control I find myself in dire need of financial aid. I simply cannot meet my debts. I ask for the ability to meet my current financial obligations and provide for my family's needs. Please plead with your Son to provide a way for me through this current financial crisis. I know that nothing is impossible for Him and I trust He will take care of me in every way. Thank you, sweet Mother for your generosity, kindness, and intercession. Amen.

Prayer of Thanksgiving for Financial Stability
(Ann Fitch)

Ever loving and gracious God, I give You thanks for all the blessings of this life, especially for financial stability. I know that You have provided everything that I have and I am eternally grateful. So many are without financial stability and I realize what a gift it is. Help me to always remember that You have blessed me abundantly in Your infinite love and mercy. Help me to share what You have given me with those who are in need and faithfully support my church community. May I always praise You and give You thanks for Your goodness to me. Amen.

Tithing Prayer
(Ann Fitch)

O infinite and loving God, I turn to You seeking Your help in knowing how much You wish for me to tithe. You have blessed me abundantly and I know that I am called to share what I have been given. I ask You to give me conviction of heart and mind in knowing how much You would have me faithfully give to my church community. Please lead me to the charities I am called to support and help me to know how much I am to give them. I know that You cannot be outdone in generosity and I know You will abundantly bless whatever I give in love. Thank You for leading me. Thank You for blessing me. Thank You for allowing me to share what I have been given. Amen.

Prayer When Applying for a Loan
(Ann Fitch)

Lord, I am applying for a loan and ask that You bless the entire process from beginning to end. I pray that I will have all documents needed for the loan prior to application and that all the loan paperwork will be filed correctly, that the loan processors will review it quickly, and that it will go through underwriting or any other process needed for final loan approval in a timely fashion. You know my needs and why I am applying for this loan. I ask that You help me not to become impatient, frustrated or anxious as my loan is in process. I trust that You are with me, blessing me and that this whole process will come to a fruitful end. Amen.

Prayer When Applying for Financial Aid, Scholarships or Grants

(Ann Fitch)

Lord I come to You today seeking Your assistance as I apply for scholarships/financial aid and/or grants. Guide me to which forms of aid I should apply for, help me to acquire all the appropriate paperwork that will need to be completed, and guide my answers as I fill out the applications. Let Your Spirit guide my paperwork through the application process. Bless the men or women who will review my applications. If it be Your will that I am granted aid, open their hearts and minds and encourage them to accept, process and respond promptly to my applications. Keep me free from anxiety, worry, and stress as I go through the application process and wait for responses. I know You are with me. I trust You are blessing me. And, I believe that in Your glorious richness You will provide for every one of my school expenses in some way. May my heart be at peace and as I surrender all to You each day. Amen.

Events

As I Age

(Ann Fitch)

O my God and lover of my soul, graciously accept the humble gift of my heart. As I age I realize that You alone can satisfy my soul and bring peace to my heart. In Your infinite goodness bless me with courage and strength, patience and perseverance, wisdom and understanding. When my loved ones and friends leave this world and enter into eternal life grant me the grace to optimistically go on living my life. In the moments when I feel alone make Your presence known to me and fill me with Your reassurance and comfort. Take as a gift all my aches, pains, and sufferings and in Your boundless compassion turn them into a blessing for others. O tender and loving God, help me to age gracefully, always keeping my eyes affixed on You and my heart filled with the hope that one day I will enter into Your light and find eternal refreshment with the angels and the saints.   Amen.

Birthday Prayer
(Ann Fitch)

Heavenly Father I give thanks to You for the gift of my life. As I celebrate this day of my birth, may I be blessed with the fullness of Your love, a renewal of the gifts of the Holy Spirit, and forgiveness for my sins through Your Son, and my Lord, Jesus Christ. As I recommit myself to You today, help me to know, love, and serve You with all of my heart, mind, body, and soul. As I begin a new year of life, help me to trust that You hold me in Your arms and that You will provide for my every need. Thank You, for my life and all the blessings You have bestowed upon me. Help me draw closer to You each day and in so doing find peace and joy.   Amen.

Prayer for Someone Celebrating a Birthday
(Ann Fitch)

Lord, I give thanks to You for the gift of (*name person*). On this his/her birthday I ask Your choicest blessings upon him/her. Fill (*name person*) with every gift and grace he/she needs to know, love, and serve You in this life and be blessed to share eternal joy with You in Heaven. Fortify (*name person*) and surround him/her with loved ones and friends. Fill this day with joy and laughter. As (*name person*) embarks on a new year of life may he/she be grateful to You for every gift and blessing he/she has received and will receive from

You. Bless him/her and grant him/her a day of happiness and celebration with those he/she loves most.   Amen.

Prayer in Preparation for Visitors
(Ann Fitch)

Lord, visitors will be coming to my home. As I prepare for their coming, help me to not be worried and anxious about how clean or perfectly decorated my house is. Help me to be satisfied with what I have and how my home looks. Be with me as I prepare the food and drink we will share. Bless me with peace in knowing I have done my best to prepare for them and fill me with hope and joy as I await their arrival. I am so excited to have visitors and I am so grateful they want to share their time and love with me. May our visit be blessed and may our love for each other be strengthened and renewed.   Amen.

Prayer Before a Musical Performance
(Ann Fitch)

O Lord, You are the One Who inspires music in the hearts and minds of Your people. Thank You for the gift of music and for giving me the talent to perform it. Grant, O Lord, that as I prepare to perform musically that my thoughts be focused on You and my heart lifted in prayer so that my performance might move the souls of those who hear it and lift their hearts to praise and glorify You. Let my music be a witness to Your majesty and love and proclaim Your glory here on Earth.   Amen.

Prayer Before a Sporting Event
(Ann Fitch)

O Lord, we thank You for the opportunities we have to watch, play, and compete in sports. We pray that a healthy spirit of competition will prevail during the game today. Help each team to be its best, to be conscientious in its play and determined in its effort. Help each player to be alert, dedicated, and confident. Protect the athletes, keeping them safe from injury.

Thank You, Lord, for all those who support these teams in their efforts. Give all spectators a spirit of temperance and generosity. Bless the coaches and officials with wisdom and right judgment. And at the end of play give these teams joy and fulfillment in victory, and in defeat, the courage and determination to improve.   Amen.

Prayer When Going on Retreat
(Ann Fitch)

Lord, I ask You to bless my retreat. May it be a time of refreshment and growth. May I be open to receiving all the blessings You have in store for me. Help me to quiet my heart, still my mind, open up my soul, and be present to You. May I listen with an open mind and hear what I am meant to hear so that I am drawn more deeply into Your love for me.

Calm any fears I have, remove any anxiety I am experiencing, and fill me with the grace to rest in Your presence. As I take time away from my busy life to be with You, renew me, transform me, and fill me with the gifts of Your Spirit. Thank You for hearing my prayers and for allowing me this time to come away with You and enter more fully into Your love.   Amen.

Pilgrimage Prayer
(Ann Fitch)

Heavenly Father, as we set off on pilgrimage be with us leading, guiding, and directing our footsteps. Open our eyes to see You in ourselves and those around us. Open our ears to hear Your voice speaking to us. Open our hearts to ways in which we can love You more each day.

Lord, may this pilgrimage not only be a physical journey but a journey of heart, mind, and soul. May our hearts be moved and challenged, our thoughts focused prayerfully on You, Your will for us, and Your unconditional and infinite love and mercy towards us, and our souls touched and converted so that we are transformed into the faithful followers You wish us to be.

O Holy Spirit, descend upon us and enflame our hearts with the fire of divine love. As we travel pour out Your grace upon us, keep us safe from all harm, and allow us to return home refreshed, renewed and recreated in Your image and likeness.   Amen.

Pilgrim's Prayer
(Ann Fitch)

Lord, You have brought me on this pilgrimage to renew and recreate me in Your image and likeness. Help me to prayerfully focus on You and Your will for me today. Open my heart and allow me to feel Your presence. Open my eyes and show me ways I need to change so that I am a reflection of Your love and presence in the world. Open my mind to new thoughts and new ways of understanding myself and others. Provide experiences on this journey that will help me grow in grace and in the virtues of faith, hope, love, humility, charity, compassion, patience, understanding, wisdom, and joy. Thank You for being with me today converting my heart, blessing my soul, and filling my mind with thoughts of You and Your power and majesty. May I honor and glorify You today and grow in my love for You.   Amen.

Prayer for a New Year
(Ann Fitch)

As this new year approaches, Lord, I look back on all the blessings You have graciously bestowed upon me and those I love and care for. Thank You for all You have provided us with and for all that You will supply in the coming year. You have mercifully and patiently walked with us through the past year. Stay by our side as a loving Shepherd as we place our trust in You and lead us and guide us to that which will bring us peace, joy, and happiness in this coming year. As the old year ends and a new one begins give us the grace and strength we need to be faithful to You and be Your presence in the world. Grant us humble hearts of love and service that wish only to generously share Your kindness. Heal any wounds we carry within us and refresh us with the gifts of Your Holy Spirit. Thank You for the hope and promise of this new year. May it truly be blessed and fruitful. Amen.

Family

Prayer for Love in My Family
(Ann Fitch)

Lord, I present to You everyone in my immediate and extended family. Bless each one of us with Your love and fill us with grace and understanding. Help us to love one another as You love us. May our love for each other be selfless, giving, and constant. May we put the highest and best interests of others before ourselves and treat one another as we wish to be treated. May each member of my family feel loved, nurtured, and treasured and may we as a family be united in Your love. Amen.

Prayer for My Parents
(Ann Fitch)

Thank You, Lord for my parents. They have nurtured me and provided for my needs throughout my life. I am so grateful for their love, attention, guidance, help, understanding, and wisdom. They have sacrificed so much for my good. Help me to be as loving to them as they have been to me. Open my eyes to ways that I can be a blessing to them. Grant that I would be a source of joy for them and that I can honor them as they deserve to be honored. As they age, keep them healthy and strong and surround them with loving friends and family to support them and bring them joy. May Your peace reign in their hearts and Your love always encompass them. Amen.

Prayer for My Mother

(Ann Fitch)

Heavenly Father, I ask You to bless my mother and fill her with Your love. She has cared for me patiently, loved me tenderly, delighted in my successes, and comforted me when I needed her gentle love. She is an amazing woman and I ask You to bless her with every happiness. Send Your Spirit upon her and continue to fill her with strength and grace, peace and wisdom, compassion and understanding. Bless her with good health and send her wonderful friends with whom she can laugh and enjoy life. Lord, my mother has blessed me immeasurably. May I always let her know how much I truly appreciate, love and cherish her. Amen.

Prayer for My Father

(Ann Fitch)

Lord, I ask You to bless my father with the fullness of Your love. Touch his heart and fill him with Your peace. Send forth Your Spirit upon him and bless him with every gift and grace he needs to live his life fully and with joy. Bless him with good health and loving friends with whom he can enjoy life. Help me be aware of and attentive to his needs and love him as he deserves to be loved. May I never cease showing him how much I treasure and respect him. Amen.

Prayer for My Brother(s)

(Ann Fitch)

Lord, I come before You seeking Your blessing upon my brother(s), (*name here*). Touch him/them with Your love and fill him/them with every gift and grace necessary to live his/their life in faithful service to You and Your Church. Bless his/their work. May it be fulfilling and provide financial stability for him/them. Send loving and supportive friends into his/their life. May his/their days be filled with joy, peace, and laughter and when troubles come, may he/they turn to You with faith and trust. May (*name brother(s) here*) always know that I am here for him/them and that I love him/them and only want what will be best for him/them in time and in eternity. Thank You, Lord, for caring for and blessing my brother(s) and for allowing us to love one another in You.   Amen.

Prayer for My Sister(s)
(Ann Fitch)

Lord, I come before You seeking Your blessing upon my sister(s), (*name here*). Touch her/them with Your love and fill her/them with every gift and grace necessary to live her/their life in faithful service to You and Your Church. Bless her/their work. May it be fulfilling and provide for her/their needs. Send loving, understanding, wise, and supportive friends into her/their life with whom she/they can share her/their thoughts, feelings, hopes and dreams. May her/their days be filled with joy, peace, and laughter and when troubles come, may she/they turn to You with faith and trust. May (*name sister(s) here*) always know that I am here for her/them and that I love her/them and only want what will be best for her/them in time and in eternity. Thank You, Lord, for caring for and blessing my sister(s) and for allowing us to love one another in You.   Amen.

Prayer for My Grandmother
(Ann Fitch)

Lord, I ask You to bless my grandmother today and fill her with Your peace. Take her in Your loving arms and place her within Your most Sacred Heart. There let Your Spirit be poured out upon her filling her with wisdom, strength, gentleness, health, hope, and joy. Surround her with loving friends who will laugh with her at life's joys and cry with her during life's sorrows, and who will enjoy all that life has to offer with her. She is such a blessing and I pray that she knows how loved, cherished, and admired she is.   Amen.

Prayer for My Grandfather
(Ann Fitch)

Lord, I pray that You fill my grandfather with every gift and grace he needs today. May he know and feel Your love for him and have peace in his heart. Bless him with caring friends who respect him, enjoy spending time with him, and value his wisdom. Strengthen him, fortify him, and in Your infinite mercy bless him with health, happiness, and hope all the days of his life. May he always be surrounded by the love of his family and know how beloved, respected, and treasured he is. Amen.

Prayer for a Family Gathering
(Ann Fitch)

Ever loving God we thank You for bringing us together as a family. We ask You to bless our time together with happiness, peace, and joy. If there are any differences between us let them be put aside. May we laugh together and celebrate the beauty and uniqueness of each member of our family. Please be with us and help us to be a reflection of Your love for one another. May we enjoy our time together and safely journey back to our homes when our gathering is through. Amen.

Fertility, Infertility & Adoption

Prayer When Undergoing Fertility Treatments
(Ann Fitch)

Lord, we are seeking help from fertility specialists in order to help the process of conception. You know we have fertility issues and we have chosen to undergo treatments in order to enhance our chances of becoming pregnant. Help us to make choices for treatment that are ethical, moral and in line with the teachings of the Church. We wish to be obedient and pray that our choices become a blessing for us and for others. You know our hearts and how deeply we desire to have children. We ask that You bless our bodies and help them to function correctly so that we can achieve a healthy pregnancy and have a healthy child.

We ask You to pour out Your Spirit upon the doctors and nurses who will be treating us and assisting us. Fill them with wisdom, knowledge, understanding, and compassion. May they help us achieve our goal and be supportive of our choices of treatment. May all our efforts be undertaken with the realization that life is a precious gift from You and that if and when You choose to create life that is in Your hands alone. We trust You, we love You, and we wish to be faithful to You as we go through this process. We place ourselves in Your loving hands and ask You to give us strength, courage, peace, hope and the joy that comes from faithfulness to You.   Amen.

Prayer of Acceptance of Infertility
(Ann Fitch)

O gracious and ever-loving God we turn to You in our brokenness. Infertility treatments, tests, pregnancy losses and/or failed attempts have taken their toll on our hearts, minds and relationship. We are exhausted emotionally, depleted financially, and we don't know what the future holds for us. We had hoped to become parents and nurture and love a child, but that has not happened. We are so tired of trying and we are grieving the loss of the dream of being parents to our own biological child. At times anger, resentment, jealousy, envy, hopelessness and feelings of failure are overwhelming. We don't want to let these emotions take over and pray that You bless us with a new sense of hope for the future, understanding, empathy and compassion for one another, and patience, joy and love as we strive to love one another through our pain and grief to acceptance and peace.

You know our hearts. You know our deepest desires. You know what You have in store for us and we trust that You are working all that we have gone through for our good and Your glory. Help us to rebuild our lives with new dreams. If we are to parent, lead us to how we are to do that and if not give us peace in our hearts with being a childless couple. Renew us, strengthen us, and help us to face the future together, united in love, with joyful expectation. You have so much in store for us and we are open to You leading us and guiding us each day to that future. Amen.

Prayer for Birthmothers
(Ann Fitch)

O Lord of life and love we ask You to bless all birthmothers today. Strengthen them and fortify them and fill them with the courage and clarity they need to make the decision to place their beloved children in adoptive homes. Be with them as they choose families to raise their precious children. Fill their minds with peace in knowing they have made the best and most loving choice for themselves and their children. Console and comfort them when their hearts are heavy with grief. Surround them with loving family and friends who are supportive, understanding, compassionate, and wise who will help them move forward in a positive ways with their lives working towards achieving their goals.

Give them the strength to go through labor and delivery and lovingly place their children when the time for relinquishment comes. Wipe away their tears of sorrow and heal their broken hearts when they miss the children they bore. Reassure them that their beloved children are being cared for, nurtured and loved in happy, healthy homes among people who adore and cherish them.

May they know how grateful their chosen adoptive families are for their selflessness and for choosing them as families for their children. And Lord, we pray a special blessing on all birthmothers on birthdays, holidays, and especially Mother's Day. May they have peace in their hearts, joy in knowing their children are adored and being brought up in loving, safe, and nurturing environments, with all the happiness that can be had in life. Amen.

Prayer While Waiting to be Chosen to Adopt
(Ann Fitch)

Mary, my Mother, I hope one day to love a child as you loved Jesus. It is difficult to trust and be patient as I wait to be chosen as an adoptive parent. I ask you to place my desire to be a parent in your Son's Sacred Heart. Ask Him to send His Spirit upon me and fill me with hope, joy, and love as I wait to be picked.

Dearest Mother, ask your Son to bless all birthparents who are lovingly choosing families for their babies. May they be filled with peace and have complete trust in whomever they choose to raise their children. May they be blessed with the conviction that adoption is the best choice for them and have the courage and strength they need to carry through on their decision to place their babies.

Heavenly Father, I thank You for the gift of life. I ask You to bless all pregnant women with healthy, safe pregnancies and deliveries. I ask a special blessing upon birthparents as they prepare to place their babies. May they feel Your love and be at peace with their decision. Bless their extended family members and friends with understanding and help them to be a source of love and support.

Thank You, Lord, for pouring out Your love on all who are involved in the adoption process. May each one of us do what is most pleasing to You and find joy and fulfillment in that. Amen.

Prayer Once Chosen to Adopt
(Ann Fitch)

Lord, Jesus, I ask for the ability to love any birthparents you bring into my life as if I am loving You. May I give freely to them without counting the cost. Give me the grace to trust them to carry through with their promise to place their baby(ies) and walk fearlessly through the adoption process. If we are to meet, may I know in my heart what to say and do so that I am a blessing to them just as they are to me.

Dearest Mother, Mary, when the time comes for delivery and placement may these birthparents be blessed with courage, peace, and hope-filled surrender. As they grieve the loss of their child(ren) wrap them in your loving arms and carry them to the Father for His blessing and love. Ask Him to bless them with the conviction that they are making the best choice for themselves and their child(ren) and to fill them with overwhelming peace.

Lord, Jesus, I ask You to fill me with patience, peace, and understanding as I walk through the birth and placement process. May I trust You completely and surrender all my fears to You. Bless all involved in this adoption with Your courage, strength, and joy. May we be blessings to one another in You, and be forever grateful for the gift of one another. Thank You, Lord. Amen.

Prayer When an Adoption Attempt Fails
(Ann Fitch)

Lord, we are broken hearted and seeking Your help and guidance. The birthmother of the child we had been chosen to adopt and begun to love as our own changed her mind and will not be placing her baby with us. She has decided to parent him/her. Our hearts are shattered and we feel betrayed and taken advantage of. To walk away from this situation is incredibly hard because we have been so emotionally invested. Help us to let go and find peace, comfort and healing. Surround us with loving, compassionate and wise friends and family who will console us as we grieve the loss of this child. We forgive this young mother for hurting us and pray that You bless her and her baby with everything they need. May they be cared for, nurtured by, and supported in every way by their loved ones. Bless them with a future full of promise, hope, and goodness and bring them every happiness. Help us to move forward trusting that in Your goodness and in Your time we will become adoptive parents. Amen.

Prayer of Thanksgiving for an Adoption Finalization
(Ann Fitch)

Heavenly Father, we wish to thank You for bringing our sweet child (*name child*) into our lives. Loving, cherishing and nurturing him/her is even more wonderful than we had dreamed of or hoped for. (*Name child*) is the light of our lives and has brought us untold joy. We are so grateful that his/her birthparents lovingly and selflessly chose us to adopt him/her. We ask You to bless them and their families and keep them in Your tender care. Thank You for allowing this adoption to be finalized. We cannot convey in words the depth of our gratitude. May we be the best parents we can be for (*name child*) and always love him/her completely and unconditionally. Amen.

Home & Pets

Prayer When Buying a Home
(Ann Fitch)

Lord, I am in need of finding a new home. Open the door to the perfect place for me. Let it be in a safe neighborhood with good schools and kind neighbors. May it be convenient to shopping and in close proximity to my work place. I ask that it be clean, have all the space and amenities I need, and that it be reasonably priced so that I can easily afford it. Lord, I pray that all inspections be done quickly, that any loans and/or contracts be processed without complications, that there be no delays in closing, and that taking possession of this new property is easy and smooth. Thank You, Lord for leading me and guiding me to the perfect home. Amen.

House Consecration
(Ann Fitch)

Lord Jesus Christ, we consecrate this house to Your Sacred Heart and to the Immaculate Heart of Your beloved Mother. May You reign as King and Queen of this household. In Your kindness O Lord, protect our home and keep it safe from fire, flood, earthquakes, tornadoes, and theft. Bless all who live and visit here. Fill each one with the gifts of Your Spirit so that they may be faithful to You in all they say and do. Bless this home profoundly. May it be a place of peace where love abounds and virtue and grace increase. O Sacred and Immaculate Hearts watch over us, preserve us from danger, and keep us in Your tender care. Amen.

Prayer When Selling a Property
(Ann Fitch)

Heavenly Father, we are in need of selling our property. Make clear to us any changes that need to be made to the property to make it appealing to a buyer. Guide us by Your Spirit to the right agent to help us move smoothly through the selling process. May that agent be wise, knowledgeable, trustworthy, and committed to handling our listing and getting our property sold and closed. Lord, Jesus Christ You know exactly who is going to buy our property. In Your perfect timing please bring that buyer to us. May they be pre-approved for a loan, honest, eager, compliant, and willing to close in as little time as possible. Lord, we trust in You to bring about this sale and see it through to conclusion. Amen.

Blessing for a Pet
(Ann Fitch)

Blessed are You, Lord God, creator of all living creatures. You created all animals in Your love for us. I ask you to bless this pet with health and happiness all of its days. May it be a good companion, always love and bring joy, and may it live a long, loved life. May I always thank You for the gift of this animal and praise You in all You have created. Amen.

Prayer to St. Francis to Bless a Pet
(Ann Fitch)

Humble St. Francis, lover of all creatures, bless (*name pet*) with your love and affection. In your kindness present him/her to the Holy Trinity and ask Their heavenly blessing upon him/her. Pray that (*name pet*) lives a long, happy, healthy life and that he/she is a joy and comfort to me always.   Amen.

Prayer When Choosing a Pet
(Ann Fitch)

Lord, as we set out to choose a new pet to add to our family we ask that You pour out Your Spirit upon us and fill us with the grace we need to choose wisely and lovingly. Bless our new pet with a sweet, docile temperament and a playful spirit.   May it give and receive love readily and be a joy to love and care for. As it comes into our home allow it to adjust easily to its new environment. Above all, Lord, bless our new pet with a long, happy, healthy life.   Amen.

Prayer for a Sick Pet
(Ann Fitch)

Lord, in Your goodness and love You have charged us with the care of our pet (*name pet*) who is ill. We trust You to guide us in providing the best possible care for (*name pet*) and that You will keep (*name pet*) in Your tender care. Help us to be sensitive to our pet's needs. Through us, comfort (*name pet*) and ease any fears we may have because of this illness. As our vet tends to (*name pet*) guide his/her hands and mind so that he/she can quickly assess what is wrong and do all that is necessary to restore (*name pet*) to full health. We ask You to keep (*name pet*) as free from pain as possible. If it is Your will, Lord, we pray for a full recovery, but if long-term care is needed we ask for the ability to provide it and for the skill and competence we will need to be the best caretakers we can be. Amen.

Prayer for a Lost Pet
(Ann Fitch)

Dear Jesus, You Who were once lost and then found, I come to You seeking Your assistance in finding my beloved and lost pet. Please keep my pet (*name pet*) from all harm. Protect (*name pet*) from cars, wild animals, or anyone who would seek to do him/her harm. Lead me to where I am to look so that I may find (*name pet*) safe and sound. I trust in You, sweet Jesus, to reunite us so that we can continue loving one another for many years to come. Thank You for caring for us and helping me in my search for (*name pet*). Amen.

Prayer When a Pet is Nearing Death
(Ann Fitch)

Lord Jesus, our beloved pet (*name pet*) is in the last phase of his/her life. (*Name pet*) has been a faithful and loving companion for many years and we pray that as he/she nears death that we will be able to give him/her the care and attention he/she needs to leave this life happy and at peace. (*Name pet*) has enriched our lives in so many ways. We thank You for allowing us to share so much time together. Touch our hearts and minds as we anticipate (*name pet*) passing from this life. May we lean on You for strength and trust You to provide us the comfort we will need when (*name pet*) is no longer with us. We hope that one day we might be reunited with (*name pet*) in Your heavenly kingdom. Amen.

Prayer When a Pet Must be Euthanized
(Ann Fitch)

Lord, You know what agony our hearts are in. We turn to You for guidance, wisdom and understanding. Our beloved pet (*name pet*) is sick and we know we must make the choice to have (*name pet*) euthanized. We don't want to, but we also do not want (*name pet*) to suffer needlessly. It is hard to make the decision to take his/her life. (*Name pet*) is so precious to us and has been a faithful and loving companion for such a long time. Lord, help us realize that we are doing the loving and humane thing by ending his/her life and allowing (*name pet*) to transition from this life into the next peacefully and without discomfort. Receive (*name pet*) into Your loving arms. May we one day be reunited with him/her and spend eternity joyfully together. Amen.

Prayer After the Loss of a Pet
(Ann Fitch)

Dear Lord, my beloved pet (*name pet*) has died and his/her death has left a void in my life and in my heart. I grieve for (*name pet*) even though I trust that he/she is in Your tender care. (*Name pet*) was a faithful companion, a source of love and joy, and he/she enriched my life in countless ways. I give You my grief and ask You to use it to bless others who are in need of Your love and mercy. Grant me the grace and strength I need to cope with his/her death. Console me and comfort me when I am missing him/her. I thank You for all the time I was blessed to share with (*name pet*) and I pray and hope that I might be reunited with him/her in Your heavenly kingdom.   Amen.

Illness

Prayer for Someone Who is Sick
(Ann Fitch)

Lord, I know You love everyone and I believe You wish health and wholeness for all. Resting in this knowledge I ask You to bring healing to (*name person*) who is not well. Stay by his/her side and comfort him/her. Keep (*name person*) as free from pain and discomfort as possible. Bless him/her and renew his/her strength and grant him/her the patience he/she needs to endure this illness with dignity and grace. Remove any fears or concerns he/she has about this illness. Fill (*name person*) and his/her family with peace and trust in Your infinite goodness. Guide the doctors who are attending to his/her care. Grant them the wisdom and knowledge they need to treat him/her effectively. May he/she recover and be restored to fullness of health. I ask this in Your holy Name.   Amen.

Prayer for a Sick Child
(Ann Fitch)

Heavenly Father, (*name child*) is ill. I lift him/her up to You for healing. You are the Doctor of all doctors. Through the power of Your Holy Spirit heal him/her. Lord, I ask You to guide the physicians attending to (*name child*) and grant them the wisdom they need to restore him/her to fullness of health. Fill the attending nurses with compassion. May they be immediately aware of his/her every need and be gentle and understanding as they assist his/her parents.

I pray that You give this child's parents strength and courage. Comfort their souls and fill their hearts with peace and joy as they care for (*name child*). Bless them and help them to place all their trust in Your merciful love. I ask You to work a wondrous miracle in this family, Lord.   Amen.

Prayer When Hospitalized
(Ann Fitch)

Lord, we ask You to bless (*name person*) with Your healing love. As he/she is hospitalized fill him/her with courage, strength, patience and peace. If he/she is in pain, take the merit of that pain, join it to Yours, and use it for the benefit of the souls in most need of Your love and mercy.

During (*name person's*) hospital stay grant that the doctors and nurses treating him/her will have the knowledge and expertise needed to quickly restore him/her to health without complications. We thank You, the Divine Physician, for Your constant presence and care and trust that You will work all together for (*name person's*) good.   Amen.

Prayer for Someone in the Hospital
(Ann Fitch)

Lord of all power (*name person*) is hurting. He/she is in the hospital and his/her body is not functioning as it should. We ask You to bless (*name person*) with wise doctors and compassionate nurses who can diagnose what is wrong and treat him/her effectively. As (*name person*) walks through this illness ease his/her suffering and bless him/her with Your peace.

Give (*name person*) patience, courage, strength, hope, and joy. When (*name person*) needs to rest allow him/her to rest peacefully and without disruption. When (*name person*) needs comfort and love may friends and family be there to provide that for him/her. If it is Your divine will for (*name person*) to be healed let him/her be quickly restored to health and wholeness. Lord, we do not know Your timing but we trust that You have heard our prayer and will answer us according to Your holy will. Amen.

Prayer When Facing Medical Testing
(Ann Fitch)

Lord, trusting in You and Your infinite goodness I turn to You and offer You every fear, anxiety, concern, and feeling of distress that I am experiencing or will experience as I face medical testing, result wait times, and actual results of the tests for Your glory and the salvation of the souls in most need of Your mercy. I believe that You will grant me Your peace which surpasses all understanding and that You will fill me with serenity. Grant me the grace and strength to face whatever I must in the way of illness and guide me to the best doctors for any treatments I must undergo. I ask You to bless my loved ones with peace and to fill them with trust in You. Together may we go through this time of testing free from anxiety and with thanksgiving in our hearts for the gifts and graces You will bestow upon us. Amen.

Prayer for Someone Before Surgery
(Ann Fitch)

Gracious Father, give (*name person*) courage and strength as he/she faces surgery. Be with him/her in Your infinite goodness. Give the surgeon a steady hand and the necessary knowledge and support to do his/her work with ease and precision. Give (*name person's*) family the assurance that You are with them all, protecting and loving them. As they wait grant them peace and tranquility. Into Your almighty hands we entrust (*name person's*) well-being.   Amen.

Prayer for Someone After Surgery
(Ann Fitch)

O merciful Father in Heaven, thank You for being with (*name person*) while he/she was in surgery. Thank You for blessing the surgeon with the skill and knowledge needed to do his/her work and for safely bringing (*name person*) through this operation. O gracious Father, bring healing to (*name person*) and bless him/her with the best care possible as he/she recovers. Continue to bless him/her with your tender care. Grant him/her patience during his/her recuperation, help him/her grow in strength each day, and bring him/her to full recovery quickly, without any setbacks.   Amen.

Prayer for Someone with Cancer
(Ann Fitch)

Lord, You are the Divine Healer, and I turn to You in prayer for (*name person*) who is sick with cancer. I ask You to bless him/her with Your healing love and if it is Your will to bring his/her cancer into remission or heal him/her of it completely. Pour out Your Spirit upon (*name person*) and fill him/her with grace, courage, strength, patience, and hope. As (*name person*) goes through any form or treatment - chemotherapy, radiation, targeted therapy, stem cell transplant or surgery – be with him/her and bless him/her with the physical strength and stamina he/she needs. Bless (*name person*) with a positive outlook and surround him/her with supportive, loving,

Ann Fitch

compassionate and empathetic loved ones. Let (*name person*) be as free from sadness and pain as possible. Please bless (*name person*) with courage when he/she is afraid, comfort when he/she is upset, and hope-filled perseverance when things seem bleak. May (*name person*) be strong in You, have inner peace, and be blessed with all the love and support he/she needs.   Amen.

Prayer for Someone with Heart Disease
(Ann Fitch)

   All powerful and ever loving God, I trust You completely and believe that You are with (*name person*) whose heart is not functioning correctly and is in need of healing. I ask You to touch his/her heart especially in the areas afflicted with illness. Heal his/her blood vessels, veins, valves and arteries so that blood can flow through them properly. Heal any infection in the nerves, muscles, and tissues in and around his/her heart. If (*name person*) is in pain please ease his/her suffering. Keep his/her family close to provide comfort and support. Ease any fears (*name person*) or his/her family members have and bless them all with Your peace. Inspire the doctors and nurses who will be caring for (*name person*) with the wisdom and knowledge they need to treat him/her effectively and aide in restoring him/her to health. If surgery is needed, please guide the surgeon's hands and allow (*name person*) to recover without complications. Thank You for being with (*name person*) and blessing him/her with Your healing touch. May his/her heart be healthier, stronger and beat more steadily for many years to come.   Amen.

Prayer for those Affected by HIV & AIDS
(Ann Fitch)

   God of all creation we turn to You today in prayer for all those who are affected by and afflicted with HIV and AIDS. Bless them, strengthen them, fortify them, and fill them with Your peace. Comfort the suffering, the lonely, and depressed. Give hope to the hopeless and bless those who have lost their sense of joy. Console

98

those who have lost loved ones and are grieving, especially those who are orphaned or alone. Heal the hearts of those who have been discriminated against, faced rejection, been misunderstood or judged, or dealt with loss of livelihood. Take them in Your loving arms and fill them to overflowing with Your unconditional love and acceptance.

In Your infinite mercy be with those who will die from HIV or complications due to AIDS today. May they be surrounded by loved ones and be treated with dignity and respect as they leave this life and enter into eternal life. Pour out Your Spirit upon all HIV and AIDS caregivers. Fill them with compassion, understanding, patience, and love. May they be profoundly blessed as they tend to those in their care. Inspire the researchers and doctors who are working towards finding effective treatments for HIV and AIDS and give them the knowledge and wisdom they need to find a cure. May their work prove fruitful and bring about the eradication of HIV & AIDS. Amen.

Prayer for Someone Diagnosed with HIV
(Ann Fitch)

Lord, (*name person*) has been diagnosed with HIV and I am turning to You in prayer for him/her. I know this is not a life sentence but his/her world has flipped upside down and (*name person*) needs You to help calm his/her spirit and so he/she is able to take in all the information and treatment options that are available to him/her. As (*name person*) shares the news that he/she has tested positive for HIV with loved ones and friends I pray that they be understanding, compassionate and supportive of (*name person*).

As (*name person*) seeks treatment direct his/her doctors to the best treatment options for him/her. Help them to know exactly how to treat (*name person*) so that he/she stays stable and does not develop AIDS. (*Name person*) is scared and I ask You to bless him/her with Your peace and to remove his/her fear and replace it with courage and strength.

Lord, I pray that (*name person*) does not see himself/herself as his/her status, HIV positive, but as a person who is unconditionally loved and accepted by You and who is living with HIV. I know You have a plan for his/her life. May (*name person*) allow that plan to unfold in a way that gives honor and glory to You. I believe that You are with (*name person*). I trust You completely and I place him/her in Your hands. Amen.

Prayer of One Living with HIV or AIDS
(Ann Fitch)

Ever loving and merciful God, I turn to You asking You to bless me with health, courage and strength. When I am rejected or not treated with dignity, compassion or understanding I ask for the grace to quickly forgive from my heart so that I do not become angry, bitter, or resentful. I give You my loved ones and ask You to touch their hearts. I know they are worried and concerned about me and I pray that You turn their anxiety to trust in You.

Lord, I believe that You are holding me safe within Your arms and blessing me with Your peace. Be with me as I move forward living with this illness. Direct me and guide me to the best treatment options for me. Provide ways for me to support my loved ones and myself and to be able to afford treatment. I pray for encouragement and understanding from those around me. May I be lifted up in prayer by those who love me and filled to overflowing with every gift and grace I need to live with this illness. Thank You for accepting me and loving me unconditionally. Thank You for always being with me, blessing me and strengthening me. May I live my life with joy and hope, serving You, and fulfilling Your will for me. Amen.

Prayer for Someone Who Has Had a Stroke
(Ann Fitch)

Lord, I come to You seeking Your blessing upon (*name person*) who has had a stroke. I pray that (*name person*) will not have any paralysis, loss of muscle control or spasticity, slurred speech, speaking difficulties or loss of speech, mental confusion or dizziness, eye damage, or difficulty swallowing. If (*name person*) must undergo surgery I pray that the surgeon is able to bring him/her relief and mitigate damage to his/her brain. Lord, if (*name person*) must rely upon others for his/her basic care I pray that he/she be patient, kind, loving and willing to graciously accept the help of others. If he/she must go through rehabilitation to recover and become independent and self-sufficient grant him/her the strength, courage, fortitude, and hope he/she needs to go through the recovery process. Please bless (*name person*) profoundly and bring him/her to the best and healthiest outcome possible. Amen.

Prayer of a Person with Dementia
(Ann Fitch)

Lord help me face this ever changing disease with grace and dignity and in a way that doesn't burden and upset others. I pray that I can make arrangements for my continued care and welfare and be content with who I have chosen to be responsible for decision making when I no longer can make decisions for myself. There are so many things to consider. Bless me with independence for as long as possible and lead me to medical help that will provide care that prolongs the quality of my life and keeps me vital, involved and capable of caring for myself. When and if the time comes that I can no longer remain at home caring for myself, send loving caregivers into my life who will treat me with gentleness, kindness, dignity, and respect.

As my mind and body begin to give way to the later stages of dementia, help me to be patient and compassionate towards those who are caring for me. Grace me with courage and tenacity and remove any fears I have. Lord, I trust in You and know that You will be with me every moment of every day. Allow me to always feel Your presence and rest in Your comforting love. I especially ask for a grateful heart for every moment I can recognize those I love and recall the experiences of my life. And, I pray that You bless me with humble acceptance of this disease and its many stages. Allow me to live as full a life as possible and grant that those I love not suffer because of me and my needs. Instead, draw us closer together as a family and bless our love for one another.   Amen.

Prayer of a Caregiver of Someone with Dementia
(Ann Fitch)

Lord I come to You today asking You to touch my heart which is hurting because each day (*name person*) slips a little further away due to dementia. I miss the relationship we once had but understand we must move forward and that I must accept the changes in our relationship. At times my heart pines for who (*name person*) once was but I am grateful for every moment of lucidity we have together. Let me not grow weary of explaining who I am or why I am caring for him/her.

Lord, keep me from getting angry at this illness or frustrated because (*name person*) has no idea who I am or cannot find words to express his/her thoughts and needs. I understand he/she is trapped inside this illness and that he/she cannot control how it is affecting him/her. Do not let me lament over what (*name person*) can no longer do but be grateful for what he/she can still do. I beg You to pour out Your Spirit upon me and fill me with patience, gentleness, kindness, compassion, strength, hope, and joy.

Lord, instead of me getting angry, bless me with the ability to laugh at life and it's twists and turns and find reasons to have joy each day I get to spend with (*name person*). When (*name person*) is agitated, upset or being difficult help me to remember his/her emotions and behaviors are being distorted by his/her illness. May I be willing, compassionate and understanding when (*name person*) is completely dependent upon me to care for, feed, change, and bathe him/her. No matter what is happening or needs to be done may I always treat (*name person*) with dignity and respect.

Help me to trust in You, Lord, and not be anxious or worried about what the future holds for (*name person*). Fill me with peace in knowing that I am doing my best to care for him/her. I believe You are holding (*name person*) in Your arms and that You are working everything together for his/her good and Your glory. Continue to bless our time together, fill us with Your grace, and in spite of this disease bring us closer together in Your love.   Amen.

Prayer for a Chronically Ill Spouse
(Ann Fitch)

Most loving God, my husband/wife, (*name spouse*), is living with chronic illness and struggling to regain his/her health. I see a decline in his/her ability to function normally and I try to encourage him/her to patiently strive for the strength to overcome the obstacles he/she is facing. There are moments when I am frustrated and impatient and I am not as gentle or kind as I should be. May (*name spouse*) not suffer at my hands because of my inability to be compassionate and understanding. Help me to place his/her needs before my own and live out my promise to care for him/her in good times or bad, in sickness and in health. Bless me with a heart that is selfless and giving, dedicated and steadfast. And, Lord, if it is Your holy will, restore (*name spouse*) to complete health. If it is not, then grant us the grace and courage to face this illness united with You for Your honor and glory and for the salvation of souls.   Amen.

Prayer When Terminally Ill
(Ann Fitch)

O my Lord and my God, I turn to You Who are all-loving and all-gracious. I know my life is coming to an end and I ask for the ability to forgive anyone who has hurt me in any way during my life. I want to let go of any anger, bitterness or resentment I have. I also ask that You forgive me for any times I have turned away from You or harmed others. Bless me with peace as I approach my death. Fill me with renewed hope in the resurrection and trust that You will carry me to eternal peace and joy with You.

Lord, I ask a special blessing of comfort on those I love and whom I leave behind. Give them the grace and strength they need to let me leave this life and enter into eternal union with You. Fill them with acceptance and peace. In their grief, comfort them and bless them with the conviction that when I am graced to enter into Your heavenly kingdom that I will be interceding for them before Your eternal throne.

Thank You for always loving me, caring for me, blessing me, supplying my every need, and for the great gift of salvation. I love You, Lord. And, I am ready to come home to You. Amen.

Prayer When Watching Someone Suffer
(Ann Fitch)

Ever loving and gracious God, (*name person*) is suffering and my heart breaks for him/ her. It is so hard to watch as he/she struggles. Bless me with patience, courage, strength, and above all kindness and gentleness. I know that You are blessing (*name person*) in the midst of his/her suffering but I am distressed when I think of all he/she is enduring. Please use the grace of his/her suffering to bless those who are in need of Your love and compassion.

Lord, help me to keep my eyes on You and be Your presence for (*name person*). When I feel overwhelmed touch my heart and fill me with Your peace. When I am afraid help me to trust more fully in You. I know You are carrying me in Your tender arms and that You are always with me, loving me. Thank You for sustaining me thus far and for filling me with compassion for (*name person*). Bless us both and fill us with every gift and grace we need to persevere. Amen.

Prayer for Someone with an Eating Disorder
(Ann Fitch)

Heavenly Father, I come before You on behalf of (*name person*) who is struggling with an eating disorder. I ask You to pour out Your Spirit upon (*name person*) and fill him/her with the grace and strength he/she needs to overcome this disorder. Open his/her eyes to see how harmful what he/she is doing is to his/her body. Grant that (*name person*) is convicted of the need to eat in a healthy way. Help (*name person*) to see food as a means of fuel for his/her body and necessary to keep his/her body healthy and strong.

Please help (*name person*) to see himself/herself as the beautiful person he/she is not in a distorted way. Guide any doctors or therapists who are helping (*name person*). May they be truly wise and capable of helping (*name person*) change for the better and find healing, health, and wholeness. May I be a help to (*name person*) in whatever ways I can. I pray he/she realizes how much I love him/her and that I am here anytime he/she needs a listening ear or a hug of comfort. Thank You for blessing (*name person*) and keeping him/her in Your tender care. Amen.

Prayer for the Mentally Ill
(Ann Fitch)

Lord, Jesus, touch those afflicted with mental illness with Your healing love. Give them the courage and strength to face their illness through the power of Your Holy Spirit. Bestow upon them the grace to bear their cross in a way that brings honor and glory to Our Father. If it is Your Divine Will, heal them of their affliction.

St. Benedict Joseph Labre and St. Dymphna, patron saints of the mentally ill, intercede before the throne of God on behalf of all those who suffer in mind and heart, especially, (*name person*). Present all the mentally ill lovingly to God and ask Him to bless each one with peace. In Jesus' Name we pray. Amen.

Prayer of the Mentally Ill
(Ann Fitch)

Lord Jesus, I offer You my mental illness and ask You to bless me with the courage and strength I need to endure it patiently with grace. Send Your Holy Spirit upon me and grant me clarity of mind so that I do not disparage myself for being ill, but accept my illness and seek appropriate treatment. Lord, help me to not be a burden to those who love and care for me. May we be patient with one another and treat one another with respect. If it is Your will, Lord, take this cross from me and bring me complete healing. Amen.

Prayer Against Depression
(St. Ignatius Loyola)

O Christ Jesus when all is darkness and we feel our weakness and helplessness, give us the sense of Your presence, Your love and Your strength. Help us to have perfect trust in Your protecting love and strengthening power, so that nothing may frighten or worry us, for, living close to You, we shall see Your hand, Your purpose, Your will through all things. Amen.

Prayer When Depressed
(Ann Fitch)

Lord, I am depressed, without joy, without hope, anxious and struggling to find peace and rest for my weary heart, mind and soul. I turn to You and ask if it is Your will that You take away this heavy burden of depression and anxiety. If not, I ask that You grant me the grace to courageously face it with You. Hold me close, Lord. Wipe away my tears, calm my fears, and lead me to a place of peace in You. I yearn to feel Your light again, to feel true joy. Envelop me in Your love and heal me of my pain. I no longer want to feel lonely, unworthy, and hopeless. Bless me with self-acceptance, loving friends and family who understand and support me, and the knowledge that I am Your beloved and precious to You. Help me to reach out to others when needed and never let me feel so alone that I contemplate harming myself. Let me feel Your presence with me today and allow me to rest in the gentle assurance of Your love.   Amen.

Prayer for Someone Who is Depressed
(Ann Fitch)

Lord, (*name person*) is depressed and feeling hopeless. He/she is struggling to find some sense of peace. I ask You to bless (*name person*) with rest for his/her weary heart, mind, and soul. If it is Your will I ask You to lift this darkness of depression and anxiety from (*name person*). If it is not Your will for (*name person*), grant him/her the grace and strength to bear this cross with patience and courage. Guide (*name person*) to wise doctors and/or therapists who will help him/her deal successfully with his/her depression on a daily basis. I pray that (*name person*) will reach out to family and friends when in need of understanding and support and never do anything to harm himself/herself.

May I always be wise, understanding and helpful to (*name person*). May Your Spirit guide me in all the ways I can be a source of comfort and support for him/her. Lord, let (*name person*) feel Your presence with him/her today and allow him/her to feel the gentle reassurance of Your merciful love. Strengthen him/her. Hold (*name person*) in Your loving arms and calm his/her fears. Fill (*name person*) with self-acceptance, self-love, tranquility, hope and joy. I know You love (*name person*) more than I can even imagine and that You want him/her to be happy, healthy, and at peace. I trust that You are taking care of (*name person*) and that You will be with him/her in his/her darkest moments blessing him/her with Your light and peace. Thank You, for caring for (*name person*) and blessing him/her with every gift and grace he/she needs today.   Amen.

Prayer for Someone with Social Anxiety
(Ann Fitch)

Lord, I see how hard any kind of social interaction is for (*name person*) and I pray that You bless him/her with a peaceful, calm and tranquil heart, mind and body. Take away his/her fears. Help (*name person*) to not feel judged or scrutinized by others. Bless him/her with the ability to partake in conversations and interact with others without feeling embarrassed or distressed. You are the Divine Healer and I ask for healing for (*name person*). Bless him/her with freedom, confidence, and self-acceptance. Fill him/her with the courage, grace and strength he/she needs to get through the day and keep him/her close to Your Sacred Heart. Amen.

Prayer of Someone with Social Anxiety
(Ann Fitch)

Lord, I feel overly anxious, uncertain and hesitant about interacting with others. Please take away my fears and bless me with a calm and peaceful heart, mind and body. Help me to not feel as if everyone is judging, evaluating, or thinking badly of me. I want to be open, friendly and sociable. Please take away my feelings of apprehension and bless me with the ability to share my thoughts with others without questioning myself or fearing I will say something wrong. When I feel embarrassed or humiliated take me in Your loving arms and comfort me. I no longer want to live my life in extreme fear of social interactions and I give You permission to move within my heart and mind blessing me and healing me.

Lord, bless me with the ability to perceive myself as lovable, accepted, capable, and intelligent. I know and believe that You love and accept me as I am and that I can always talk to You without being judged or rejected. I thank You for always being with me, strengthening me and blessing me with Your love and grace. Send loving, understanding and compassionate people into my life with whom I can fearlessly be myself and bless me with inner peace and self-confidence. Amen.

Prayer for Someone Who Self-Harms
(Ann Fitch)

Lord, I come before You asking for the grace to be wise, understanding, compassionate and empathetic with (*name person*) who is harming himself/herself. I want to be a means of support for him/her and I hope to be a person he/she can trust with his/her deepest thoughts and feelings. Help me to listen lovingly and be available whenever he/she needs me. Instead of seeking relief through self-harm let (*name person*) feel the relief that comes from knowing he/she is loved by You and being held in Your loving arms. He/she is bright, creative, and talented. Help him/her to recognize the things that cause him/her to self-harm and turn to appropriate coping skills in order to be free of this addiction. Bless (*name person*) with self-control, self-acceptance, courage and strength. Help him/her express himself/herself in healthy ways and to stop giving in to the urge to self-harm. Thank You for blessing (*name person*) and for filling him/her with Your love and grace, peace and hope. Amen.

Prayer to Stop Harming Oneself
(Ann Fitch)

Heavenly Father, I turn to You asking for the grace and strength to stop harming myself. At times I feel out of control and the urge to inflict pain on myself is overwhelming. In those moments when I am tempted to hurt myself grant me the courage and strength to choose to love myself and do something that is healthy and life-giving instead of destructive. In those moments fill me with self-acceptance and self-love and let me feel Your love for me. Send people into my life who will help me be freed from this addiction. Open my heart and give me the courage I need to share my deepest feelings and thoughts, especially when I have the urge to hurt myself so that with their help and Your grace I can overcome the urges and find relief in other ways. Thank You, Lord for Your love and for blessing me with health, peace, and hope. Amen.

Prayer for Someone Who is Suicidal
(Ann Fitch)

Lord, I come before You seeking help for (*name person*) who is depressed and suicidal. I ask You to give him/her the understanding that he/she has a future that is blessed and wonderful, filled with possibility. I truly care for (*name person*) and I know he/she is in a very dark place and is struggling to see any good reason to continue on with his/her life. Give me the wisdom I need to help him/her and the words to break through his/her darkness and bring relief to him/her. Guide me in what I can do to help him/her realize that taking his/her life is not the answer to his/her problems.

Bless (*name person*) with the courage to face today and the inner strength to overcome his/her thoughts of suicide. Bless him/her with moments of peace and joy today so that he/she experiences new hope for the future. Touch his/her heart and mind with the life-giving power of the Holy Spirit. Instill in (*name person*) a new will to live, to fight the good fight, to accept that life can be beautiful and peaceful. Grant him/her the courage to reach out for help when he/she is feeling overwhelmed and is tempted to end his/her life. I know You love and care for (*name person*) more than I ever could and I trust that You will continue to fill him/her with the fullness of Your love and assure him/her that You are always there for him/her. Thank You for Your love and help. Amen.

Life, Abortion & the Unborn

Prayer for Life's Journey

May God the Father who created you, guide your footsteps, may God the Son who redeemed you, share your journey, may God the Holy Spirit who sanctifies you, lead you on life's pilgrimage, and may the blessing of God, Father, Son and Holy Spirit be with you wherever you may go. Amen.

Prayer for Life
(Ann Fitch)

O God, our Creator, all life is in Your hands from conception until natural death. Help us to cherish our children, especially the yet to be born and to reverence the awesome privilege we have in sharing in the lives of the handicapped and elderly. May all people live fully and die a natural death with dignity surrounded by loved ones. Bless all who tend to the care of and defend the rights of the unborn, the handicapped, and the aged. Enlighten and be merciful toward those who fail to love and allow them to live a dignified life. Let personal freedom be tempered by responsibility, integrity, and morality. May we recognize the beauty and uniqueness of every individual and fight for each person to have a life of liberty and happiness. Amen.

Prayer for the Unborn
(Ann Fitch)

Lord we know that every child is a gift of love from You, a wondrous miracle of life. Bless every mother with profound love for and an intense need to protect her unborn child. Pour out Your grace upon each pregnant woman and fill her to overflowing with joy. We ask You to embrace any woman considering abortion and fill her with peace in carrying her baby full term. May any pregnant woman in turmoil and confusion choose life for her child and find peace and hope in You. Remove any fears or concerns that pregnant women might have and fill them with Your comfort and reassurance. Lord, send Your angels to protect each unborn child and in Your infinite power surround every womb and bring each baby to a safe, healthy delivery. Amen.

Prayer to End Abortion
(Ann Fitch)

Heavenly Father, I come before You asking You to touch the hearts of any women who are contemplating abortion. Through the power of the Holy Spirit enlighten their minds so that they realize they are carrying a precious life inside them that they need to protect, nurture and cherish.

Lord, Jesus, in Your infinite mercy, fill the hearts of any women seeking an abortion with unconditional and overwhelming love for their children. Open their eyes to see their babies as they are, living children who deserve to be born and cared for. Soften the hearts of those around them. May they encourage these mothers to have their babies and provide them with the emotional, spiritual, and financial support they need to provide and care for their children both before and after they are born.

O Blessed Virgin Mary, our Mother, intercede for any women contemplating abortion and their babies. Ask the Lord to fill them with every gift and grace. Pray that they have the courage and strength to carry their infants to full term and either parent or place them in loving homes. Ask that God bless these women with peace and that He send loving, encouraging, and helpful people into their lives who will support and love them in every way.

O loving Mother, we also ask your intercession for all abortion practitioners. Pray that the Holy Spirit opens their eyes to recognize abortion for the atrocity it is. Pray that they have a complete change of heart and mind and that they no longer can take the lives of those who are yet to be born. May God bless them with the desire to protect life, especially before birth. We ask all this in Jesus' Holy Name. Amen.

Prayer for Aborted Babies
(Ann Fitch)

O Loving God, we ask You to bring the souls of all aborted babies into the joy of eternal union with You. Hold them close to You and grant them rest. May these innocent victims rejoice forever with Mary, the Mother of God, and all the angels and saints. We ask this through Christ our Lord. Amen.

Prayer After an Abortion
(Ann Fitch)

Heavenly Father, I am so ashamed that I chose to abort my baby. The guilt I feel is overwhelming. Each time I see a pregnant woman or infant my heart breaks a little more. The emptiness I feel has become unbearable. Regret, anger and grief bombard me and I am full of remorse. I feel alienated from You, my family, my friends and wonder if after what I have done I deserve to be loved at all. Please take all the emptiness within me and fill it with Your loving presence.

Lord Jesus, in Your infinite mercy please forgive me. I am truly sorry for what I have done. I now know how wrong the choice was. Because of it I feel abandoned and alone. In my heart of hearts I know You forgive me, but I still feel horribly guilty. I ask You to help me give my guilt to You and accept Your comfort. Lord, I choose to forgive myself, those who counseled me to seek an abortion, as well as, those who performed it. I ask You, Lord, to bring peace and wholeness back to me and I beg You to carry my child to Heaven and fill him or her with eternal hope and joy. Please allow my baby to rest in eternal peace with You and all the angels and saints.

O Holy Spirit, take away the darkness that has enveloped me. Help me to walk in the light of Your truth and love. Please grant me the courage, grace, and strength I need to go through the spiritual, emotional and relational healing processes I need to go through to be at peace with myself and others. I give myself entirely to You. Guide me, teach me, and bless me with new hope and new joy. Amen.

Marriage & Divorce

Prayer for a Newly Married Couple
(Ann Fitch)

Lord God, we give thanks for the union of (*name bride*) and (*name groom*) and we pray for that they may be strengthened always to keep the covenant which they have made. May they be a blessing and a comfort to each other, the sharers of each other's joys, consolers to each other in sorrow, helpers to each other in all the chance and change of this life. May they encourage each other to pursue their hopes and dreams and strive to help one another become their best. May they trust each other and, trusting You as well, live their lives with hope and joy. May they not only accept but give affection to one another, and together share their love with those who will be part of their family. Thank You, Lord for all they will be for one another and grant them peace in all their days.   Amen.

A Prayer for Married Couples

Father of life and love, You created us in Your image – woman and man. We rejoice and thank You for the gift of each other. Sustain us in our love and lead us to a deeper understanding of Your love.

Jesus, we come before You, seeking Your guidance and direction in our relationship. In marriage You call and challenge us to a permanent, exclusive and sacred friendship. Be our strength and support, therefore, as we continue this journey together.

Holy Spirit, help us to strive towards a lasting, honest commitment united in love. Give us Your strength to carry each other in times of darkness, Your joy in times of happiness, and Your gift of awe in the uniqueness and sacredness of each other. May our love be a reflection and sign of Your love in the world.   Amen.

Prayer of Spouses for Each Other
(Ann Fitch)

Lord Jesus, grant that my spouse and I may have a true and understanding love for each other. Grant that we may both be filled with faith and trust. Give us the grace to live with each other in peace and harmony. May we always bear with one another's weaknesses and grow from each other's strengths. Help us to forgive one another's failings and grant us patience, kindness, cheerfulness and the spirit of placing the well-being of one another ahead of one's self. May the love that brought us together grow and mature with each passing year. Bring us ever closer to You through our love for each other. Amen.

Prayer for My Wife
(Ann Fitch)

Thank You, Heavenly Father, for my amazing wife whom I cherish and adore. She is my best friend and the love of my life and I ask Your blessing upon her. Through the power of Your Holy Spirit fill her with hope, peace, joy, courage, strength, and wisdom.

Lord, Jesus, help me to be patient, encouraging, and always considerate of my wife's needs, wants, and desires. May I listen to her and value her advice. May I be kind, gentle, and affectionate. May my wife feel my love for her and know that I treasure her. May my passion for her grow and may she realize how much I desire her and love her. Remind me to tell her daily how special she is to me and how much I appreciate all she does for me and for our family.

Lord, help me to be forgiving, understanding, and compassionate. Help me to willingly admit when I have been wrong and to humbly seek my wife's forgiveness when needed. May our relationship grow and mature with each passing year and may we enjoy health, prosperity, and happiness. Amen.

Prayer for My Husband
(Ann Fitch)

Thank You, Heavenly Father, for my incredible husband whom I cherish and adore. He is my best friend and the love of my life and I ask Your blessing upon him. Through the power of Your Holy Spirit fill him with hope, peace, joy, courage, strength, and wisdom.

Lord, Jesus, help me to be patient, encouraging, and always considerate of my husband's needs, wants, and desires. May I listen to him and value his advice. May I be kind, gentle, and affectionate.

May my husband know I love him dearly. Let my passion for him grow and let him realize how much I desire him. May I remember to tell him daily how much I appreciate all he does for me and for our family.

Lord, help me to be forgiving, understanding, and compassionate. Help me to willingly admit when I have been wrong and to humbly seek my husband's forgiveness when needed. Bless our relationship and allow it to grow and mature with each passing year and bless us with health, prosperity, and happiness.   Amen.

Anniversary Prayer
(Ann Fitch)

Lord, we thank You for (*name the couple*) and for all the ways they have shared Your love with one another and those around them in the past year. Today, as we celebrate their anniversary, our prayer is that You will continue to bless them with every gift and grace they need to live out faithfully the sacrament of marriage. May they grow in love for one another. Let their testimony of love and forgiveness be an inspiration to other couples and may their commitment to each other and to You provide them with many more years of happiness together.   Amen.

On Our Anniversary
(Ann Fitch)

We thank You Lord for the gift of our marriage which You have blessed and strengthened in the past year. As we celebrate the day of our wedding we thank You for Your constant mercy, love, and forgiveness and for all the graces and gifts You have bestowed upon us. Continue to fill our lives with happiness and joy and may our commitment to one another be fortified as the coming year unfolds. Keep our trust in one another strong and let nothing come between us that could dim our love for one another.   Amen.

Prayer for the Restoration of a Marriage
(Ann Fitch)

Gracious and ever loving God I come before You seeking Your help. My husband/wife and I are separated and in need of reconciling. You made us one flesh, one spirit on the day we entered into holy matrimony. I believe in the sanctity of marriage and will do all I possibly can to see that our marriage is restored.

Heavenly Father, pour out Your Spirit upon us and fill us with the burning desire to rebuild our marriage. Wipe away any anger, bitterness, or resentment we feel towards one another and fill us with love, joy, peace, kindness, gentleness, compassion, sympathy, understanding, and wisdom. Help us to forgive one another whatever wrongs we have committed and help us begin to trust each other again. Please take away any hurt we have in our hearts and fill us with a deep abiding love for one another. Instill in us a fervent need to be faithful to one another and the desire to live together in peace and harmony.

Lord, You are the God of hope and I believe that You will help us reconcile and move forward with our marriage fully restored. As we work towards reconciliation don't let us become discouraged or feel defeated. May we be committed to supporting and loving one another as we face our issues, struggles, and differences. Help us to be honest with one another and treat one other with dignity and respect. May we truly listen to each other, recognize and acknowledge each other's needs, and be willing to change in order for our relationship to grow and become all it is meant to be. May our passion for one another be rekindled and may we find true happiness in loving one another as husband and wife. Amen.

Prayer During a Divorce
(Ann Fitch)

O God, my heart is broken and tattered. I feel rejected, abandoned, and unloved. At times fear, anger, and resentment overwhelm me. I'm not sure what to do or how to navigate this time in my life. So, I am turning to You Who are all-good and all-loving.

Lord, help me to trust You with all that bothers, upsets or concerns me. Help me to turn to You when I feel unsure, lost or afraid. Bless me with the patience, wisdom, and courage I need to face each new day as I go through the divorce process. Heal me of any anger, resentment or bitterness I have within me. Heal my hurts and help me to rely fully on Your love and grace. Restore my self-esteem and help me to go through this divorce with dignity and a healthy sense of self-love and acceptance. Help me to be loving, forgiving, and understanding. And, help me to move forward in faith with trust and renewed hope.

I give myself to You, Lord, and I accept Your guidance. Make clear to me what You will for my life. Thank You for Your infinite love, forgiveness, mercy and complete acceptance of me. Thank You for blessing me and strengthening me with Your Spirit and for keeping me close to Your Heart. Amen.

Prayer for My Children During a Divorce
(Ann Fitch)

Lord, You alone know the extent to which my children are broken because of my divorce. May they never blame themselves for or feel they are the cause of it. Please Lord, embrace them and heal them of any rejection, abandonment or sense of being unloved that they may feel. Take away any fears they have and bless them with a sense of security in the midst of this trauma. Bless them with the knowledge that they are precious to You and to me and cherished no matter the state of our family.

Lord, grant my children the grace and strength they need to face the challenges that come with living between two homes. Help them adjust to our new life and help them thrive within the new parameters of our family. Lord, help them be loving, patient, and understanding with me and with one another. May they give You any anger or resentment they have and find it in their hearts to forgive me and my soon to be ex-spouse. Lord, hold them close to Your Heart and fill them with peace, hope, and trust in You. Thank You, Lord. Amen.

Prayer for Another During a Divorce
(Ann Fitch)

Lord, You alone are the One Whose love can heal and restore the brokenhearted. Knowing this I give (*name person*) to You for healing. Take away any anger, resentment or bitterness he/she feels. Remove his/her fears and replace them with a renewed trust in You and in Your providence. Grant him/her the courage, grace, and strength to face the challenges ahead and fill him/her with peace, hope and new joy. Bless (*name person*) with a forgiving heart and with infinite patience as he/she adjusts to a new way of life. I thank You for Your love and trust that You will bless (*name person*) with wholeness and the fullness of Your love. Amen.

Military & First Responders

A Prayer for the Armed Forces
(Ann Fitch)

All-powerful and ever-loving God, I offer to You all those who are serving in the armed forces at home and abroad. Be with them, guiding their footsteps and protecting them from harm. May they courageously and loyally serve their country and meet every challenge with grace and strength. Whether in active duty or in training be with them, encouraging them and blessing them with Your love. May they have the complete support of their loved ones and without reservation fulfill their duties. May they serve the cause of justice and peace and protect the freedoms of our country valiantly. In Your infinite mercy assure them of Your presence and guide them by the power of Your Spirit. Bless each one to overflowing with every gift and grace needed to fulfill their duties and return safely to their loved ones.   Amen.

Prayer for the Armed Forces
(Ann Fitch)

O God of love and mercy I ask You to protect all the men and women in the armed forces both here and abroad who protect and defend my freedoms and the country I love. Bless them and care for them. Defend them, strengthen them, and encourage them. If they are tired grant them strength. If they are lonely grant them Your love. If they are conflicted by doing their duty grant them Your wisdom and clarity. If they are anxious or afraid grant them Your peace. If they are ill, wounded or suffering in any way grant them Your healing and comfort. O Lord, bless their selfless service and keep them safe from all harm.   Amen.

Prayer of Someone Serving in the Armed Forces
(Ann Fitch)

Heavenly Father, I come to You asking for Your blessing. As I serve my country may I always have the strength and fortitude necessary to do my duty without reservation. Grant me the courage I need to fearlessly complete every task assigned to me. Send Your angels to watch over me and keep me safe from all harm. Help me to treat every person with whom I come in contact with compassion, dignity and respect and keep my mind sharp, clear, and free from distraction. May I serve my country valiantly and help to promote justice and peace in all that I do. Bless my loved ones with Your peace and keep them free from anxiety and fear. May they know my love for them and trust that You are with me, guiding me and blessing me with Your grace and strength.   Amen.

Prayer for Military Families

(Ann Fitch)

Heavenly Father, bless the immediate and extended families of our military personnel. Take away their anxieties and fears and replace them with the knowledge that You are keeping their loved ones safe and that You have blessed them with angels who guard and protect them. Send Your Spirit upon them and fill them with Your joy, love, and comfort. And as You promised, let Your peace, which surpasses all understanding, guard their hearts and minds in Christ Jesus. Amen.

Prayer of a Military Spouse with Children During Deployment

(Ann Fitch)

Dear Lord, I turn to You Who are all loving and all merciful, for guidance while my loved one is deployed. I am now responsible for all our family's needs and at times I feel overwhelmed with all that requires of me. Grant me the wisdom, knowledge and discernment I need to make healthy, life-giving decisions for our family.

Lord, sometimes I am exhausted because of the struggles I am facing with our children and handling household chores. Help me to not take their tantrums, anger, anxiety or acting out personally. Give me the ability to help them adjust to our family's separation in a way that is positive and effective. May they feel comfortable turning to me for advice and support instead of to harmful behaviors. Help me to listen to their fears and anxieties and bless me with words of comfort and understanding for them. May I give them all the love, care, guidance and encouragement they need to continue growing and developing in a healthy way.

Lord, when I find myself feeling alone and lonely comfort me with Your loving presence. Bless me with the support I need from others to get through this separation in a way that is positive and helps me grow and become a better spouse and parent. When I am anxious or afraid regarding the welfare of my loved one bless me with Your peace and the gentle assurance that You have him/her safely in Your care. Never let me become resentful, angry or bitter because my loved one is away, serving his/her country. Instead, give me a grateful heart that is full of love, pride, and thanksgiving for all he/she does to secure our freedoms.

Lord, keep my loved one safe from all harm. Strengthen him/her and grant him/her the courage he/she needs to perform all his/her duties well. Send Your angels to protect him/her and bring him/her home healthy in mind, body, and soul. May he/she feel my love for him/her and know beyond a shadow of a doubt that I am committed to our love and marriage even though we are far apart.

I thank You, Lord, for all You do for me each day and I praise You for all You are doing in the lives of those I love.   Amen.

Prayer of a Military Spouse During Deployment
(Ann Fitch)

O Lord, I turn to You Who are all loving and all merciful, for guidance while my loved one is deployed. Grant me the wisdom, knowledge and discernment I need to make healthy, life-giving decisions for us. When I find myself feeling alone and lonely send family and friends to encourage and comfort me. Bless me with the support I need to get through this separation in a way that is positive and allows me to become a better spouse. When I am anxious or worried about the welfare of my loved one, bless me with Your peace and grant me the gentle assurance that he/she is safely in Your care. Never let me become resentful, angry or bitter because my partner is away, serving his/her country. Instead, give me a grateful heart that is full of love, pride, and thanksgiving for all he/she does to secure our freedoms.

Lord, I humbly ask You to keep my spouse safe from all harm. Strengthen him/her and grant him/her the courage he/she needs to do all his/her commanding officers ask of him/her. Send Your angels to protect him/her and bring him/her home healthy in mind, body, and soul. May he/she know with certainty that I support him/her in every way, may he/she feel my love for him/her, and know that I am committed to our love and marriage every minute of every day. Amen.

Prayer at the Death of Military Men and Women
(Ann Fitch)

Heavenly Father, we pray for the peaceful repose of all military men and women who have given their lives in the line of duty. We are profoundly grateful for their service, bravery and commitment and we grieve their loss.

Grant to them, O Lord, Your mercy, Your forgiveness, and Your peace. Bring them into Your Heavenly presence and bless them with eternal rest with You.

Lord, send Your comforting Spirit upon the families and friends of these valiant military men and women who have given their lives to preserve and defend our freedom. Grant them, O God, Your peace and healing grace for You alone can fill their emptiness with hope. We entrust them to Your tender care. May we never forget the invaluable sacrifice of their loved ones, nor the nobility and honor . with which they served. Amen.

Prayer for Police Officers
(Ann Fitch)

Almighty God and Father, I ask You to watch over all police officers and law enforcement officers. With Your mighty arm protect them from all harm as they carry out their duties to stop crime, keep the peace, and protect society. Bless them with the courage, strength, and dedication they need to do their job effectively and efficiently. Bless them with empathy and compassion for their fellow man and help them to always do that which is honorable. Keep them in Your loving care and daily renew their desire to serve and protect. Amen.

Prayer for Firefighters and Paramedics
(Ann Fitch)

Heavenly Father, I humbly come before You asking for Your protection over all firefighters and paramedics. Keep them safe as they daily risk their lives for the health and protection of others. Grant them the courage and skills they need to fulfill their duties safely and diligently. Be by their sides as they face the dangers of fire and smoke and as they assist the sick and those suffering due to accidents. May they have the wisdom to make crucial decisions, save lives, and quickly and efficiently extinguish any flames. Lord, keep them in Your tender care and encourage them daily as they aid and protect others. Amen.

Parenting

A Parent's Prayer to Their Children's Guardian Angels
(Ann Fitch)

O Heavenly guardians, thank you for your ever-present care of my children and for your constant intercession on their behalf. Please continue to bless them with your protection and lead them ever closer to God. Inspire them with good thoughts, works and words, and preserve them from all evil. Continue to guide them and lead them in doing that which is God's will. And, at the end of their lives, escort them into God's glorious presence and rejoice with them for all eternity. Amen.

Parent's Prayer
(Ann Fitch)

Dear Lord, bless our children. Keep them safe and protected, healthy and happy, and uplifted and supported. Afford them every opportunity to thrive and may their basic needs always be met. Grant them loyal friends. Help them to be loving, empathetic, wise, and understanding. Fill their days with joy and laughter. Bless their hearts, minds and souls, and guide them in Your ways. May they always know our love for them and have peace in their hearts. Amen.

Prayer for My Children (Grandchildren)
(Ann Fitch)

Dear Lord, I ask a special blessing upon my children (*grandchildren*). Fill them with Your grace and bless them with every gift they need to live their lives in faithful obedience to You. Touch their hearts and minds and fill them with wisdom, knowledge, hope, and understanding. Help them to be loving, kind and compassionate. Be their protector and send holy angels to lead them and guide them as they go through their day. Bless their lives with peace, joy, and true happiness. Send loving friends into their lives who will be blessings to them. Keep them healthy and whole spiritually, relationally, emotionally and physically. Let Your light shine brightly in them and may they bring love and joy to all they meet. Bless them with healthy self-images and may they always know how precious they are to You and to me. May they grow to be responsible, generous, humble people of integrity and good sense. Lord, I place them in Your loving care and trust that You will always lead them, guide them, and love them.   Amen.

Parenting Prayer
(Ann Fitch)

Dear Lord, help me to be a better parent to my children. Help me to have patience with them when they behave badly, are disrespectful, or thoughtless. Grant me the grace and wisdom to correct and discipline them when necessary. Give me the strength to accept them as they are and love them through their struggles and disappointments. Help me to guide them lovingly to a personal relationship with You and by my example keep them faithful to Your teachings. Keep me from speaking to them harshly, judging them, or criticizing them for their choices. Please help me to be a good example to them in all that I say and do.   Amen.

Prayer of Grandparents Raising Grandchildren
(Ann Fitch)

Heavenly Father, You know how much I love my grandchild(ren) and how much I want him/her/them to be happy, healthy and whole. I give him/her/them to You today and ask You to bless him/her/them with Your healing touch. So much has happened in his/her/their life and I pray he/she/they not be negatively affected by what has happened and that he/she/they have a healthy sense of self-love and self-acceptance. Heal any hurts that are buried in his/her/their heart(s) and fill his/her/their mind(s) with positive and life-giving thoughts.

In Your infinite goodness bless him/her/them with peace, hope and joy. Send Your holy angels to protect him/her/them and keep him/her/them safe from all harm. I pray that our home is one of peace, love, healing, happiness, and hope for him/her/them. May he/she/they know that I love him/her/them completely, without condition, and that I am always here to listen, guide, help, and care for him/her/them. Help me, Father, to be a good example for him/her/them and may my words and actions be a reflection of Your love. Pour out Your Spirit upon me and help me be the best parent I can be for him/her/them. Fill my heart with compassion, understanding, gentleness, patience, and above all, love.

When I must discipline or admonish him/her/them may I have the wisdom and strength I need to do so with love. May he/she/they know that I love him/her/them and that no matter what happens in our lives, I will do all I can to protect, nurture, cherish, and help him/her/them grow up to be loving, caring, kind, and compassionate. Amen.

Prayer of a Working Mom
(Ann Fitch)

Lord as I go to work today I ask You to bless me with the strength that I need to get through the day. Help me to be the best mother and worker possible. Fortify me with the gifts of patience, kindness, wisdom, understanding, gentleness, and compassion. Help me to not be impatient, rude, angry or anxious. I trust that You are with me and with my child(ren) as we go through our day. Keep my child(ren) safe from all harm and send loving care givers and teachers to watch over, guide, and help him/her/them grow into the loving, generous, and kind person/people You created him/her/them to be. Bless my aching heart and take away the guilt I feel in leaving my child(ren) in someone else's care and fill me with peace in knowing that I am doing my best to provide a loving, safe home for him/her/them. Thank You for my job. Thank You for my child(ren). Thank You for all the blessings You have bestowed upon us. May I be a blessing to my child(ren) and to those with whom I work. Amen.

Prayer for Foster Parents
(Ann Fitch)

Lord we come before You seeking Your blessing upon all the loving men and women who serve children as foster parents. Bless them with courage and strength and never let them lose heart as they daily care for, protect, and nurture the children they are fostering. May their homes be places of peace, love, refuge, healing and joy. When their foster children are struggling or hurting may they provide love, understanding, comfort and wisdom. Lord, let the unconditional love they give be a healing balm for the wounds these children carry in their hearts and minds. May they be equally committed to reunification and adoption dependent upon which is in the best interest of the children. When they must say, "Good-bye," to children they are fostering, comfort and console them and help them to make the children's transition from their home to another happen with as little disruption, pain or trauma as possible. Lord, profoundly bless these men and women and fill them with every gift and grace they need to be Your loving presence for the children in their care.   Amen.

Prayer for a College Student
(Ann Fitch)

Eternal Father, I come before You asking Your blessing upon (*name student*). Fill him/her with Your grace and help (*name student*) be mature and responsible while in college. Fill (*name student*) with self-confidence and help him/her be diligent in applying himself/herself to his/her studies. Help (*name student*) to properly manage his/her time so that he/she can successfully complete all coursework in a timely manner. May he/she study effectively so that he/she can recall facts or information and do well on all tests and exams. May (*name student*) have professors who are passionate about their field of study, ethical, wise and moral, and who challenge (*name student*) to be and do his/her very best. Keep (*name student*) happy and healthy. Lead (*name student*) to good friends who will encourage him/her to be mature, healthy, and responsible. May (*name student*) be strong when faced with temptations and make sound moral choices when it comes to activities he/she chooses to be involved with. May his/her time in college be blessed and lead (*name student*) to wonderful opportunities in the future. Amen.

Prayer for a Child in Trouble
(Ann Fitch)

Dear Lord, my child is in serious trouble. Come to my aid and help me to handle this situation in a way that honors and glorifies You. My child needs me now more than ever. Help me to be available to him/her with a patient, understanding, and loving heart. Grant me the courage and strength I need to walk through this situation with my child until it is resolved. Help me not blame myself for this situation or be judgmental of my child, and help me be forgiving and wise. Please resolve this situation in a way that brings us closer to one another and to You. Thank You, Lord.   Amen.

A Prayer for a Sick Child
(Ann Fitch)

Lord Jesus, we praise You and thank You for Your love and compassion. You have a special love for children. Knowing Your love for children we place our child (*name child*) in Your loving arms. In Your merciful love, touch (*name child*) and bless him/her with Your healing love. Let it permeate every cell in his/her body. You are the Divine Physician and nothing is impossible for You. Confident in Your power we ask You to bless our child (*name child*) with every gift and grace needed to walk through this illness. Fill (*name child*) with courage, strength, hope, happiness, patience, perseverance, and joy.

If (*name child*) must continue to suffer illness we pray that we are able to work with the best specialists and nurses available, that we have peace knowing that our child (*name child*) is getting the best care possible and that everyone is doing what they can to make sure he/she is happy, comfortable and loved. May (*name child*) know how deeply we love him/her and be free from anxiety, worry and fear. Amen.

Prayer for a Missing Child
(Ann Fitch)

O Lord, (*name child*) is missing and our hearts are full of anguish and fear for him/her. Be with (*name child*) and fill him/her with Your strength, courage, and hope. Please protect (*name child*) from being abused or exploited in any way. We pray that (*name child*) knows that he/she is loved immeasurably and unconditionally and that we will never stop searching for him/her. We believe that You love (*name child*) even more than we do and we pray that You will keep (*name child*) in Your loving care while he/she is far from us. Please, Lord, let (*name child*) be found alive and healthy and returned safely to us. Amen.

Prayer for the Family of a Missing Child
(Ann Fitch)

O Holy Spirit we ask You to be with the family of (*name child*) who is missing. Fill them to overflowing with Your peace, wisdom, patience, courage, strength, and hope. They are terrified for (*name child*) and are concerned for his/her safety and welfare. Touch their hearts and minds and ease their fears. Bless them with trust that You are with (*name child*) and that You are doing all that You can to keep (*name child*) safe and free from harm. Help them as they search for (*name child*). Lead them to men and women who can help them in their search for (*name child*) and who have connections with groups whose main goal is to find children and reunite them with their families. May their search lead them to (*name child*) and end happily with (*name child*) being returned home healthy and unharmed. Amen.

Personal & Emotional

Serenity Prayer
(Reinhold Niebuhr)

God, grant me the serenity to accept the things I cannot change, the courage to change the things I can, and the wisdom to know the difference. Amen.

A Prayer for Peace
(Ann Fitch)

Heavenly Father I turn to You seeking peace. I pray for peace in my heart, mind and soul. I pray for peace in my family, my community, my country, and throughout the world. Bless me profoundly with Your peace and help me to allow You to love through me those I encounter each day. Make me a bearer of the peace of Christ, which surpasses all understanding. May my face shine with His peace and may Your Spirit of truth guide me, transform me, and lead me to everlasting peace. Amen.

Prayer for Joy
(Ann Fitch)

Gracious and ever-loving God, I thank You for the gift of true joy, the deep and lasting joy that comes from allowing Your Spirit to dwell in me. I pray that my heart be cheerful and that it delight in Your love and presence. May my face shine with joy and my smile be a reflection of Your loving presence within me. You are my joy, my hope, my happiness. I choose to rejoice in You always.   Amen.

A Prayer for Hope
(Ann Fitch)

Gracious and ever-loving God, I turn to You in the midst of my darkness. All seems bleak and lost. I feel helpless and I am struggling to cling to You. I know in my heart of hearts that You are with me but I do not feel Your presence. I will trust in You, my Rescuer, and believe that You will carry me through this present darkness and back into Your own wonderful light. Let Your light penetrate my darkness. Illuminate my heart, mind, and soul. In Your goodness bless me with the grace and strength I need to trust in You, to hope in You, to believe in Your love for me. I wait on You with hope filled expectation.   Amen.

Prayer for Charity
(Mary Stewart)

Keep us, O God, from all pettiness. Let us be large in thought, in word, in deed. Let us be done with fault-finding and leave off all self-seeking. May we put away all pretense and meet each other face to face, without self-pity and without prejudice. May we never be hasty in judgment, and always be generous. Let us always take time for all things, and make us to grow calm, serene and gentle. Teach us to put into action our better impulses, to be straightforward and unafraid. Grant that we may realize that it is the little things of life that create differences, that in the big things of life, we are as one. And, O Lord God, let us not forget to be kind!   Amen.

Lord, Help Me Be Kind

Lord, help me be for everyone the one who waits for the other without becoming impatient, who listens without becoming tired, who accepts with thanks and gives with love, who is always available when needed, the one to whom others can go when they are in need, who radiates peace from within and who belongs totally to You and is therefore kind to others. Thank You, Lord. Amen.

Forgive Me, Lord

(Ann Fitch)

For the times I did not put You first in my life, forgive me Lord.

For taking Your Name in vain, forgive me Lord.

For disclosing confidences or gossiping, forgive me Lord.

For lying, forgive me Lord.

For using inappropriate language, forgive me Lord.

For talking out of turn or interrupting more than listening, forgive me Lord.

For any ways in which I hurt others, forgive me Lord.

For the times I did not respect others or myself, forgive me Lord.

For being envious or jealous, forgive me Lord.

For lashing out in anger or frustration, forgive me Lord.

For the times I didn't show compassion or concern for others, forgive me Lord.

For holding grudges or harboring resentment, forgive me Lord.

For being critical or judgmental, forgive me Lord.

For being selfish or greedy, forgive me Lord.

For being prejudiced, biased, or discriminatory in any way, forgive me Lord.

For not consoling or comforting others when I could have, forgive me Lord.

For not sharing my time, talents, and riches, forgive me Lord.

For not caring for myself, physically, relationally, psychologically, emotionally or spiritually, forgive me Lord.

For any sins of the flesh, forgive me Lord.

For failing to see and help You in the homeless and needy, forgive me Lord.

For not loving others or myself as You love, forgive me Lord.

For not forgiving others or myself as You forgive, forgive me Lord.

For not living fully submitted to You, forgive me Lord.

For doubting that You forgive me unconditionally, forgive me Lord.

For doubting You love me without condition, forgive me Lord.

For not embracing Your mercy and forgiveness, forgive me Lord.

For not allowing You to love me completely, forgive me Lord.

And for any other sins I have committed, forgive me Lord.

Prayer of Humble Surrender
(Ann Fitch)

Lord, You said, *"He who exalts himself will be humbled and he who humbles himself will be exalted."* I choose to turn away from my selfish pride and seek to know, love and serve You in humble surrender. I wish to do that which is Your will in my life and to embrace the graces You are pouring out upon me through Your Spirit. I desire to humbly walk in truth and wisdom and I ask Your forgiveness for the times when my pride has caused me to turn away from You, Your will for me, and Your gifts of grace. You are my Creator and my God and I am Your servant who wants to only do that which will bring You honor and glory. May my life exalt You and be forever submitted in obedience to You and Your commands. Amen.

Prayer to Forgive Oneself
(Ann Fitch)

Heavenly Father, I am struggling to forgive myself for the things I have said and done. I know in my head and in my heart that if I have sought Your forgiveness with a truly contrite heart that You have

133

forgiven me, but I cannot seem to forgive myself. I know it is pride that is keeping me bound with attitudes of self-abasement, shame, guilt and unworthiness.

Help me to humble myself before You and grant me the grace to believe that once You have forgiven me I am truly forgiven. Open my eyes to see that once You have forgiven me You remember my sins no more, they are forgotten. I want to choose to forgive myself and make a choice that is life giving for me.

Bless me with the courage and strength to truly, completely forgive myself and accept with total thanksgiving Your gift of forgiveness. I no longer wish to punish myself for what I have done or hold myself bound by unforgiveness. I give myself completely to You and accept with all my heart Your gift of forgiveness. Thank You for blessing me, pouring out Your grace upon me, and for forgiving me in Your infinite love and mercy. Amen.

Prayer for Peace of Mind
(St. Frances Xavier Cabrini)

Fortify me with the grace of Your Holy Spirit and give Your peace to my soul that I may be free from all needless anxiety, solicitude and worry. Help me to desire always that which is pleasing and acceptable to You so that Your will may be my will. Amen.

Prayer When Stressed
(Ann Fitch)

Lord there is so much going on in my life. I feel stressed, anxious and overwhelmed. I know You will guide me through all that is happening and strengthen me as I walk with You, but I struggle to trust You completely. Help me to entrust all that concerns me to Your care. I know You will work everything out for my greater good and Your glory, but I am still impatient, so bless me with patience. Grant me the courage I need to face the challenges in my life and send supportive family and friends to listen to me, understand me, and lift me up in prayer. When I feel alone or afraid let me feel Your love and presence. I surrender everything to You and ask for the grace to rest in Your peace. Amen.

Prayer When Overwhelmed
(Ann Fitch)

Ever powerful and all mighty God I feel overwhelmed. I am tired and the weight of my burdens is crushing me. I turn to You seeking comfort and solace. I trust You completely and I give You everything that is weighing me down. Lift these heavy burdens off my shoulders and let me rest in You. Hold me in Your loving arms and soothe my weary soul. Allow me to feel Your presence. Let the waves of Your love and mercy flow over me, refreshing me, filling my heart and mind with Your peace. Thank You for pouring out Your Spirit upon me and blessing me with the strength and grace I need to get through today. Thank You for being with me, caring for me, and restoring my peace. Amen.

Prayer When Anxious
(Ann Fitch)

Pray the first half of each sentence as you breathe in slowly and the second half as you breathe out.

Come Holy Spirit, calm my heart and mind.
Come Lord Jesus, fill me with Your peace.
Come Heavenly Father, bless me.

(Repeat as often as needed.)

Prayer When Having a Panic Attack
(Ann Fitch)

O my God, I am full of fear. My heart is racing, I am sweating and shaking, and it's hard for me to focus or breathe. My mind is racing and I feel the need to run and hide but there is nowhere to go except to You. So, Lord, I turn to You and ask You to tuck me safely within

Your Sacred Heart and allow Your love and mercy to permeate every fiber of my being. Steady my heartbeat and take away my fears and replace them with trust in Your goodness. I know that You only want what is best for me and I give myself to You. Send Your Spirit of peace and tranquility upon me. Grant me the courage and strength I need to face my fears with You and realize that in You I am safe. Amen.

Prayer When Tempted
(Ann Fitch)

O Lord, You know the temptation I am facing. In the midst of it I ask for the wisdom and clarity to see Your way out of it, the grace to refrain from sinning, and the fortitude to be obedient to You. I throw myself on Your mercy and trust in Your grace to see me through. Thank You for being my faithful deliverer and my strength when I am weakest. Amen.

Prayer When Struggling Spiritually
(Ann Fitch)

Good and ever loving God, I turn to You in my time of need. I am struggling and feel as if I am far away from You. I feel alone even though I know You are with me every moment of every day. I truly trust that You are carrying me even though I do not feel Your presence. Help me to remain faithful to You. Help me to continue trusting in Your guidance. May this time of struggle draw me closer to You and help me grow in wisdom and grace. Help me to continue serving You in those around me. I know that one day I will once again feel Your love for me and my joy will return. Until that day comes I pray that I will be faithful, obedient, loving, kind, hopeful and patient. I pray that as I persevere through this time of spiritual dryness, that I will become more faithful to You and Your Holy Church, more loving towards myself and others, and trust more completely in You and Your love for me. Amen.

Prayer When Feeling Like a Failure
(Ann Fitch)

Lord, I have failed again. I do the very things I hate and wish with all my heart that I could stop myself from stumbling so frequently. I want to love You and honor You with my thoughts, words, and actions, but I keep failing and falling into sin. I ask for the grace and strength to truly believe that You love me, no matter what I have said, done or not done. I want to believe that Your love for me is unconditional and to love myself as You love me – completely, failures and all.

Pour out Your Holy Spirit upon me Lord and fill my heart and mind with peace, self-acceptance, and self-love. I plead with You for the grace to not succumb to feelings of guilt. For I know that guilt is not from You. Instead, help me to seek Your forgiveness immediately upon faltering and to embrace Your loving mercy, believing that You have forgiven me completely. I choose to forgive myself and ask for the grace to offer You my temptations to sin so that I am strengthened in the moment of temptation and can stand strong against it.

Thank You, Lord, for Your infinite mercy. Thank You for Your unconditional love. Thank You for the grace and strength to stand firm in my resolve to seek You when I am tempted and embrace Your love and forgiveness when I falter. Amen.

Prayer for Forgiving Specifically
(Ann Fitch)

O Merciful Lord, I forgive (*name person*) for _____. I choose to let go of all anger, bitterness, and resentment I am harboring regarding this event and I ask You to transform my heart and bless me with charity and understanding. Please forgive me for any ways in which I hurt (*name person*) knowingly or unknowingly. Bless both of us with Your forgiveness and Your healing love. Thank You, Lord. Amen.

Prayer for Self-Acceptance
(Ann Fitch)

Dear Lord, I come before You asking for the grace to accept and love myself as You love and accept me - unconditionally. Help me to be kind, compassionate and understanding towards myself. Bless my heart with the grace to embrace who I am as a child of God, precious and loved beyond measure. May I have peace and joy as I strive to embrace myself and live my life according to Your will for me. I choose to accept myself, as I am, where I am, and I accept the courage and strength I need to continue to transform my heart and mind and grow in self-love and self-acceptance. Amen.

A Prayer for Self-Love
(Ann Fitch)

Lord You have commanded me to love myself as I love others and as You love me, but I find that so hard to do because I see all my faults and imperfections. Help me to love myself as You love me - completely, unconditionally, and without limits. Help me to be as kind, gentle, merciful, understanding, compassionate, patient, loving, and forgiving with myself as I am with others.

You have designed and created me as one of a kind, a unique reflection of Your love and presence in the world. I choose to embrace myself as I am and to nurture, cherish, and love myself unreservedly. I reject all negative feelings I have had towards myself and embrace Your love for me without condition. I will no longer listen to any negative or unloving words I hear inside my heart and mind. I choose to replace those words with all the compliments and positive things people have said to and about me. I will embrace myself completely as Your child, precious and loved beyond measure and do all that I can to grow in self-love. Thank You for blessing me, for loving me, and for accepting me without condition. I am full of gratitude and thanksgiving. Amen.

Prayer When Afraid

(Ann Fitch)

Heavenly Father, I turn to You in my time of need. I am afraid and I wish to give You all my fears so that I can rest in Your amazing love. I do not wish to dwell on that which frightens me, but rather to dwell on the reality of Your presence with me. Hold me in Your loving arms and wash away my fears with Your peace which quells all concerns, worries and fears. Pour out Your Spirit upon me and fill me with every grace I need to fully trust in You, Your goodness, Your love for me.

Bless me with a calm heart and a peaceful mind. Take all the thoughts that are running through my head and transform them into thoughts of Your infinite love for me and Your desire for me never to fear because You are with me. Lord, Jesus You said, *"Peace I leave with you; my peace I give you...Do not let your hearts be troubled or afraid."* I cling to these words of truth and choose with every fiber of my being to give my every fear to You, Who are all-knowing and all-loving. I give You my fear of _____. It is Yours now, do with it as You please. I also give You my fear of _____. Take it and transform it in Your love. I choose freedom in You, to trust in Your love for me that surpasses anything I could hope for or imagine. Thank You for blessing me. Thank You for helping me find freedom from my fears. I love You and truly wish to walk hand in hand with You through my day. Amen.

Prayer When Suffering

(Ann Fitch)

Lord I am suffering and in need of Your love, compassion and consolation. You know all that is causing my discomfort and I give each and every problem to You knowing that You are working everything together for my good and Your glory. Let me not become so immersed in my suffering that I take my eyes off You who are all good and all loving. Instead, accept my suffering as a gift to You for those in most need of Your merciful love. Do not allow my current distress to overwhelm me but rather help me to persevere believing that I will be blessed by You with patience and hope. Help me to trust that my sufferings are nothing compared to the glory that will be revealed to me in time. I turn to You, O Lord, and thank You for sustaining me, strengthening me, filling me with the graces I need to hold fast to You. I praise You for helping me carry my crosses and thank You for easing my burdens and blessing me with Your peace. Amen.

Prayer When Having a Bad Day
(Ann Fitch)

Heavenly Father I am having a bad day. I don't know where to turn except to You, Who are all good and all loving. Turn this unpleasant day into a gift that leads me ever closer to You. I know that You are working everything together for my good and Your glory. Pour out Your Spirit upon me and fill me with peace, hope and joy. Draw me into Your loving arms and keep me safe from all harm. Thank You for the graces You have bestowed upon me today and for being with me, blessing and caring for me.   Amen.

Prayer When Feeling Lonely
(Ann Fitch)

Lord, I feel so alone. I have no one to hug, kiss, laugh with or talk to. I miss the comfort of companionship. It's hard to be alone and have no one with whom to share my thoughts, my joys, my worries, my life. I don't want to feel empty and alone. I know You are with me, but I do not feel Your presence. I truly want to feel Your love. Pour out Your Spirit upon me and allow me to feel Your love and comfort. Inspire those I love to call me and chat or come and visit with me. Thank You for caring for me, always being with me, and loving me.   Amen.

Prayer When Misunderstood
(Ann Fitch)

Lord, I feel completely misunderstood. I feel awkward and uncomfortable. I'm hurt, frustrated, and a bit angry, but I know You have a lesson in this for me. Touch my heart and mind and heal the hurt within me. Pour out Your Spirit upon me and allow me to see this situation as an opportunity to grow in grace and selflessness. You were misunderstood, but You responded with forgiveness and love, patience and kindness. So I choose to do the same.

Misunderstandings are going to happen and how I respond to them is what matters. It's not essential that I be understood, only that I am kind, loving, forgiving, and patient when I'm not. Thank You for blessing me in this moment. Thank You for accepting me as I am, for understanding me, and for helping me be honest with myself so that I can grow in charity, humility and understanding. I love You and I am grateful for Your unconditional love. Amen.

Prayer When Angry
(Ann Fitch)

Dear Lord, I am so infuriated I can't think straight. I'm feeling overwhelmed with anger and I turn to You asking for the gift of self-control. I do not want to say or do anything I will regret. Pour out Your Spirit upon me and fill me with Your peace. Calm my heart and mind and bring tranquility and clarity of mind back to me. Please help me focus on Your presence within me and in so doing embrace Your love and turn the ugliness of anger into an opportunity to love as You love. Transform my heart and mind and bless me with gentleness, kindness, and serenity. Amen.

Prayer When in a Bad Mood
(Ann Fitch)

O Lord, I am in a bad mood. Everything seems to bother me and cause me irritation. I cannot seem to shake feeling annoyed. I do not like the way I feel so I choose to surrender to You all that is bothering, irritating or annoying me. In Your merciful love, touch my heart and mind with the power of Your Holy Spirit and change them so that I am at peace with myself and with life. I choose to feel love. I choose to embrace joy. I choose to be at peace. Thank You for blessing me and for granting me Your peace.   Amen.

Prayer When You Cannot Sleep
(Ann Fitch)

Heavenly Father, my mind is racing and I cannot seem to fall asleep. I am tossing and turning thinking about what happened today and worrying about tomorrow. The needs of those I love seem to be bombarding my thoughts. So I turn to You and with trust in Your infinite goodness I give You all that is worrying me. Rescue me from my swirling thoughts and bless me with a calm and tranquil mind. I know there is nothing I can do about what happened today. Today is over and done. But, I do ask You to forgive me for any wrongs I committed and for the grace embrace Your forgiveness. Help me to relax and rest in Your loving presence. Let the waves of Your love and mercy wash over me and lull me to sleep. As I rest, revive me physically and mentally so that when I awake I am restored and refreshed and ready to face a new day loving and serving You. Thank You, Father for being with me, blessing me, calming me, and filling me with Your peace so that I can rest fully in Your love.   Amen.

Prayer in Times of Change
(Ann Fitch)

Eternal and ever living God, my life is changing, and it is unsettling. I know that change is part of life so I willingly choose to embrace it. Help me to see Your hand in all that is happening. I choose to be adaptable and submissive to Your holy will in the midst of it all. May these changes bring me ever closer to You and help me grow in love and grace.   Amen.

Prayer of Complete Trust in God
(St. Francis de Sales)

Be at peace. Do not look forward in fear to the changes of life; rather look to them with full hope as they arise. God, Whose very own you are, will deliver you from out of them. He has kept you hitherto, and He will lead you safely through all things; and when you cannot stand it, God will bury you in His arms. Do not fear what may happen tomorrow; the same everlasting Father Who cares for you today will take care of you then and every day. He will either shield you from suffering, or will give you unfailing strength to bear it. Be at peace, and put aside all anxious thoughts and imagination. Amen.

A Prayer for a New Start
(Ann Fitch)

Lord, You are a God of new beginnings, help me and be with me as I begin this new phase in my life. Guide me in any decisions I will need to make and strengthen me with Your Spirit so that I am able to cope with any difficulties life brings. Reassure me as I adjust to different demands and bless me with Your loving presence as I face new situations. Thank You for the new opportunities You are blessing me with. Help me embrace them with hope and courage. When I feel uncertain, help me to remember that You are with me, the God of all wisdom, protecting me and filling me with every gift and grace I need to move forward. Lord, I place all my trust in You and in Your Divine Providence. Thank You for whatever lies ahead. May I welcome my future with grace, humor, and dignity. Amen.

Prayer When in Need
(Ann Fitch)

Almighty and ever-loving God, I have a need that I ask You to bless and resolve according to Your will for me. I know that You can do all things. All I ask is for the patience to accept Your timing and the grace to embrace Your will. I trust in You. I wait on You. I believe that You will take care of this need as You see fit. Amen.

Prayer When Making a Decision
(Ann Fitch)

Lord, I have to make a difficult decision and I am not sure what to do. Send forth Your Spirit upon me that I might have the grace to choose wisely. You have given me the freedom and intelligence to weigh every option and then make a choice. May the decision I make honor and glorify You, reflect Your will for my life, and in so doing bring me peace and contentment. Amen.

Prayer During Difficulty
(Ann Fitch)

O God, You are my help. Be with me as I face this difficulty. I believe that if I humbly face this trial with You I will become stronger and grow in grace. Grant me the courage I need to endure this problem for You alone are my hope and refuge, my source of comfort. I trust fully in Your infinite love and compassion. Walk with me and keep me in Your tender care. Make clear to me through the power of Your Spirit what I am to say and do in order to accomplish Your will through this time of trouble. I believe You are working all together for good and that You will make a way for me to come through this trial whole and at peace. Thank You for Your assistance. Amen.

Prayer When Needing to Resolve a Problem
(Ann Fitch)

Blessed Lord, I have a problem that needs to be resolved. I am not sure how You would have me handle this situation. Open my eyes to see Your way through this and open my ears to hear Your gentle voice speaking in my heart. In Your love and compassion lead me in Your holy will for me. I know that You are working everything together for my good and for Your honor and glory but I do not see clearly which way to go. I ask for patience as You work in the hearts of all involved in this situation and put into place all that needs to happen for this issue to be resolved. I trust in Your timing and in You. Help me to be loving, compassionate, understanding and wise with my words and actions. No matter what happens with this situation I know You are with me, blessing me, guiding me in Your infinite mercy. Thank You for being with me, filling me with Your peace, and showing me how to best resolve this issue.   Amen.

Prayer When Struggling with Same Sex Attraction
(Ann Fitch)

Heavenly Father, I am struggling with same sex attraction and I am concerned about how those in my life will treat me if I share my struggle with them. I know that I may face rejection and I ask that You fill me with the grace to be forgiving and understanding when those I love and care for are not accepting and compassionate.

I know You love me without condition. Help me to love and accept myself as You do - without condition. I desire to be faithful to You in every way and I ask You to pour out Your Spirit upon me and fill me with the grace and strength I need to be chaste and pure in heart, mind, and body. Help me to love as You love and be kind, compassionate, and understanding no matter how others behave towards me.

May I live my life obedient to You, Your Church, and her teachings. And, may my heart belong to You and remain steadfast and true. Amen.

Prayer to Know Your Vocation

Lord, my God and my loving Father, You have made me to know You, to love You, to serve You, and thereby to find and to fulfill my deepest longings. I know that You are in all things, and that every path can lead me to You.

But of them all, there is one especially by which You want me to come to You. Since I will do what You want of me, I pray You, send your Holy Spirit to me: into my mind, to show me what You want of me; into my heart, to give me the determination to do it, and to do it with all my love, with all my mind, and with all of my strength right to the end. Jesus, I trust in You.   Amen

Purity Prayer
(Ann Fitch)

Jesus, font of purity, I come to You seeking Your help. I desire to be pure in thought, word and deed in imitation of Your holy purity. May I always be aware that I am a temple of the Holy Spirit and as such I am called to live a life of grace and virtue. Instill in me, Lord, a deep reverence for the human body, created in Your image and likeness. Protect me from anything that would tempt me to be impure so that I may love and serve You all the days of my life with unsullied purity. When I am confronted with temptation have mercy upon me and bless me with the courage and strength I need to fend off temptation and avoid sin. O merciful, Lord, I surrender my life and will to You that I might worthily serve and glorify You in pureness of heart, mind, body and soul.   Amen.

Prayer to be a Good Friend
(Ann Fitch)

Lord help me to be the best friend I can be. Help me to accept my friends as they are, respect them, encourage them, and be supportive of them when they need support. May I laugh and cry with them and be empathetic and compassionate. Let me never judge them. Help me to immediately forgive them if they hurt me or upset me in any way. May I be truly wise, understanding and patient with them. May I give of myself unconditionally and always be available to them when they are in need. May my friends know how much I love, value and treasure them and may they always know they can count on me to be there for them.   Amen.

Prayer for a Female Friend
(Ann Fitch)

Heavenly Father, I thank You for (*name person*). She has been such a blessing to me and I ask You to bless her with every gift and grace. Surround her with loved ones who respect, cherish, and nurture her and who are sources of joy and comfort to her. May she enjoy good health and be full of energy and exuberance for life.

Lord Jesus, when (*name person*) needs encouragement may my words lift her up. When she confides in me may I allow her the freedom to express herself without feeling judged. When she comes to me seeking advice may I give wise counsel. In times of happiness and sorrow may I be there to laugh and cry with her.

O Holy Spirit, please continue to bless our friendship. Fill us both with kindness, gentleness, patience, understanding, and wisdom. May we continue to be blessings to one another.   Amen.

Prayer for a Male Friend
(Ann Fitch)

Heavenly Father, I ask You to bless (*name person*). Fill him with every gift and grace. Surround him with loving family and friends and let him enjoy good health in body, mind and spirit.

Lord Jesus, help me to be the best friend I can be. May (*name person*) know that I respect him, that he can depend on me, and that I accept him as he is. May I be there for him when he needs someone to listen, support him when he needs encouragement, and laugh with him about life and all it entails.

O Holy Spirit, fill (*name person*) with wisdom and help him to make choices that fulfill him and bring him success and prosperity. Bless him in his workplace. May he feel valued, challenged, and confident.

Lord, continue to bless our friendship and keep us in Your loving care.   Amen.

Prayer When Excluded
(Ann Fitch)

O Heavenly Father, my heart is broken because I was not included. There has been an event from which I was definitely excluded. I feel angry, upset, judged, rejected, and unwanted. My immediate response is to want to lash out at those who excluded me. But I know I cannot do that. I'm frustrated because I want to know why I was excluded. But I suppose that doesn't really matter. What matters is that You always accept me, love me, care for me, bless me, encourage me, want me, believe in me, and embrace me.

So I turn to You seeking healing for my heart and mind. Take my anger and turn it to good will towards those who excluded me. Help me to forgive them. Take my hurt and frustration and use that to bless the hearts of those who left me out. Take my feelings of being judged and rejected and use that pain to bless those who are in most need of Your mercy and forgiveness. Help me to focus not on what has been done to me but rather on how powerfully You are moving in me at this moment. I am so grateful, humbled, and overwhelmed by Your love and acceptance. Thank You, Father for blessing me so profoundly. Amen.

Prayer When Feeling Left Out
(Ann Fitch)

Dear Lord, my feelings are hurt and I come to You seeking solace. I know You understand how it feels to be an outsider or to feel rejected and alone. I don't know if I was excluded on purpose or if there was a good reason for me not being included. All I know is I am saddened and feeling left out. Help me to be understanding and to not be offended. Let me see this situation from the perspective of others and bless me with a forgiving heart. I do not want to be angry, hold a grudge or let this situation disrupt relationships. I choose to let this go and place the entire situation in Your hands. Amen.

Prayer When Rejected
(Ann Fitch)

Lord, my heart is aching because I was vulnerable and gave love and kindness that was not welcomed or returned. I believed that there was more to our relationship than there was. Clearly the one I loved didn't love me as deeply as I loved. I know that You completely understand how I am feeling because You constantly give of the fullness of Your love and so often it is not returned. Bless me with the grace and strength to move past this rejection without being further embarrassed, angry or upset. I give this relationship to You and ask You to lead me to a relationship in which my love will be reciprocated. Amen.

Prayer Before A Trip
(Ann Fitch)

Lord, I ask You to go before me with Your angels and make safe the way I will be travelling. Protect me and keep me safe from all harm. Bless my time travelling. May I truly enjoy the company of others and may my relationships be deepened and strengthened. And as I journey home, send Your Spirit to pave the way for me so that I reach my home safe and sound. Thank You, Lord. Amen.

Prayer When Travelling Alone
(Ann Fitch)

Heavenly Father, today I will be travelling alone. I ask that You send kind people to help me when I have the need for help, interesting people for me to talk to and share my thoughts with, and above all wise professionals to carry me safely to my destination. I know that You go before me with Your angels, paving the way for me to go. Fill my heart with peace and bless me with the conviction that You are protecting me as I journey far from home. Thank You for watching over me and keeping me safe from all harm. Amen.

Prayer After an Accident
(Ann Fitch)

Lord, I lift up everyone involved in this accident. You know the needs of each and every one. If anyone has been injured, send wise doctors and caring nurses to bring about healing quickly, with minimal discomfort, and without complications. If anyone lost their life bring them into the fullness of Your joy and fill their loved ones with Your comfort and peace. If repairs need to be made may they be done affordably and with little disruption.

May the men and women who will be working with those involved in this accident be understanding, kind, gentle, honest and fair. And may those who have rendered help in any way be profoundly blessed. Amen.

Prayer in Time of Tragedy
(Ann Fitch)

Lord, I turn to You in this time of tragedy. I am truly broken. My life has been shattered and I need You to help me see my way through this terrible time. I know that You are with me, blessing me but I feel lost and weary. My life seems to be in such turmoil and the pain I feel is overwhelming. Pour out Your Spirit upon me and grant me the courage, understanding, patience, and strength I need in the wake of this catastrophe. In Your boundless love calm my troubled heart and mind and fill me with Your peace. Hold me in Your arms and carry me through this difficulty. I trust in You and know that I need not be anxious or afraid because You are with me comforting me, guiding me, and protecting me. With compassion I ask You to heal my brokenness. Lord, I place all my hope in You and trust that everything I need will be provided for me. Amen.

Prayer To Find Something

Little Jesus, lost and found, please bring (*name thing*) around. Amen.

Prayer Before a Meeting
(Ann Fitch)

Good and loving God, source of every grace and blessing, I turn to You before I enter this meeting. Be present with me. Send Your Spirit upon me to guide my words and actions. I trust You to give me the wisdom and understanding I need to be of benefit to those present. Grant that everyone be respectful and kind. May we listen to each other and make wise decisions. Bless our work and let this meeting be productive and successful. Amen.

Prayer When Preparing for a Test or Exam
(Ann Fitch)

Dear Lord, I am preparing for a test/exam. Pour out Your Spirit upon me as I study and direct me to the facts I need to learn and recall. Open my mind and help me absorb the information I am studying. Keep me alert and bless me with the ability to recall facts so that I am able to convey what I have learned clearly and concisely. Amen.

Prayer Before a Test or Exam
(Ann Fitch)

Come Holy Spirit with all Your gifts and graces. Help me to recall the facts I have studied for this test/exam. Guide my thinking process and fill my mind with the ideas and concepts I need to know in order to do well. Illuminate my mind and make clear the answers I am supposed to give for each question. As I answer, keep my thoughts clear and concise. Replace any anxiety I feel with peace in knowing that You are with me to assist me and guide my responses. Amen.

Dieter's Prayer
(Ann Fitch)

Heavenly Father, I know You want me to be a healthy weight. Today, I choose to be resolute, to take care of my body and in so doing become healthier and happier. I ask You to bless me with the wisdom to make healthy eating decisions and the determination to stick with my fitness program. Help me to stay positive as I endeavor to lose weight and get in shape. When I am tempted, fill me with the tenacity I need to overcome and succeed at living a fuller, healthier life. Thank You for the inner strength and will power I need to take care of myself as I seek to reach my goal. I know You are with me today and I am so grateful for Your encouragement, love, and guidance. Amen.

Prayer for Healthy Eating
(Ann Fitch)

Lord Jesus Christ, I know that nothing is impossible with You. Trusting in this truth, I give You my eating habits. I ask that You bless me with the grace I need to see and use food in ways that display self-respect and that honor my body as the temple of Your Spirit. Today I choose only to eat that which will fuel my body, nourish it, and make it strong and healthy. I stand firm and resist the need to use or abuse food to satisfy non-physical hungers. I embrace the gifts of self-control and moderation and choose to be healthy, happy, and whole. Help me to accept myself and see myself as You see me – loved, cherished, and beautiful. Thank You for blessing me, strengthening me, and filling me with Your peace. Amen.

Pregnancy & Birth

Prayer to Become Pregnant
(Ann Fitch)

Heavenly Father, Creator of all, we come before You and ask that You send Your Holy Spirit upon us and grant us the gift of a child. We are open to the gift of life and desire to be parents. We dedicate to You the child(ren) You will bless us with and promise, as best we can, to be examples of Your love. Grant us patience as we wait to become parents and bless us with the ability to trust fully in Your timing, love and divine plan for us.   Amen.

Prayer to St. Gerard for Others
(Ann Fitch)

Good St. Gerard, powerful intercessor before the throne of God, I call upon you and seek your assistance. You know how much (*husband's name*) and (*wife's name*) desire to become parents. Present their fervent prayers to God the Father, the Creator of all life. Implore Him to send forth His Holy Spirit upon them and bless them with the gift of new life. Intercede for them asking that God grant them the fulfillment of their dreams, a baby to cherish and protect, a child to teach and guide, a blessing to their family.   Amen.

Prayer of Expectant Mothers

Lord Jesus, I bring to You with love the sweet hope that I carry within my womb. You have given me the gift of this tiny living being within me. I thank You for choosing me as your instrument of love. As I wait in expectation, help me to surrender myself joyfully to Your will. Make my heart pure, strong and generous. To You I offer my preoccupation about what is to come, along with my fears, anxieties and expectations about this little child whom I do not as yet know fully. Grant that my baby may be born healthy. Keep every bodily illness away from my baby and above all preserve it from all spiritual harm. O Mary, you who experienced the ineffable joys of a holy motherhood, obtain for me a heart capable of transmitting a life of ardent and living faith. Sanctify my expectation, bless my joy-filled hope so that the fruit of my womb may grow in virtue and holiness with your prayers and the grace of Your Son.   Amen.

Prayer for an Expectant Mother
(Ann Fitch)

Heavenly Father, I thank You for the gift of life, the miracle of love that (*name mother*) carries within her womb. Hold both mother and child in Your almighty arms and fill them with Your unbounded love. Bless (*name mother*) with hope filled expectation. Ease any worries or concerns she may have for her unborn child and fill her with peace and joy. Allow this pregnancy to be healthy and progress without complications. When the time for delivery comes allow this new life come into the world safely. I know this little one will always be loved, nurtured and cherished. May (*name mother*) always praise You and thank You for this child and may their guardian angels keep watch over them all the days of their lives. Amen.

Pregnancy Prayer
(Ann Fitch)

Heavenly Father, I give thanks for the child(ren) I carry within my womb. Bless us with health as this pregnancy progresses. Hold us in Your tender arms and grant that we feel Your love and presence at all times. I dedicate my child(ren) to You and promise to raise him/her/them to know, love and serve You.

Lord Jesus, I ask You to send Your Spirit upon us. Enlighten every fiber of our beings and fill us with every gift and grace. In Your mercy and love grant us a safe and happy pregnancy and delivery.

Dearest Mother, I ask you to place us within your Immaculate Heart. Fill my heart to overflowing with love for my baby(ies). May I love him/her/them as you love Jesus and never forget what a precious gift life is.

Thank You, Lord for the child(ren) you have blessed me with. May I always praise You and thank You for the gift of his/her/their life. Amen.

Prayer in Anticipation of Birth
(Ann Fitch)

O God, Creator of all, I turn to You as the time for labor and delivery approaches. I believe it is a wondrous privilege to carry a child within my womb and I am full of joyful anticipation for the time when I will meet my child face-to-face. You created this little one in Your image and likeness and I pray that his/her delivery will be swift, smooth, safe, and without complications. I believe You created me to do this and I trust in the birthing process. As I endure each contraction I ask for patience and fortitude. Bless me with wise doctors and caring nurses to help me labor and deliver this little miracle of Your love. Thank You for filling me with Your peace and keeping me calm as I await the birth of this precious child.   Amen.

Prayer in Anticipation of the Birth of Multiples
(Ann Fitch)

O God, Creator of all, I turn to You as the time for labor and delivery approaches. I believe it is a wondrous privilege to carry children within my womb and I am full of joyful anticipation for the time when I will meet my children face-to-face. You created these little ones in Your image and likeness and I pray that their delivery will be swift, smooth, safe, and without complications. I believe You created me to do this and I trust in the birthing process. As I endure each contraction I ask for patience and fortitude. Bless me with wise doctors and caring nurses to help me labor and deliver these little miracles of Your love. Thank You for filling me with Your peace and keeping me calm as I await the birth of these precious children. Amen.

Prayer for Another During Labor
(Ann Fitch)

Gracious Lord, I ask You to bless (*name person*) as she labors and gives birth. I am so excited and happy for her and eagerly await the birth of her child(ren). Pour out Your Spirit upon (*name person*) and fill her with patience, strength, courage, and perseverance. As she labors help her to not focus on her pain but on You and Your love for her and her child(ren). Remove any anxiety or fear (*name person*) has and help her to relax her body and breathe effectively so that she can bring forth her child(ren) swiftly, smoothly, and without complications. Thank You for being with (*name person*) as she labors and delivers her precious child(ren) and for blessing them profoundly. Amen.

Prayer During Labor
(Ann Fitch)

Lord God, thank You for the gift of this child who is waiting to be born. Fill me with Your peace as I labor. May my love for this precious baby give me the strength I need to endure every contraction calmly. May I stay focused on the task at hand and realize that each contraction is bringing me closer to the moment when I will meet this little baby face-to-face. Help me to keep my body relaxed so that this miracle of Your love can come into the world swiftly, smoothly and without complications. Thank You for blessing me beyond my wildest imaginings. Amen.

Prayer During Labor With Multiples
(Ann Fitch)

Lord God, thank You for the gift of these children who are waiting to be born. Fill me with Your peace as I labor. May my love for these precious babies give me the strength I need to endure every contraction calmly. May I stay focused on the task at hand and realize that each contraction is bringing me closer to the moment when I will meet these little ones face-to-face. Help me to keep my body relaxed so that these miracles of Your love can come into the world swiftly, smoothly and without complications. Thank You for blessing me beyond my wildest imaginings. Amen.

Prayer Before a C-Section
(Ann Fitch)

Lord, I turn to You as I enter into surgery and await the birth of my precious child(ren). Take away my fears and fill me with Your peace, which surpasses all understanding. Bless me with skillful and experienced doctors and nurses. May they be wise and caring and provide for all our needs. As the moment for delivery arrives fill me with joyful anticipation. Let my child(ren) be delivered swiftly and smoothly and may he/she/they be happy, healthy, and whole. In Your goodness, bless me with an uncomplicated and quick recovery. Amen.

Prayer After the Loss of a Pregnancy
(Ann Fitch)

Lord, we do not understand why this life, which we had hoped to bring into this world, is now gone from us. We only know that where there was sweet expectation, now there is bitter disappointment; where there were hope and excitement, there is a sense of failure and loss. We have seen how fragile life is, and nothing can replace this life, this child, whom we have loved before seeing.

In our pain and confusion we look to You, Lord, in Whom no life is without meaning, however small or brief. Let this loss draw us closer to You and closer to one another. We lay our broken hearts open to You and ask You to bless us with Your healing grace. Amen.

Protection & Conversion

Prayer of Protection
(Ann Fitch)

Lord, I know You are my Savior and that You have overcome death and defeated Satan. I place myself in Your hands and ask You to surround me with Your light and presence. No matter how Satan comes against me I know that You are with me protecting me. I denounce any patterns of evil in my life and turn to You in full submission. Please pour out Your Spirit upon me and fill me with every gift and grace I need to be faithful to You in every moment of every day. Thank You for loving me and sending Your angels to guide me and keep me safe from harm. I trust in You and believe that You will deliver me from all evil. Amen.

Prayer to be Defended by the Most Precious Blood

Almighty and everlasting God, You who have appointed Your only-begotten Son to be a Redeemer of the world, and have willed to be appeased by His Blood, grant, we implore You, that by our solemn worship, we may so venerate the price of our redemption, and by Its power, be so defended from the evils of this present earthly life, that we may enjoy its fruits forevermore in Heaven. Through the same Christ our Lord. Amen.

Prayer to the Precious Blood for Conversion or Return to the Faith

O God, all hearts are in Your hands. You can bend, as it pleases You, the most stubborn, and soften the most obdurate. I beseech You by the Holy Name, the Precious Blood, the merits, wounds and Divine Heart of Jesus, Your beloved Son, to grant the conversion of (*name person*). Amen.

Marian Offering of the Precious Blood for Conversion

Immaculate Heart of Mary, offer to the eternal Father the Precious Blood of our Lord Jesus Christ, for the conversion of sinners, especially (*name people*). Amen.

For the Conversion of a Child

(Ann Fitch)

O Sacred Heart of Jesus, I humbly kneel before You, adoring You. Listen to my prayer for grace and salvation for my child who has strayed. From all eternity You have loved him/her. Have mercy on him/her now. I know You want my son/daughter to be converted and live a life in faithfulness to You and Your Church. You have bought him/her at a great price; take possession of Your property. Lead him/her to the Sacrament of Penance, the fountain of pardon and grace which You have opened in Your Church that he/she may receive new life.

Sacred Heart of Jesus, listen to the prayers of Your Blessed Mother and of Your saints for my child. Hear my prayers joined with theirs. I trust You will be moved by our prayers for my child. Grant me what is dearest to me on Earth, the salvation of my child. Thank You, Lord. Amen.

Prayer for Return to the Church
(Ann Fitch)

Eternal and merciful Father, I give You thanks for the gift of Your Divine Son Who suffered, died and rose for the salvation of all mankind. I thank You also for my Catholic faith and ask that with Your help I may grow in fidelity by prayer, by works of charity and penance, by reflection on Your Word, and by regular participation in the Sacrament of Reconciliation and frequent reception of Holy Eucharist.

Heavenly Father, You gave St. Monica a spirit of selfless love that manifested in her constant prayer for the conversion of her family. Inspired by her boundless confidence in Your power to move hearts, and by the success of her prayers, I ask for the grace to imitate her perseverance in my prayers for (*name(s)*) who is/are far from the Church. Grant through my prayers and example of Christian living, that he/she/they may be open to the promptings of Your Holy Spirit, and return to full and faithful union with Your Church. I ask this through Christ, our Lord, Who lives and reigns with You, one God, forever in Heaven. Amen.

Prayer for Conversion to the Catholic Faith
(Ann Fitch)

Merciful and blessed Lord, I know the soul of (*name person*) is in Your all-powerful hands and I believe that You desire his/her conversion more than I do. You have called (*name person*) and have loved him/her from the beginning of time. You paid the ultimate price for his/her salvation. I ask for the gifts of patience and perseverance as I pray for his/her heart, mind, and soul, to be fully opened to You, Your commands, and Your holy Church. I beg of You to fill him/her with every grace needed to freely choose to want to know, love and serve You faithfully as a Roman Catholic. Help me to never give up hoping, believing, trusting that (*name person*) will one day be converted and live a life of faithfulness to You and Your Church. If it is Your will, allow me the joy of celebrating his/her full union with the Catholic faith. Thank You for keeping (*name person*) in Your grace and continuously blessing him/her with Your merciful love. Amen.

Prayer for Turning Back to God
(Ann Fitch)

Heavenly Father, I love You, I praise You, I adore You. I come before You with true contrition in my heart. I am sorry for seeking spiritual experiences outside of You. I choose to turn back to You and be faithful to You alone for You are my God. I know You forgive me for turning away from You and I thank You for pouring out Your Spirit of truth and wisdom upon me, making clear to me my transgressions. Direct my ways and through my faithful participation in the sacraments, meditation on Sacred Scripture, and prayer time show me how to live my life in accordance with Your will.

Lord Jesus, I place myself at the foot of Your cross and ask You in Your love and mercy to pour forth Your Precious Blood upon me and wash me completely clean, removing any spirit of darkness and severing any influence evil has had in my life. Replace all darkness in my life with the light of Your Spirit. I place my trust completely in You and ask for an infilling of Your grace and love. I invite You into my life and ask You to rule and reign over my heart and soul from this day forward.

Come Holy Spirit and bind my mind to the mind of Christ. Transform me as I offer myself to You. Change my attitude, mindset, thought patterns, habits and beliefs. Fill me with Your holy light and illuminate any areas of my life that have been influenced by false doctrines or philosophies. Come into me and sanctify my thoughts, my actions, and my words. Thank You for blessing me and always drawing me into Your love and goodness.

Holy Mary, my mother, continue to intercede for me before the throne of God. Watch over me with all the holy angels, and by your example, inspire me to live my life in humble service to God. Amen.

Prayer in Proxy for Someone to Turn Back to God
(Ann Fitch)

Heavenly Father, I come before You standing in proxy for (*name person*) who has been involved with and influenced by false doctrines and philosophies. I ask You to pour out Your Spirit of truth and wisdom upon (*name person*) and make his/her transgressions clear to him/her. Bless him/her and instill in him/her the desire to only do that which is Your will for him/her.

Lord Jesus, I place (*name person*) at the foot of Your cross and ask You in Your infinite mercy to pour forth Your Precious Blood upon him/her. Sever all influence evil has upon (*name person*) and forgive him/her all his/her sins. I ask You to be Lord of his/her life and to bring him/her Your peace.

O Holy Spirit, fill (*name person*) with Your light, power, and wisdom. Help him/her realize that he/she is Your temple. Change his/her attitude, mindset, thought patterns, habits and beliefs and sanctify his/her thoughts, words, and actions.

Thank You, Lord for Your love for (*name person*). Thank You for blessing (*name person*) with Your strength and grace. Thank You for bringing (*name person*) under Your dominion and power and for setting him/her free to love and serve You both now and forever. Amen.

Prayer to Resist Satan
(Ann Fitch)

Heavenly Father, I know that it is written, *"Submit yourselves to God. Resist the devil, and he will flee from you. Draw near to God, and he will draw near to you."* (James 4:7-8) So I choose to reject Satan and all his works and empty promises. I choose to draw near to You Who are all good and deserving of all my love. I trust that as I draw near to You that You will draw near to me and bless me with every gift and grace I need to resist the devil.

Lord Jesus Christ, let Your Precious Blood pour forth upon me cleansing, sanctifying, and transforming me. You said, *"Peace I leave with you, my peace I give you. Not as the world gives do I give it to you. Do not let your heart be troubled or afraid."* (John 14:27) Holding fast to your promise of peace I choose to not be afraid of Satan and all his works. You have defeated him and I know that Your victory over sin and death is also my victory. You have promised to be faithful to me and protect me from the evil one. I trust in You to fulfill that promise to me now. I cling to You, to Your power, to Your majesty.

Lord, allow Your Holy Spirit to descend upon me and fill me with wisdom, understanding, knowledge, courage, strength, holiness, gentleness, peace and tranquility. May You be glorified in my life and may I always walk in faithful obedience to You, Your laws, and Your Church. Amen.

Prayer to Protect Another from Satan
(Ann Fitch)

Lord Jesus Christ, Satan is working hard in the life of (*name person*) and I come before You asking Your help in keeping him/her safe from harm. You know all the ways in which he/she is being tempted. I ask that You pour out Your Precious Blood upon him/her and cleanse, sanctify and transform him/her and by the power of that Blood to vanquish all forces of evil from his/her life. Allow Your Spirit to fall upon (*name person*) and fill him/her with wisdom, understanding, knowledge, courage, strength, holiness, and peace so that he/she can resist every tactic of the devil. I trust in You to protect (*name person*) and keep him/her safe within the confines of Your Sacred Heart. There may he/she be filled with every gift and grace he/she needs to glorify You in his/her life and hold faithfully on to You, Your laws, and the teachings of Your Church. Amen.

Servants of the Church

Prayer to the Sacred Heart for the Church

O most holy Heart of Jesus, shower Your blessings in abundant measure upon Your holy Church, upon the Supreme Pontiff, and upon all the clergy; to the just grant perseverance; convert sinners; enlighten unbelievers; bless our relations, friends, and benefactors; assist the dying; deliver the holy souls in Purgatory; and extend over all hearts the sweet empire of Your love. Amen.

Prayer for the Pope
(Ann Fitch)

O God, Divine Shepherd of all the faithful, look favorably on Your servant (*name pope*), whom You have set at the head of Your Church. Grant, we pray, that by word and example he may be of service to those over whom he presides and build Your Church into a sacrament of unity, love and peace for all the world. May he be blessed with every gift and grace in this life and together with the flock entrusted to his care come to the joy of everlasting life. We ask this through our Lord Jesus Christ, Your Son, Who lives and reigns with You in the unity of the Holy Spirit, one God, forever and ever. Amen.

A Prayer for Vocations through the Intercession of St. John Vianney

O God our Father, You promised, *"I will appoint shepherds for My sheep who will shepherd them so that they need no longer fear and tremble: and none shall be missing."* (Jeremiah 23:4-5) Hear my prayers. Through the intercession of Your beloved priest, St. John Vianney, I beg You to call to the sacramental priesthood generous men who will desire nothing more than to serve You in imitation of Your Son, Our Lord Jesus Christ, our High Priest.

And after You call them, I pray that You sustain the doubtful, console the discouraged, strengthen the weak, enflame the hearts of each with a true zeal for the salvation of souls, encourage those who doubt, and embrace and sanctify each one as he progresses through the long and demanding preparation for the priesthood.

Mary, Mother of priests, and example of faithful, humble, and joyful acceptance of God's will, help all those who are called to the priesthood to open their hearts to the gentle call of the Holy Spirit and respond with a resounding, "Yes!"   Amen.

Litany for Seminarians

(Ann Fitch)

That all seminarians have great love for the Holy Trinity. *I beseech You, Lord.*

That all seminarians are filled with the gifts and fruits of the Holy Spirit. *I beseech You, Lord.*

That all seminarians are filled with a burning zeal for the salvation of souls. *I beseech You, Lord.*

That all seminarians are filled with every gift and grace. *I beseech You, Lord.*

That all seminarians have open, humble, and generous hearts. *I beseech You, Lord.*

That all seminarians are men of prayer. *I beseech You, Lord.*

That all seminarians are obedient to the Church and their superiors. *I beseech You, Lord.*

That all seminarians are holy in body, mind, heart and soul. *I beseech You, Lord.*

That all seminarians are the light of Christ to those around them. *I beseech You, Lord.*

That all seminarians have an intense love for the Holy Eucharist. *I beseech You, Lord.*

That all seminarians who are ill are restored to health. *I beseech You, Lord.*

That all seminarians who are sad are comforted and consoled. *I beseech You, Lord.*

That all seminarians who are anxious or worried are filled with peace and joy. *I beseech You, Lord.*

That all seminarians who feel lonely find loving friends to uplift them. *I beseech You, Lord.*

That all seminarians who are questioning their vocation find clarity and conviction. *I beseech You, Lord.*

That all seminarians burn with love for God and all His people. *I beseech You, Lord.*

That all seminarians have great love for Mary and all the saints. *I beseech You, Lord.*

That all seminarians do all for the glory of God. *I beseech You, Lord.*

O God, hear the prayer I am offering for all seminarians. Give them all clarity and conviction when it comes to their vocation. Help them to be men of faith, hope, and love. Draw them ever closer to You and fill them with the grace and strength they need to be faithful and true to You and Your holy Church. May they answer Your call with open, humble, and generous hearts and be dedicated to joyfully serving and loving You all through their lives. Amen.

Daily Prayer for Priests
(St. Therese of Lisieux)

O Jesus, I pray for Your: faithful and fervent priests; for Your unfaithful and tepid priests; for Your priests laboring at home or abroad in distant mission fields; for Your tempted priests; for Your lonely and desolate priests; for Your young priests; for Your dying priests; for the souls of Your priests in Purgatory.

But above all, I recommend to You the priests dearest to me: the priest who baptized me; the priests who absolved me from my sins; the priests whose Masses I attended and who gave me Your Body and Blood in Holy Communion; the priests who taught and instructed me; all the priests to whom I am indebted in any other way especially (*name priest(s)*).

O Jesus, keep them all close to Your heart, and bless them abundantly in time and in eternity.   Amen.

Prayer for Holy Priests
(St. Charles Borromeo)

O Holy Mother of God, pray for the priests your Son has chosen to serve the Church. Help them by your intercession, to be holy, zealous and chaste. Make them models of virtue in the service of God's people. Help them to be prayerful in meditations, effective in preaching, and enthusiastic in the daily offering of the holy sacrifice of the Mass. Help them to administer the sacraments with joy.   Amen.

Prayer for Priests
(Ann Fitch)

Heavenly Father, I come before You in prayer for all priests. I ask that through Your Holy Spirit You fill them with Your: love and compassion; wisdom and knowledge; understanding and counsel; integrity and justice; humility and generosity; patience and peace; gentleness and kindness; happiness and joy; strength and courage;

passion and zeal. Grant them every grace they need to fulfill their calling and have total dedication to You.

Lord Jesus, inflame their hearts with burning love for You and a deep desire for the salvation of souls. Imbue them with renewed faith and hope. Inspire them to be merciful and empathetic. Sanctify, guide and renew them. Bless them with health and wholeness. Enkindle in them intense love and reverence for You in the Eucharist, loyalty and obedience to their superiors or bishops and the Church, and true holiness in body, mind and spirit.

Lord, may their eyes reassure, their words inspire, and their hands be instruments of healing. May they hear You speaking to them in the quiet of their hearts and feel Your constant presence with them as they minister in Your love. May Your holy angels keep them safe from all harm. And, may they know Your Mother's love, have her constant intercession on their behalf, and be safeguarded in the confines of her Immaculate Heart. Amen.

Litany for Priests

Jesus, meek and humble of heart, give all priests Your spirit of humility.

Jesus, poor and worn out for souls, give all priests Your spirit of zeal.

Jesus, full of patience and mercy for sinners, give all priests Your spirit of compassion.

Jesus, victim for the sins of the world, give all priests Your spirit of sacrifice.

Jesus, lover of the little and the poor, give all priests Your spirit of charity.

Mary, Queen of the Clergy, pray for us; and obtain for us numerous and holy priests and religious. Amen.

A Prayer for Priests
(St. Therese of Lisieux)

O Jesus, eternal Priest, keep Your priests within the shelter of Your Sacred Heart, where none may touch them. Keep unstained their anointed hands, which daily touch Your Sacred Body. Keep unsullied their lips, daily purpled with Your Precious Blood. Keep pure and unearthly their hearts, sealed with the sublime mark of the priesthood. Let Your holy love surround them and shield them from the world's contagion. Bless their labors with abundant fruit and may the souls to whom they minister be their joy and consolation here and in Heaven their beautiful and everlasting crown.   Amen.

Prayer for a Specific Priest
(Ann Fitch)

O Jesus, Eternal High Priest, live in (*name priest*), act in him, speak in and through him. Think Your thoughts in his mind, love through his heart. Give him Your own dispositions and feelings. Teach, lead and guide him always. Correct, enlighten and expand his thoughts. Possess his soul and direct his life. Replace him with Yourself. Incline him to constant adoration and thanksgiving; pray in and through him. Let him live in You and keep him in intimate union with You always.

O Mary, Mother of Jesus and Mother of Priests, pray and intercede for (*name priest*).   Amen.

Litany for Priests

Let us pray for the Holy Father: fill him with courage and grace, Lord.
Cardinals, archbishops, and bishops: give them a shepherd's heart, Lord.
Diocesan priests: fill them with your Spirit, Lord.
Priests in religious orders: perfect them in their calling, Lord.
Priests who are ill: heal them, Lord.
Priests who are in danger: deliver them, Lord.
Priests who are weak: strengthen them, Lord.

Priests who are poor: relieve them, Lord.

Priests who have lost their zeal: renew them, Lord.

Priests who are sad: console them, Lord.

Priests who are worried: give them peace, Lord.

Priest who are old: sustain them, Lord.

Priests who are alone: accompany them, Lord.

Missionary priests: protect them, Lord.

Priests who are preachers: enlighten them, Lord.

Priest who direct souls: instruct them, Lord.

Priests who have died: bring them to glory, Lord.

For all priests: give them Your wisdom and knowledge.

For all priests: give them Your understanding and counsel.

For all priests: give them reverence and awe of You.

For all priests: give them patience and love.

For all priests: give them obedience and kindness.

For all priests: give them a burning zeal for souls.

For all priests: give them virtues of faith, hope and love.

For all priests: give them an intense love for the Eucharist.

For all priests: give them loyalty to the Holy Father and their Bishops.

For all priests: give them respect for life and human dignity.

For all priests: give them integrity and justice.

For all priests: give them humility and generosity.

For all priests: give them strength in their labors.

For all priests: give them peace in their sufferings.

For all priests: give them great love for the Trinity.

For all priests: give them great love for Mary.

For all priests: let them be the light of Christ.

For all priests: let them be the salt of the earth.

For all priests: let them practice sacrifice and self-denial.

For all priests: let them be holy in body, mind and spirit.

For all priests: let them be men of prayer.

For all priests: may faith shine forth in them.

For all priests: may they be concerned for our salvation.

For all priests: may they be faithful to their priestly vocation.

For all priests: may their hands bless and heal.

For all priests: may they burn with love for You.

For all priests: may all their steps be for the glory of God.

For all priests: may the Holy Spirit fill them, and give them His gifts in abundance.

Father, Son, and Holy Spirit, hear the prayer I am offering for priests. Let them know clearly the work that You are calling them to do. Grant them every grace to answer Your call with courage, love, and lasting dedication to Your will. Amen.

Prayer for Joyful Priests and Religious

Heavenly Father, give the Church today many, holy, prayerful and joyful priests and religious. May their enthusiasm and good humor inspire the faithful, transform our hearts, extend Your Kingdom and bring You glory. We ask this through Jesus Christ, Your Son. Amen.

Prayer for the Repose of the Soul of a Priest

O God, You raised Your servant, (*name priest*), to the sacred priesthood of Jesus Christ, according to the Order of Melchisedech, giving him the sublime power to offer the Eternal Sacrifice, to bring the Body and Blood of Your Son Jesus Christ down upon the altar, and to absolve the sins of men in Your own Holy Name. We beseech You to reward his faithfulness and in Your mercy to forget his faults, admitting him speedily into Your Holy Presence, there to enjoy forever the recompense of his labors. This we ask through Jesus Christ Your Son, our Lord. Amen.

A Prayer for Deacons
(Ann Fitch)

Heavenly Father, we come to You asking Your blessing upon all deacons. You have called them to serve You and Your Church and they are an extraordinary blessing. May they be filled with the wisdom of Your Spirit as they teach, lead, and guide Your people. As they proclaim and preach the Gospel, assist at Holy Mass, administer the Sacrament of Baptism, witness marriages, and conduct wake and funeral services may they be the Light of Christ for others. May they be filled with every grace as they balance their service as a deacon with their work and family life. By their witness may they lead countless souls to know, love, and serve You. Amen.

Prayer for a Specific Deacon
(Ann Fitch)

O Holy Spirit, giver of all gifts, bless (*name deacon*) with every gift and grace he needs to fulfill his duties as deacon. Fortify him, strengthen him, and fill him with patience, peace, hope and joy. Fill his heart to overflowing with love for God, His people, and His holy Church. Fill his mind with wisdom and knowledge so that he is a blessing to those who seek his counsel and guidance. May he, by the example of his life, draw others to Christ. Bless (*name deacon*) each day with renewed zeal, a deepened love for the Holy Eucharist, and a profound desire to serve the Lord in those he encounters. Thank You for calling (*name deacon*) to serve as deacon. Bless his family for selflessly and generously sharing him with the Church. May they together grow in faith and love. Amen.

Prayer for Vocations to Religious Life
(Ann Fitch)

Heavenly Father, we thank You for calling faithful men and women to live a consecrated life and for choosing them before they were born to fulfill Your call to spread Your love and spend their lives for the salvation of souls throughout the world. Thank You for calling them through grace to a holy life and for deeming them worthy to serve You.

Bless these men and women whom You have called and set apart and through Your loving kindness draw them into the vocation of consecrated life. Fill them with courage and strength as they faithfully dedicate themselves to You in service within the Church. Pour out upon them the gifts of the Holy Spirit and bless them with the virtues of charity, humility, meekness, patience, and wisdom.

In Your love bless the works they are called to do and keep them ever faithful to You and Your Church. May they be lights shining in the darkness, beacons of hope and joy, men and women of integrity, faith, and love. Thank You for setting them apart and using them for Your honor and glory. Amen.

Prayer for Religious Men and Women
(Ann Fitch)

Gracious and ever-loving God, I ask You in Your infinite goodness to bless all religious men and women. Fill them to overflowing with every gift and grace they need to live out Your call to a life of poverty, chastity and obedience with courage, devotion, and perpetual dedication. Be for them, O generous Lord, their joy, their comfort, their support, and their strength.

Send forth Your Spirit upon them Lord, and fortify them, fill them with joy, and enflame their hearts and souls with a burning love for You. Let them be living signs of Your presence in the world and bless them with steadfast faith, true humility, firm hope, and burning zeal for the salvation of souls. May their fidelity to You and Your Church provide them with peace and contentment and may their loving service be fruitful and rewarding. Amen.

A Prayer for Catechists

(Ann Fitch)

Lord we thank You for the men and women who have stepped forward to be catechists. Fill them to overflowing with zeal for Your Church and with a deep abiding love for You and those they will catechize. Pour out Your Spirit upon them and bless them with wisdom, knowledge, compassion, kindness, gentleness and patience.

May Your Spirit guide their words and actions and may they inspire those they catechize to desire to know, love and serve You faithfully throughout their lives. May they be true blessings to the people they serve, as they share their love for You, be witnesses to the Gospel, and be true reflections of Your love. Amen.

Thanksgiving

Prayer of Thanks

O my God, I thank You for all the favors You have bestowed upon me. I give You thanks from the bottom of my heart for having created me, and for all the joys of life, and its sorrows, too, for the home You gave me, for the loved ones with which You have surrounded me, for the friends I have made through life.

My Lord, I thank You for guarding me always and keeping me safe; I thank You for giving me so often in the Sacrament of Penance forgiveness for my sins; for offering Yourself in Holy Mass with all the infinite merits to the Father for me; for coming to me in Holy Communion, in spite of the coldness of my welcome; for the patient waiting in the adorable Sacrament of the Altar.

My Jesus, I thank You for having lived, suffered, and died for me. I thank You for Your love. I thank You, Lord, for preparing a place for me in Heaven where I hope to be happy with You, and to thank You for all eternity. Amen.

Thanksgiving Prayer
(Ann Fitch)

Almighty God, I humbly give You thanks for all Your goodness and loving kindness, and all the blessings of this life. But above all, I thank You for Your unspeakable gift of love in the redemption of the world through Your Son, Jesus Christ - the source of hope and the means of grace. Instill in me awareness of all Your goodness, that my heart may be overflowing with gratitude, that I might sing Your praise, not only with my lips, but with my life, giving myself wholly to Your service and walking in Your sight with humility and grace. Amen.

In Thanksgiving for Prayers Answered
(Ann Fitch)

Lord, I am grateful that You are with me, loving me, every moment of every day. I know that You only want what is best for me. You know what I need even before I ask. You are always faithful and I am humbled by Your faithfulness. I have trusted in You completely and placed myself in Your generous and loving hands. Thank You for Your infinite love and immeasurable mercy. Thank You for listening to and answering my prayers. My heart is full of joy that You have answered me so beautifully. Receive my thanks. You know that I love You and that I will continue to seek Your help and praise You all the days of my life. Amen.

Prayer of Thanksgiving for Restored Health
(Ann Fitch)

Almighty and ever loving God, I give You thanks for having restored (*name person*) to fullness of health. In Your infinite love and kindness, You, the Divine Physician, have reached down, touched him/her with Your healing love, and graced him/her with healing and wholeness. For this I praise You and give You thanks my Lord and my God. I cannot extol You enough or find words to express the depth of my gratitude. May You be praised, honored, and adored always. Amen.

Thank You Prayer

Dear Lord,

For all that You have given to me, thank You.

For all that You have withdrawn, thank You.

For all that You have withheld, thank You.

For all that You have permitted, thank You.

For all that You have prevented, thank You.

For all that You have forgiven me, thank You.

For all that You have prepared me for, thank You.

For all my strengths, thank You.

For all my weaknesses, thank You.

For the death that You have chosen for me, thank You.

For the place You have prepared for me in Heaven, thank You.

For having created me to love You for all eternity, thank You.   Amen.

Litany of Thanksgiving

(Ann Fitch)

For the beauty of creation. *I thank You, Lord.*

For the gift of life and breath. *I thank You, Lord.*

For this day. *I thank You, Lord.*

For the gift of free will. *I thank You, Lord.*

For the gift of faith. *I thank You, Lord.*

For the ability to know, love, and serve You. *I thank You, Lord.*

For my relationship with You in Your Triune form. *I thank You, Lord.*

For Your faithfulness, love, and unconditional acceptance. *I thank You, Lord.*

For the gift of my salvation. *I thank You, Lord.*

For Your mercy, love, and forgiveness. *I thank You, Lord.*

For the Church, her sacraments, her guidance, and her wisdom. *I thank You, Lord.*

For my immediate family whom I love. *I thank You, Lord.*

For my extended family whom I love. *I thank You, Lord.*

For my friends who love, support and care for me. *I thank You, Lord.*

For the gifts and talents I have been given. *I thank You, Lord.*

For my job and the financial stability it brings me. *I thank You, Lord.*

For my home which provides shelter and safety. *I thank You, Lord.*

For the food I have to eat that nourishes and sustains me. *I thank You, Lord.*

For my health and the health of those I love. *I thank You, Lord.*

For the joys, challenges and difficulties of life. *I thank You, Lord.*

For all the varied answers to my prayers. *I thank You, Lord.*

For my many freedoms. *I thank You, Lord.*

For every grace and blessing You have bestowed upon me. *I thank You, Lord.*

NOVENAS

The word novena comes from the Latin word "novem" which means nine. It is a prayer or set of prayers said over the course of nine consecutive hours, nine days, or nine weeks on the same day of the week. It is a prayer of confidence and perseverance that is usually said for a special intention or special grace that is an immediate need or a need with a sense of urgency for oneself or another. A novena may be said privately or publicly. When a novena is prayed in anticipation of a feast day it is started 10 days before the feast so that the novena ends on the day before the feast day.

Novenas find their origin in ancient tradition. Originally, they were a Greek and Roman custom of praying for nine days after the death of a loved one followed by a feast or celebration. The practice of praying a novena was adopted by those in the early Church and was associated with Mary and the apostles praying for nine days in the Upper Room until the Holy Spirit descended on Pentecost.

Novenas can be a source of great consolation and are a way to take immediate action when a special need or intention arises. Here is a collection of novenas for many different needs that may comfort you and help you commit your intentions to God. Remember, novenas are prayers of confidence in God, trust in His holy will, and perseverance for special intentions.

"Devote yourselves to prayer, keeping alert in it with thanksgiving." (Colossians 4:2)

Novena of Urgent Need to the Sacred Heart

O Jesus, Who has said, *"Ask and you shall receive, seek and you shall find, knock and it shall be opened,"* through the intercession of Mary, Your Most Holy Mother, I knock, I seek, I ask that my prayer be granted (*state your intention*).

O Jesus, Who has said, *"All that you ask of the Father in My Name, He will grant you,"* through the intercession of Mary, Your Most Holy Mother, I humbly and urgently ask Your Father in Your Name that my prayer will be granted (*state your intention*).

O Jesus, Who has said, *"Heaven and Earth shall pass away but My word shall not pass away,"* through the intercession of Mary, Your Most Holy Mother, I feel confident that my prayer will be granted (*state your intention*).

O Sacred Heart of Jesus, for Whom it is impossible not to have compassion on the afflicted, have pity on us poor sinners and grant us the grace which we ask of You, through the Sorrowful and Immaculate Heart of Mary, Your tender Mother and ours.

Pray the **Hail Holy Queen**.

Novena of Confidence to the Sacred Heart

O Lord Jesus Christ, to Your most Sacred Heart I confide this intention (*state your intention*). Only look upon me, then do what Your love inspires. Let Your Sacred Heart decide. I count on You. I trust in You, I throw myself on Your mercy. Lord Jesus, You will not fail me.

Sacred Heart of Jesus, I trust in You.
Sacred Heart of Jesus, I believe in Your love for me.
Sacred Heart of Jesus, Your kingdom come.

O Sacred Heart of Jesus, I have asked You for many favors, but I earnestly implore this one. Take it, place it in Your open Heart. When the Eternal Father looks upon it, He will see it covered with Your

Precious Blood. It will be no longer my prayer but Yours, Jesus. O Sacred Heart of Jesus, I place all my trust in You. Let me not be disappointed. Amen.

Novena to the Infant Jesus of Prague

Dear Jesus, little Infant of Prague, how tenderly You love us! Your greatest joy is to dwell among us and to bestow Your blessing upon us. So many who turned to You with confidence have received graces and had their petitions granted. I also come before You now with this special request (*state your intention*).

Dear Infant Jesus, rule over me and do with me and mine as You will, for I know that in Your divine wisdom and love You will arrange everything for the best. Do not withdraw Your hand from me, but protect and bless me forever.

Dear Infant Jesus, help me in my needs. Make me truly happy with You in time and in eternity, and I shall thank You forever with all my heart. Amen.

Novena to St. Jude for Others

(Ann Fitch)

O most holy apostle, St. Jude, faithful servant and friend of Jesus, the Church honors and invokes you universally, as the patron of difficult cases. Please pray for (*name person*). Intercede with God for him/her that He will come to his/her assistance particularly with (*state your intention*) and that He will answer according to His will and for (*name person's*) greater good. Thank you, St. Jude for your help. May (*name person*) in time enjoy the promise of Heaven and there praise God with you and all the saints forever and ever. Amen.

Novena to St. Jude for Oneself

(Ann Fitch)

O most holy apostle, St. Jude, faithful servant and friend of Jesus, the Church honors and invokes you universally, as the patron of difficult cases. Please pray for me. Intercede with God for me that He will come to my assistance particularly with (*state your intention*) and that He will answer according to His will and for my greater good. Thank you, St. Jude for your help. May I in time enjoy the promise of Heaven and there praise God with you and all the saints forever and ever. Amen.

St. Jude Novena

Most holy St. Jude – apostle, martyr and friend of Jesus, today I ask that you pray for me and my intentions!

(*State your intentions here.*) You are the patron of the impossible. Pray for me and my intentions! O St. Jude, pray that God's grace and mercy will cover my intentions. Pray for the impossible if it is God's will. Pray that I may have the grace to accept God's holy will even if it is painful and difficult for me. St. Jude, pray for me that I will not lose faith. O St. Jude, pray for me that I may grow in faith, hope and love and in the grace of Jesus Christ. Pray for these intentions, but most of all pray that I may join you in Heaven with God for all eternity.   Amen.

May the Most Sacred Heart of Jesus be adored, and loved in all the tabernacles until the end of time.   Amen.

May the most Sacred Heart of Jesus be praised and glorified now and forever.   Amen.

St. Jude pray for us and hear our prayers.   Amen.

Blessed be the Sacred Heart of Jesus. Blessed be the Immaculate Heart of Mary. Blessed be St. Jude Thaddeus, in all the world and for all eternity.   Amen.

Pray an **Our Father** and a **Hail Mary**.

A Precious Offering Novena

O Mary, Mother of Sorrows, I beseech you, by the inexpressible tortures you did endure at the death of your Son, offer to the Eternal Father, in my stead, your beloved Son all covered with Blood and Wounds, for the grace of (*state your intention*). Amen.

Novena to the Father

Eternal Father, I offer You the Precious Blood of Jesus Christ, the merits, love and sufferings of His Sacred Heart, the tears and sorrows of our Immaculate Mother, as the price of the favor I wish to obtain (*mention request here*), if it is for Your glory and my salvation.   Amen.

Novena to the Holy Spirit

Holy Spirit, third Person of the Blessed Trinity, Spirit of truth, love and holiness, proceeding from the Father and the Son, and equal to them in all things, I adore You and love You with all my heart.

Dearest Holy Spirit, confiding in Your deep, personal love for me, I am making this novena for the following request, if it should be Your will to grant it (*state your intention*).

Breathe in me, Holy Spirit, that all my thoughts may be holy. Act in me, Holy Spirit, that all my work may be holy. Fill my heart, Holy Spirit, that I may love only what is holy. Strengthen me, Holy Spirit, ever to defend what is holy. Guard me always, Holy Spirit, that I may ever remain holy. Preserve me, Holy Spirit, that my body may remain Your dwelling place. In my last hour, call me, Holy Spirit, to enjoy the holiness of Heaven.   Amen.

Novena in Honor of the Sorrows of the Blessed Virgin Mary

Most holy and afflicted Virgin, Queen of Martyrs, you stood beneath the cross, witnessing the agony of your dying Son. Look with a mother's tenderness and pity on me, who kneel before you. I venerate your sorrows and I place my requests with filial confidence in the sanctuary of your wounded heart. Present them, I beseech you, on my behalf to Jesus Christ, through the merits of His own most sacred passion and death, together with your sufferings at the foot of the cross. Through the united efficacy of both, obtain the granting of my petition. Intercede for me and obtain for me from Jesus (*state your intention*) if it be for His honor and glory and for my good. Amen.

Novena to the Precious Blood

Lord Jesus, by the power of Your Precious Blood, I ask You to hear my prayers and answer them. So many graces, so many mercies have come forth from Your Precious Blood that I shall not cease to hope even to the end, in Its efficacy. O Jesus, by Your Precious Blood seven times shed for the welfare of man, I entreat You to hear my prayer (*state your intention*).

O Sweet Jesus, Who during Your mortal life consoled the suffering, healed the sick, encouraged so many who were disheartened, I know that in Your infinite mercy You will not fail to have pity on a me as I cry out to You from the depth of my soul through the merits of Your Most Precious Blood. Thank You for hearing and answering my prayer in a way that honors and glorifies Our Father in Heaven.   Amen.

Novena to Your Guardian Angel

O holy angel, whom God, by the effect of His goodness and His tender regard for my welfare, has charged with the care of my conduct, and who assists me in all my wants and comforts me in all my afflictions, who supports me when I am discouraged and continually obtains for me new favors, I return to you profound thanks, and I earnestly beseech you, O most amiable protector, to continue your charitable care and defense of me against the malignant attacks of all my enemies. Keep me away from all occasions of sin. Obtain for me the grace of listening attentively to your holy inspirations and of faithfully putting them into practice. In particular, I implore you to obtain for me the favor which I ask for by this novena (*mention your petition*). Protect me in all the temptations and trials of this life, but more especially at the hour of my death, and do not leave me until you have conducted me into the presence of my Creator in the mansions of everlasting happiness. Amen.

Novena to St. Padre Pio

Dear St. Padre Pio, God blessed you with the gifts of the Spirit. Your body was marked with the five wounds of Christ crucified and you were a powerful witness to the saving passion and death of Jesus. God endowed you with the gift of discernment, and you labored endlessly in the confessional for the salvation of souls. With reverence and intense devotion you celebrated Mass, and invited countless men and women to enter into greater union with Jesus Christ in the Sacrament of the Holy Eucharist. Through your intercession, countless healings and miracles have occurred. So, I confidently ask God to grant me the grace of (*state your intention*), through your intercession. Amen.

Novena to the Immaculate Heart of Mary

Immaculate Heart of Mary, full of love for God and mankind, and of compassion for sinners, I consecrate myself entirely to you. I entrust to you the salvation of my soul. May my heart be ever united with yours, so that I may hate sin, love God, and my neighbor, and reach eternal life together with those whom I love. Mediatrix of all graces and Mother of Mercy, remember the infinite treasure which your Divine Son has merited by His sufferings and which He has confided to you for us, your children.

Filled with confidence in your motherly Heart, which I venerate and love, I come to you with my pressing needs. Through the merits of your loving Heart, and for the sake of the Sacred Heart of Jesus, obtain for me the favor I ask (*state your intention*).

Dearest Mother, if what I ask for should not be according to God's Will, pray that I may receive that which will be of greater benefit to my soul. May I experience the kindness of your motherly Heart and the power of your intercession with Jesus during life and at the hour of my death. Amen.

Novena to Our Lady of the Rosary

My dearest Mother Mary, behold me, your child, in prayer at your feet. Accept this Holy Rosary, which I offer you in accordance with your requests at Fatima, as a proof of my tender love for you, for the intentions of the Sacred Heart of Jesus, in atonement for the offenses committed against your Immaculate Heart, and for this special favor which I earnestly request in my Rosary Novena (*mention your request*).

I beg you to present my petition to your Divine Son. If you will pray for me, I cannot be refused. I know, dearest Mother, that you want me to seek God's holy will concerning my request. If what I ask for should not be granted, pray that I may receive that which will be of greater benefit to my soul.

I offer you this spiritual "Bouquet of Roses" because I love you. I put all my confidence in you, since your prayers before God are most powerful. For the greater glory of God and for the sake of Jesus, your loving Son, hear and grant my prayer. Sweet Heart of Mary, be my salvation. Amen.

Pray the *Rosary*.

Novena to St. Joseph

O glorious St. Joseph, you were appointed by the eternal Father as the guardian and protector of the life of Jesus Christ. You were the comfort and support of His holy mother, and the instrument in His great design for the redemption of mankind. You had the happiness of living with Jesus and Mary, and of dying in their arms.

Be moved with the confidence we place in you, and procure for us from the Almighty, the particular favors which we humbly ask through your intercession (*state your intention*). Pray for us, O great St. Joseph, and by your love for Jesus and Mary, and by their love for you, obtain for us the supreme happiness of living and dying in their love. Amen.

Novena to St. Joseph in Times of Difficulty

O glorious St. Joseph, you who have power to render possible even things which are considered impossible, come to my aid in my present trouble and distress. Take this important and difficult affair under your protection and pray that it may come to a happy ending (*state your intention*).

O dear St. Joseph, all my confidence is in you. Since you are so dear to Jesus and Mary, place my intention in their hands and in your goodness continue to plead my case with them. Thank you, St. Joseph for your love and intercession. Amen.

Novena to the Holy Angels

Bless the Lord, all you His angels. You who are mighty in strength and do His will, intercede for me at the throne of God. By your unceasing watchfulness protect me in every danger of soul and body. Obtain for me the grace of final perseverance, so that after this life I may be admitted to your glorious company and with you may sing the praises of God for all eternity.

All you holy angels and archangels, thrones and dominions, principalities and powers and virtues of Heaven, cherubim and seraphim, and especially you, my dear guardian angel, intercede for me and obtain for me the special favor I now ask (*state your intention*).

Pray one **Glory Be**.

Novena to St. John Paul II
(Ann Fitch)

Dear St. John Paul II, you urged us to open wide our hearts to Christ and conquer hatred with love. You led the Church faithfully and fearlessly, trusting in God's infinite mercy and the intercession of the Blessed Virgin Mary. I come before you seeking your intercession. Please take this need (*mention request*) and with Mary deliver it to God the Father, God the Son, and God the Holy Spirit. Place it before Them asking that if it be Their will and for Their honor and glory that They answer favorably.

Through your example of love, humility, peace, hope and joy countless lives were drawn to the love of God and countless men and women dedicated themselves to His service. You drew the youth of the world together and inspired them to serve the Church and be faithful to her. Thank you, St. John Paul II, for your service to the Church and for your intercession on my behalf. Amen.

Novena to St. Therese, The Little Flower

O Little Therese of the Child Jesus, please pick for me a rose from the heavenly gardens and send it to me as a message of love. O Little Flower of Jesus, ask God today to grant the favors I now place with confidence in your hands (*state your intention*).

St. Therese, help me to always believe as you did, in God's great love for me, so that I might imitate your "Little Way" each day. Amen.

Novena to St. Anne
(Ann Fitch)

O glorious St. Anne, filled with compassion for those who invoke you and love for those who suffer, heavily laden with the weight of my troubles, I throw myself at your feet and humbly beg of you to take under your special protection that which I commend to you (*state your intention*).

Recommend it to your daughter, the Blessed Virgin Mary, and lay it before the throne of your grandson, Jesus, so that He may bring it to a happy outcome. Cease not to intercede for me until God in His infinite wisdom answers my request. Above all, obtain for me the grace of one day beholding my God face to face, and, with you and Mary and all the saints, may I praise and bless Him for all eternity.

Good St. Anne, mother of Mary who is our life, our sweetness and our hope, and grandmother to our Lord, Jesus, intercede for me and obtain my request if it be the will of God. Amen.

Novena to St. Monica
(Ann Fitch)

Dear St. Monica, troubled wife and mother, many sorrows pierced your heart during your lifetime. Yet, you never despaired or lost faith. With confidence, persistence, and profound faith, you prayed daily for the conversion of your children and husband. Inspired by your faithfulness I ask you to intercede for me with Mary, the Mother of God, on behalf of (*state name(s) here*) that God will grant his/her/their conversion.

Dear St. Monica, I have full confidence, that your prayers and the prayers of our Blessed Mother will gain favorable hearing in Heaven. Mother of a sinner turned saint; obtain for me patience, perseverance, and total trust in God's perfect timing. In God's appointed hour, in His merciful way, may He respond to your prayer and mine, which I offer through you and the Blessed Virgin Mary for His greater honor and glory. Amen.

Novena to St. Monica

Dear St. Monica, you were once the mournful mother of a prodigal son. Your faithfulness to prayer brought you and your son so close to God that you are now with him in eternity. By your intercession and God's grace, your son St. Augustine became a great and venerable saint of the Church. Please take my request to God with the same fervor and persistence with which you prayed for your own son (*state your intentions*).

With your needs, worries and anxieties, you threw yourself on the mercy and providence of God. Through sorrow and pain, you constantly devoted yourself to God. Pray for me that I might join you in such a deep faith in God's goodness and mercy. Above all, dear St. Monica, pray for me that I may, like your son, turn from my sin and become a great saint for the glory of God. Amen.

Mother's Novena

Cherished Virgin, Heaven's Queen, chosen before all women to be the mother of the Son of God, Mary, my Mother, who in your maternity so sanctified the state of holy motherhood, imploringly I come to you; humbly I beseech you; confidently I trust in you (*mention your request*). I know that, by your powerful intercession, you can help me in my need. In you I take refuge, dear Virgin, my Mother. Poor and needy, I turn devoutly to you and place all confidently in your hands. Accept my humble trust, hear my petitions and come to my aid, dear Mother of Mothers. Amen.

Novena to St. Anthony

O Holy St. Anthony, gentlest of saints, your love for God and charity for His creatures made you worthy, when on Earth, to possess miraculous powers. Miracles waited on your word, which you were ever ready to speak for those in trouble or anxiety. Encouraged by this thought, I implore of you to obtain for me (*state your intention*).

The answer to my prayer may require a miracle, even so, you are the saint of miracles. O gentle and loving St. Anthony, whose heart was ever full of human sympathy, whisper my petition into the ears of the sweet Infant Jesus, who loved to be folded in your arms, and the gratitude of my heart will ever be yours. Amen.

Novena to St. Dominic

O Holy Priest of God, St. Dominic, beloved son and confidant of the Queen of Heaven, on Earth you opened your heart to the miseries of your fellow man, and your hands were strong to help them. Now in Heaven, pray for me to Mary, Mother of the Rosary, and to her divine Son, Jesus, for I have great confidence that through your assistance I shall obtain the favor I desire (*state your intention*).

O glorious Mother of God, Queen of the Most Holy Rosary, you who did love St. Dominic with the affection of a mother, and were most tenderly loved and honored by him, look upon me, for his sake, with an eye of pity, deign to join with him in presenting my petition to your beloved Son, Jesus. I sincerely desire from this moment to love Him with all my heart, and serve Him with all my strength, and now place myself under your powerful protection, as a sure means of obtaining all the graces necessary to serve Him faithfully on Earth, that I may eternally rejoice with Him in Heaven. Amen.

Novena to St. Gerard
(Ann Fitch)

Dear St. Gerard, patron saint of pregnancy, I ask you to lovingly place (*name person*) and her unborn child(ren) in the Blessed Mother's arms. Ask her, as a mother, to plead for their health and safety, before the Holy Trinity with you. Pray that (*name person*) will be patient and trusting during her pregnancy and delivery and that she will have no fears. I thank you for your continued prayers for (*name person*) and her unborn child(ren) and for your constant intercession on their behalf. Amen.

Novena to St. Peregrine
(Ann Fitch)

Dear St. Peregrine, patron saint of those with cancer, I ask your intercession for (*name person*) who is suffering with cancer. Ask God to relieve him/her of this illness if that be His holy will. Plead with the

Blessed Virgin Mary, whom you loved so tenderly, to carry him/her to the throne of God and intercede on his/her behalf. Help (*name person*) to imitate you, St. Peregrine, in accepting suffering and to unite his/her suffering with Jesus crucified as you did for God's greater glory and the salvation of souls. Thank you, St. Peregrine, for your intercession. Amen.

Exaltation of the Holy Cross Novena

Jesus, Who because of Your burning love for us willed to be crucified and to shed Your Most Precious Blood for the redemption and salvation of our souls, look down upon us and grant the petition we ask for (*state your intention*).

We trust completely in Your mercy. Cleanse us from sin by Your grace, sanctify our work, give us and all those who are dear to us our daily bread, lighten the burden of our sufferings, bless our families, and grant to the nations, so sorely afflicted, Your peace, which is the only true peace, so that by obeying Your commandments we may come at last to the glory of Heaven. Amen.

Novena to the Precious Blood for the Souls in Purgatory

O gentlest Heart of Jesus, ever present in the Blessed Sacrament, ever consumed with burning love for the poor captive souls in Purgatory, have mercy on the soul of Your departed servant (*name person*). Be not severe in Your judgment but let some drops of Your Precious Blood fall upon the devouring flames and do You, O Merciful Savior send Your angels to conduct Your departed servant (*name person*) to a place of refreshment, light and peace. Amen.

Novena of Divine Mercy

During the Solemn Novena leading to Divine Mercy Sunday, the Chaplet of Divine Mercy should be offered each day for the day's intentions.

First Day

Most Merciful Jesus, Whose very nature it is to have compassion on us and to forgive us, do not look upon our sins but upon our trust which we place in Your infinite goodness. Receive us all into the abode of Your Most Compassionate Heart, and never let us escape from It. We beg this of You by Your love which unites You to the Father and the Holy Spirit.

Eternal Father, turn Your merciful gaze upon all mankind and especially upon poor sinners, all enfolded in the most compassionate Heart of Jesus. For the sake of His sorrowful passion show us Your mercy, that we may praise the omnipotence of Your mercy for ever and ever. Amen.

Second Day

Most Merciful Jesus, from Whom comes all that is good, increase Your grace in men and women consecrated to Your service, that they may perform worthy works of mercy; and that all who see them may glorify the Father of Mercy Who is in Heaven.

Eternal Father, turn Your merciful gaze upon the company of chosen ones in Your vineyard - upon the souls of priests and religious; and endow them with the strength of Your blessing. For the love of the Heart of Your Son in which they are enfolded, impart to them Your power and light, that they may be able to guide others in the way of salvation and with one voice sing praise to Your boundless mercy for ages without end. Amen.

Third Day

Most Merciful Jesus, from the treasury of Your mercy, You impart Your graces in great abundance to each and all. Receive us into the abode of Your most compassionate Heart and never let us escape from It. We beg this grace of You by that most wondrous love for the heavenly Father with which Your Heart burns so fiercely.

Eternal Father, turn Your merciful gaze upon faithful souls, as upon the inheritance of Your Son. For the sake of His sorrowful passion, grant them Your blessing and surround them with Your constant protection. Thus may they never fail in love or lose the treasure of the holy faith, but rather, with all the hosts of angels and saints, may they glorify Your boundless mercy for endless ages. Amen.

Fourth Day

Most compassionate Jesus, You are the light of the whole world. Receive into the abode of Your most compassionate Heart the souls of those who do not believe in God and of those who as yet do not know You. Let the rays of Your grace enlighten them that they, too, together with us, may extol Your wonderful mercy; and do not let them escape from the abode which is Your most compassionate Heart.

Eternal Father, turn Your merciful gaze upon the souls of those who do not believe in You, and of those who as yet do not know You, but who are enclosed in the most compassionate Heart of Jesus. Draw them to the light of the Gospel. These souls do not know what great happiness it is to love You. Grant that they, too, may extol the generosity of Your mercy for endless ages. Amen.

Fifth Day

Most Merciful Jesus, Goodness Itself, You do not refuse light to those who seek it of You. Receive into the abode of Your most compassionate Heart the souls of those who have separated themselves from Your Church. Draw them by Your light into the unity of the Church, and do not let them escape from the abode of Your most compassionate Heart; but bring it about that they, too, come to glorify the generosity of Your mercy.

Eternal Father, turn Your merciful gaze upon the souls of those who have separated themselves from Your Son's Church, who have squandered Your blessings and misused Your graces by obstinately persisting in their errors. Do not look upon their errors, but upon the love of Your own Son and upon His bitter passion, which He underwent for their sake, since they, too, are enclosed in His most compassionate Heart. Bring it about that they also may glorify Your great mercy for endless ages.   Amen.

Sixth Day

Most Merciful Jesus, You Yourself have said, *"Learn from Me for I am meek and humble of heart."* Receive into the abode of Your most compassionate Heart all meek and humble souls and the souls of little children. These souls send all Heaven into ecstasy and they are the Heavenly Father's favorites. They are a sweet-smelling bouquet before the throne of God; God Himself takes delight in their fragrance. These souls have a permanent abode in Your most compassionate Heart, O Jesus, and they unceasingly sing out a hymn of love and mercy.

Eternal Father, turn Your merciful gaze upon meek souls, upon humble souls, and upon little children who are enfolded in the abode which is the most compassionate Heart of Jesus. These souls bear the closest resemblance to Your Son. Their fragrance rises from the Earth and reaches Your very throne. Father of mercy and of all goodness, I beg You by the love You bear these souls and by the delight You take in them: bless the whole world, that all souls together may sing out the praises of Your mercy for endless ages.   Amen.

Seventh Day

Most Merciful Jesus, Whose Heart is Love Itself, receive into the abode of Your most compassionate Heart the souls of those who particularly extol and venerate the greatness of Your mercy. These souls are mighty with the very power of God Himself. In the midst of all afflictions and adversities they go forward, confident of Your mercy; and united to You, O Jesus, they carry all mankind on their shoulders. These souls will not be judged severely, but Your mercy will embrace them as they depart from this life.

Eternal Father, turn Your merciful gaze upon the souls who glorify and venerate Your greatest attribute, that of Your fathomless mercy, and who are enclosed in the most compassionate Heart of Jesus. These souls are a living Gospel; their hands are full of deeds of mercy, and their hearts, overflowing with joy, sing a canticle of mercy to You, O Most High! I beg You O God: show them Your mercy according to the hope and trust they have placed in You. Let there be accomplished in them the promise of Jesus, Who said to them that during their life, but especially at the hour of death, the souls who will venerate this fathomless mercy of His, He, Himself, will defend as His glory. Amen.

Eighth Day

Most Merciful Jesus, You Yourself have said that You desire mercy; so I bring into the abode of Your most compassionate Heart the souls in Purgatory, souls who are very dear to You, and yet, who must make retribution to Your justice. May the streams of blood and water which gushed forth from Your Heart put out the flames of Purgatory, that there, too, the power of Your mercy may be celebrated.

Eternal Father, turn Your merciful gaze upon the souls suffering in Purgatory, who are enfolded in the most compassionate Heart of Jesus. I beg You, by the sorrowful passion of Jesus Your Son, and by all the bitterness with which His most sacred soul was flooded: manifest Your mercy to the souls who are under Your just scrutiny. Look upon them in no other way but only through the wounds of Jesus, Your dearly beloved Son; for we firmly believe that there is no limit to Your goodness and compassion. Amen.

Ninth Day

Most compassionate Jesus, You are Compassion Itself. I bring lukewarm souls into the abode of Your most compassionate Heart. In this fire of Your pure love, let these tepid souls who, like corpses, filled You with such deep loathing, be once again set aflame. O most compassionate Jesus, exercise the omnipotence of Your mercy and draw them into the very ardor of Your love, and bestow upon them the gift of holy love, for nothing is beyond Your power.

Eternal Father, turn Your merciful gaze upon lukewarm souls who are nonetheless enfolded in the most compassionate Heart of Jesus. Father of Mercy, I beg You by the bitter passion of Your Son and by His three-hour agony on the cross: let them, too, glorify the abyss of Your mercy.   Amen.

Lenten Novena

Father, all-powerful and ever-living God, during the holy season of Lent You call us to a closer union with Yourself. Help me to prepare to celebrate the Paschal Mystery with mind and heart renewed. Give me a spirit of loving reverence for You, our Father, and of willing service to my neighbor. As I recall the great events that gave us new life in Christ, bring the image of Your Son to perfection within my soul.

This great season of grace is Your gift to Your family to renew us in spirit. Give me strength to purify my heart, to control my desires, and so to serve You in freedom. Teach me how to live in this passing world with my heart set on the world that will never end. I ask for the grace to master my sinfulness and conquer my pride. I want to show to those in need Your goodness to me by being kind to all.

Through my observance of Lent, help me to correct my faults and raise my mind to You, and thus grow in holiness that I may deserve the reward of everlasting life. In Your mercy grant me this special favor (*state your intention*).

The days of the life-giving death and glorious resurrection of Jesus Christ, Your Son, are approaching. This is the hour when He triumphed over Satan's pride, the time when we celebrate the great event of our redemption. The suffering and death of Your Son brought life to the whole world, moving our hearts to praise Your glory. The power of the cross reveals Your judgment on this world and the kingship of Christ crucified. Father, through His love for us and through His sufferings, death and resurrection, may I gain eternal life with You in Heaven.   Amen.

Advent Novena

Jesus, Word made flesh, I adore You. I stand before Your mystery with faith and awe. Only Your grace makes possible my belief in You. Only Your love opens me to the profound understanding needed to appreciate Who You are. I bow in adoration.

Jesus, walk with me in the many difficulties, big and small, that I face each day. Help me to see life from Your point of view. May love be the outcome of whatever I do. Remember my special intention in this novena (*state your intention*) and fill every person with whatever good is needed.

O Jesus, be reborn in my heart and in every heart.   Amen.

Christmas Novena

This Novena is said daily from the Feast of St. Andrew, November 30, until Christmas.

Repeat the following prayer 15 times.

Hail, and blessed be the hour and moment at which the Son of God was born of a most pure Virgin at a stable at midnight in Bethlehem in the piercing cold. At that hour vouchsafe, I beseech You, to hear my prayers and grant my desires (*state your intention*). Through Jesus Christ and His Most Blessed Mother.   Amen.

Sorrowful Mother Novena for the Gifts of the Holy Spirit

Verse.   O God, hasten to my aid.
Response.   O Lord, make haste to help me.

V. Glory be to the Father and to the Son and to the Holy Ghost.
R. As it was in the beginning, is now, and ever shall be, world without end.   Amen.

I grieve for you, O Mary most sorrowful, in the affliction of your tender heart at the prophecy of the holy and aged Simeon. Dear Mother, by your heart so afflicted, obtain for me the virtue of humility and the gift of the holy fear of God. (Pray 1 **Hail Mary**.)

I grieve for you, O Mary most sorrowful, in the anguish of your most affectionate heart during the flight into Egypt and your sojourn there. Dear Mother, by your heart so full of anguish, obtain for me the virtue of generosity, especially toward the poor, and the gift of piety. (Pray 1 **Hail Mary**.)

I grieve for you, O Mary most sorrowful, in those anxieties, which tried your troubled heart at the loss of your dear Jesus in the temple. Dear Mother, by your heart so full of anguish, obtain for me the virtue of chastity and the gift of knowledge. (Pray 1 **Hail Mary**.)

I grieve for you, O Mary most sorrowful, in the consternation of your heart at meeting Jesus as He carried His cross. Dear Mother, by your heart so troubled, obtain for me the virtue of patience and the gift of fortitude. (Pray 1 **Hail Mary**.)

I grieve for you, O Mary most sorrowful, in the martyrdom, which your generous heart endured in standing near Jesus in His agony on the cross. Dear Mother, by your afflicted heart, obtain for me the virtue of temperance and the gift of counsel. (Pray 1 **Hail Mary**.)

I grieve for you, O Mary most sorrowful, in the wounding of your compassionate heart, when the side of Jesus was pierced by a lance before His body was removed from the cross. Dear Mother, by your heart thus transfixed, obtain for me the virtue of fraternal charity and the gift of understanding. (Pray 1 **Hail Mary**.)

I grieve for you, O Mary most sorrowful, for the pangs that wrenched your most loving heart at the burial of Jesus. Dear Mother, by your heart sunk in the bitterness of desolation, obtain for me the virtue of diligence and the gift of wisdom. (Pray 1 **Hail Mary**.)

Let us pray:

Let intercession be made for us, we beseech You, O Lord Jesus Christ, now and at the hour of our death, by the throne of Your mercy, by the Blessed Virgin Mary, Your Mother, whose most holy soul was pierced by a sword of sorrow in the hour of Your bitter passion, through You, O Jesus Christ, Savior of the world, Who with the Father and the Holy Ghost lives and reigns world without end.   Amen.

Novena to the Immaculate Conception

Day One

O God, Who by the Immaculate Conception of the Blessed Virgin Mary, did prepare a worthy dwelling place for Your Son, we beseech You that, as by the foreseen death of this, Your Son, You did preserve her from all stain, so too You would permit us, purified through her intercession, to come unto You. Through the same Lord Jesus Christ, Your Son, Who lives and reigns with You in the unity of the Holy Spirit, one God, world without end.   Amen.

O most Holy Virgin, who was pleasing to the Lord and became His mother, immaculate in body and spirit, in faith and in love, look kindly on me as I implore your powerful intercession. O most Holy Mother, who by your blessed Immaculate Conception, from the first moment of your conception did crush the head of the enemy, receive my prayers as I implore you to present at the throne of God the favor I now request (*state your intention*).

O Mary of the Immaculate Conception, Mother of Christ, you had influence with your divine Son while upon this Earth; you have the same influence now in Heaven. Pray for me and obtain for me from Him the granting of my petition if it be His divine will.   Amen.

Day Two

O God, Who by the Immaculate Conception of the Blessed Virgin Mary, did prepare a worthy dwelling place for Your Son, we beseech You that, as by the foreseen death of this, Your Son, You did preserve her from all stain, so too You would permit us, purified through her intercession, to come unto You. Through the same Lord Jesus Christ, Your Son, Who lives and reigns with You in the unity of the Holy Spirit, one God, world without end. Amen.

O Mary, ever blessed Virgin, Mother of God, Queen of Angels and of Saints, I salute you with the most profound veneration and filial devotion as I contemplate your holy Immaculate Conception. I thank you for your maternal protection and for the many blessings that I have received through your wondrous mercy and most powerful intercession. In all my necessities I have recourse to you with unbounded confidence. O Mother of Mercy, I beseech you now to hear my prayer and to obtain for me of your divine Son the favor that I so earnestly request in this novena (*state your intention*).

O Mary of the Immaculate Conception, Mother of Christ, you had influence with your divine Son while upon this Earth; you have the same influence now in Heaven. Pray for me and obtain for me from Him the granting of my petition if it be His divine will. Amen.

Day Three

O God, Who by the Immaculate Conception of the Blessed Virgin Mary, did prepare a worthy dwelling place for Your Son, we beseech You that, as by the foreseen death of this, Your Son, You did preserve her from all stain, so too You would permit us, purified through her intercession, to come unto You. Through the same Lord Jesus Christ Your Son, Who lives and reigns with You in the unity of the Holy Spirit, one God, world without end. Amen.

O Blessed Virgin Mary, glory of the Christian people, joy of the universal Church and Mother of Our Lord, speak for me to the Heart of Jesus, who is your Son and my brother. O Mary, who by your holy Immaculate Conception did enter the world free from stain, in your mercy obtain for me from Jesus the special favor which I now so earnestly seek (*state your intention*).

O Mary of the Immaculate Conception, Mother of Christ, you had influence with your divine Son while upon this Earth; you have the same influence now in Heaven. Pray for me and obtain for me from Him the granting of my petition if it be His divine will. Amen.

Day Four

O God, Who by the Immaculate Conception of the Blessed Virgin Mary, did prepare a worthy dwelling place for Your Son, we beseech You that, as by the foreseen death of this, Your Son, You did preserve her from all stain, so too You would permit us, purified through her intercession, to come unto You. Through the same Lord Jesus Christ, Your Son, Who lives and reigns with You in the unity of the Holy Spirit, one God, world without end. Amen.

O Mary, Mother of God, endowed in your glorious Immaculate Conception with the fullness of grace; unique among women in that you are both mother and virgin; Mother of Christ and Virgin of Christ, I ask you to look down with a tender heart from your throne and listen to my prayers as I earnestly ask that you obtain for me the favor for which I now plead (*state your intention*).

O Mary of the Immaculate Conception, Mother of Christ, you had influence with your divine Son while upon this Earth; you have the same influence now in Heaven. Pray for me and obtain for me from Him the granting of my petition if it be His divine will. Amen.

Day Five

O God, Who by the Immaculate Conception of the Blessed Virgin Mary, did prepare a worthy dwelling place for Your Son, we beseech You that, as by the foreseen death of this, Your Son, You did preserve her from all stain, so too You would permit us, purified through her intercession, to come unto You. Through the same Lord Jesus Christ, Your Son, Who lives and reigns with You in the unity of the Holy Spirit, one God, world without end. Amen.

O God, Who, by the Immaculate Conception of the Virgin Mary, did prepare a fitting dwelling for Your Son, I beseech You that as by the foreseen death of Your Son, You did preserve her from all stain of sin, grant that through her intercession, I may be favored with the granting of the grace that I seek at this time (*state your intention*).

O Mary of the Immaculate Conception, Mother of Christ, you had influence with your divine Son while upon this Earth; you have the same influence now in Heaven. Pray for me and obtain for me from Him the granting of my petition if it be His divine will.   Amen.

Day Six

O God, Who by the Immaculate Conception of the Blessed Virgin Mary, did prepare a worthy dwelling place for Your Son, we beseech You that, as by the foreseen death of this, Your Son, You did preserve her from all stain, so too You would permit us, purified through her intercession, to come unto You. Through the same Lord Jesus Christ, Your Son, Who lives and reigns with You in the unity of the Holy Spirit, one God, world without end.   Amen.

Glorious and immortal Queen of Heaven, I profess my firm belief in your Immaculate Conception preordained for you in the merits of your divine Son. I rejoice with you in your Immaculate Conception. To the one ever-reigning God, Father, Son, and Holy Spirit, three in Person, one in nature, I offer thanks for your blessed Immaculate Conception. O Mother of the Word made Flesh, listen to my petition as I ask this special grace during this novena (*state your intention*).

O Mary of the Immaculate Conception, Mother of Christ, you had influence with your divine Son while upon this Earth; you have the same influence now in Heaven. Pray for me and obtain for me from Him the granting of my petition if it be His divine will.   Amen.

Day Seven

O God, Who by the Immaculate Conception of the Blessed Virgin Mary, did prepare a worthy dwelling place for Your Son, we beseech You that, as by the foreseen death of this, Your Son, You did preserve her from all stain, so too You would permit us, purified through her intercession, to come unto You. Through the same Lord Jesus Christ,

Your Son, Who lives and reigns with You in the unity of the Holy Spirit, one God, world without end.   Amen.

O Immaculate Virgin, Mother of God, and my mother, from the sublime heights of your dignity turn your merciful eyes upon me while I, full of confidence in your bounty and keeping in mind your Immaculate Conception and fully conscious of your power, beg of you to come to my aid and ask your divine Son to grant the favor I earnestly seek in this novena if it be beneficial for my immortal soul and the souls for whom I pray (*state your intention*).

O Mary of the Immaculate Conception, Mother of Christ, you had influence with your divine Son while upon this Earth; you have the same influence now in Heaven. Pray for me and obtain for me from Him the granting of my petition if it be His divine will.   Amen.

Day Eight

O God, Who by the Immaculate Conception of the Blessed Virgin Mary, did prepare a worthy dwelling place for Your Son, we beseech You that, as by the foreseen death of this, Your Son, You did preserve her from all stain, so too You would permit us, purified through her intercession, to come unto You. Through the same Lord Jesus Christ, Your Son, Who lives and reigns with You in the unity of the Holy Spirit, one God, world without end.   Amen.

O Most gracious Virgin Mary, beloved Mother of Jesus Christ, our Redeemer, intercede with Him for me that I be granted the favor which I petition for so earnestly in this novena. O Mother of the Word Incarnate, I feel animated with confidence that your prayers on my behalf will be graciously heard before the throne of God. O Glorious Mother of God, in memory of your joyous Immaculate Conception, hear my prayers and obtain for me my petitions (*state your intention*).

O Mary of the Immaculate Conception, Mother of Christ, you had influence with your divine Son while upon this Earth; you have the same influence now in Heaven. Pray for me and obtain for me from Him the granting of my petition if it be His divine will. Amen.

Day Nine

O God, Who by the Immaculate Conception of the Blessed Virgin Mary, did prepare a worthy dwelling place for Your Son, we beseech You that, as by the foreseen death of this, Your Son, You did preserve her from all stain, so too You would permit us, purified through her intercession, to come unto You. Through the same Lord Jesus Christ, Your Son, Who lives and reigns with You in the unity of the Holy Spirit, one God, world without end. Amen.

O Mother of the King of the Universe, most perfect member of the human race, "our tainted nature's solitary boast," I turn to you as mother, advocate, and mediatrix. O Holy Mary, assist me in my present necessity. By your Immaculate Conception, O Mary conceived without sin, I humbly beseech you from the bottom of my heart to intercede for me with your divine Son and ask that I be granted the favor for which I now plead (*state your intention*).

O Mary of the Immaculate Conception, Mother of Christ, you had influence with your divine Son while upon this Earth; you have the same influence now in Heaven. Pray for me and obtain for me from Him the granting of my petition if it be His divine will. Amen.

Ann Fitch

PRAYERS TO PATRON SAINTS

Asking the intercession of the saints is a long-standing tradition in the Catholic Church. I believe the saints are wonderful intercessors and I wanted to include a section in this book that had prayers that could be prayed to the patron saints of our most common occupations, illnesses, and needs. In the book of James it is written, *"The prayer of the righteous is powerful and effective."* Other than God Himself and the Blessed Virgin Mary, there is no one more righteous than the saints in Heaven who have been perfected and spend their time praising and glorifying God. These holy men and women can and will pray with and for us with great efficaciousness if we ask them to. I hope that you utilize the prayers in this section frequently and find comfort in knowing that you have sought the intercession of the saints who are always in the presence of God in Heaven.

"So let us then confidently approach the throne of grace to receive mercy and find grace for timely help." (Hebrews 4:16)

Prayer to One's Patron Saint
(Ann Fitch)

O heavenly patron, upon whose help I rely, pray ever before God for me: that my faith be strong; my life be virtuous; my soul protected from harm; and, that at the end of my life I may join you in Heaven to praise and glorify God forever and ever.   Amen.

Prayer to St. Agatha (breast ailments)
(Ann Fitch)

St. Agatha, patroness of those with breast ailments, I come before you seeking your assistance for (*name person*) and all those who are suffering with breast ailments. Present each one to the blessed Trinity and plead their cases asking that they be healed if that is God's holy will. I trust in your help and intercession and pray that God will comfort and strengthen (*name person*) in his/her fight against breast disease. Amen.

Prayer to St. Agatha (sexual assault)
(Ann Fitch)

O blessed St. Agatha, you witnessed the horror of sexual assault and the humiliation and indignity that occur as a result. I beg of you to pray for (*name person*) who has suffered so much. You understand all that (*name person*) has been through and how it is affecting him/her. Plead with the Lord that He bless (*name person*) with healing in mind, body and heart and that He grace (*name person*) with the gift of forgiveness so that he/she can find peace and wholeness as you did. Ask the Lord to send angels to minister to (*name person*) and to guard and protect him/her. Thank you, dear saint for your understanding, help, prayers and continued intercession for (*name person*). Amen.

Prayer to St. Agnes (engaged couples)
(Ann Fitch)

Dearest St. Agnes, virgin and martyr, I come to you asking your prayers on behalf of (*name man*) and (*name woman*) who are engaged to be married. As they go through the engagement process pray that they grow in their love for one another, that they are accepting of each other's faults, weaknesses and flaws, and that they are kind, considerate and patient with one another. Plead with the Lord that they are filled with every gift and grace needed to successfully join their lives together in holy matrimony. Pray dear saint that their marriage is filled with joy and that they are always as faithful to one another as you were to Christ. Thank you St. Agnes for your prayers for (*name man*) and (*name woman*).   Amen.

Prayer to St. Alban (refugees)
(Ann Fitch)

O generous St. Alban, who took in and kept safe a holy priest who was fleeing persecution and who was martyred for your faith look kindly upon (*name person*) and all who are fleeing persecution or are seeking refuge. Pray for them, dear saint, along with the Blessed Virgin Mary, that they will have the strength, courage, and assistance they need to faithfully live each day in an unfamiliar place far from their homes. O holy martyr, keep them all in your prayers, and ask the Lord to allow them in time to either establish new homes or return to their homeland safely with the hope that they can resume their lives and livelihoods.   Amen.

Prayer to St. Aloysius Gonzaga (HIV & AIDS patients)
(Ann Fitch)

St. Aloysius, I come before you on behalf of all those suffering from HIV and AIDS, especially (*name person*). Ask God to: bless them with caregivers who are respectful and kind, and who treat them with dignity; to touch the hearts of their friends, co-workers and families so that they are embracing, compassionate, and empathetic; and to heal any hurts they have because of misunderstanding or rejection. Please plead their cases before God's heavenly throne and always assist them with your love and prayers.   Amen.

Prayer to St. Alphonsus Liguori (vocations)
(Ann Fitch)

O glorious St. Alphonsus Liguori, patron saint of vocations, I come before you asking your intercession for all those discerning a vocation to the priesthood, religious life or the deaconate in particular for (*name person*). With the Blessed Virgin Mary ask the Lord to bless the hearts and souls of those whom He has called to be set apart with every gift and grace that they might live out their lives in faithful service to Him and the Church. May they respond generously and promptly, knowing with all their hearts that they are called to Christ. Pray that they be humble and completely dedicated during their formation, steadfast in their love for Christ and His Church, zealous in their desire for the salvation of souls, and completely obedient to their superiors and the teachings of the Church. I ask this through Christ our Lord. Amen.

Prayer to St. Andre Bessette (religious brothers)
(Ann Fitch)

O holy and venerable St. Andre Bessette, I humbly ask you to pray for all religious brothers, especially (*name person*). May they be true servants of the Lord who give of themselves unconditionally. Pray that the Lord fill their hearts with zeal for the salvation of souls and with a deep abiding love for His holy Church. Ask that He bless them with strength, courage and joy as they daily serve Him in those around them. May your example St. Andre inspire them to seek to be completely submissive and obedient to their superiors and to simply live their vows of chastity, poverty and obedience. Please keep them in your prayers and intercede for all their needs. Amen.

Prayer to Sts. Anne & Joachim (grandparents)
(Ann Fitch)

Dear Sts. Anne and Joachim, patron saints of grandparents, I present to you all my grandchildren. I ask your intercession on their behalf. Please watch over them and when they are in need, plead their case before your grandson, Jesus, asking that He bless them and keep them in His tender care. I thank you for your prayers and your assistance. Amen.

Prayer to St. Anthony (elderly)
(Ann Fitch)

O loving St. Anthony, patron saint of the elderly, I ask your special prayers for (*name person*) and all elderly people. Pray, beloved saint, that they are grateful for the years they have lived, content with their place in life, have hearts and minds that are full of happy memories and thankful thoughts, that they are blessed with good health, and that they are examples of Christian living for all they love and meet. Please pray that if they are tested with illness, suffering, loneliness, or the death of loved ones that they be blessed with God's peace and comfort, strength and courage. And when their time comes to enter into eternal life, I pray you welcome them into Heaven where along with you they might praise God forever and ever. Amen.

Prayer to St. Anthony (lost articles)
(Ann Fitch)

Dear St. Anthony, you are the patron of all who seek lost articles. Help (*name person*) to find (*lost article*). I thank you in advance for your assistance and pray that I will one day join you in everlasting peace. Amen.

Prayer to St. Benedict (kidney diseases)
(Ann Fitch)

O blessed and compassionate St. Benedict, you were full of the love of God and led countless others to Him, His Word, and His holy Church. Trusting in your intercession I turn to you seeking prayers for (*name person*) and any who suffer from diseases of the kidneys. Pray dear saint that if it be God's will for them that they be healed and restored to fullness of health. If it is not God's will beg that they be strengthened and fortified so that they can patiently endure their illness. Cease not praying for (*name person*) and plead with God that he/she may one day praise God for all eternity with you, the angels and the saints. Thank you, holy St. Benedict, for your intercession on our behalf. Amen.

Prayer to St. Bernardine of Siena (respiratory illnesses)
(Ann Fitch)

St. Bernardine of Siena, you were healed of respiratory illness and preached the love and mercy of God everywhere you went. I come to you now seeking your prayers for (*name person*) and all who suffer with respiratory illnesses. Plead their cases in unison with Mary, the Mother of God, and seek healing for them if that is God's holy will. Pray, dear saint, that they suffer with joy, persevere with hope, and that they join their afflictions with Jesus' for the salvation of souls. I ask your intercession on their behalf in Jesus' holy Name. Amen.

Prayer to St. Bona of Pisa (pilgrimages)
(Ann Fitch)

St. Bona, you traveled far and wide making pilgrimages to holy places. As I set out for (*name place*) help me to desire to grow in holiness and faithfulness to the Church. I ask your protection as I journey there and back. Through your intercession may I be strengthened in my walk with Christ and fortified, as you were, to live a life of faith, hope, and love. May my journey be safe and my heart opened and converted. I ask all this through Christ our Lord. Amen.

Prayer to St. Camillus de Lellis (nurses)
(Ann Fitch)

O Good St. Camillus, I ask your intercession on behalf of all those who nurse others back to health, especially (*name person*). Ask the Lord to bless them with strength, kindness, patience, and love. Pray that they always treat those they care for with dignity and respect and that they never succumb to the illnesses from which those they treat suffer. Amen.

Prayer to St. Catherine of Siena (protection from fire)
(Ann Fitch)

O blessed St. Catherine of Siena, protectress against fire, I come before you seeking your intercession. Protect (*name person*), his/her family and property from burning flames. Ask God to keep them safe from harm and to grant them peace in this time of trial. Pray, dear St. Catherine, that all hearts are enflamed with the fire of divine love, as yours was, and that all souls are protected from the fires of Hell. Amen.

Prayer to St. Dominic Savio (delinquent or troubled youth)
(Ann Fitch)

Dearest St. Dominic Savio, you spent your short life totally for love of Jesus and His Mother. I come to you today seeking prayers for (*name youth*) and all delinquent or troubled teens. I ask you to intercede for them praying that their hearts be opened by the Holy Spirit and filled with every grace they need to turn away from bad influences, sinful endeavors, and harmful behaviors. Please pray to their guardian angels to protect them and keep them from all influences of evil. St. Dominic Savio, I trust in your prayers for (*name youth*) and all delinquent and troubled youth. May your prayers, along with those of the Blessed Virgin Mary reach God's ears and bring about a favorable outcome for (*name youth*). I pray that like you he/she may grow in virtue and grace so that he/she can find peace and joy now and forever in Heaven. Amen.

Prayer to St. Dymphna (mental illness)
(Ann Fitch)

O blessed St. Dymphna, go before the Lord and ask Him to touch those afflicted with mental illness with His healing love, especially (*name person*). Ask that He give them courage and strength to bear their illness and that He bless them with peace of heart and mind. If it is God's holy will, pray that He heal them completely and restore them to fullness of health. We ask all this in Jesus' Name. Amen.

Prayer to St. Elizabeth Ann Seton (loss of children)
(Ann Fitch)

    O holy and venerable St. Elizabeth Ann Seton, you knew the pain and anguish parents feel at the death of a child as you experienced this pain several times. I ask you to pray for (*name person*) and all who have lost children. Place them in the Blessed Mother's arms and ask her to go with you to the Holy Trinity and pray they have the grace, strength, and courage they need to grieve the loss of their beloved children and in time that they experience healing and find new joy in their memories of their children. Intercede on behalf of the children who have died before their parents and ask the Lord to welcome them into eternal peace in Heaven with Him. I ask all this through Christ our Lord.   Amen.

Prayer to St. Elizabeth of Hungary (widows)
(Ann Fitch)

    O blessed St. Elizabeth of Hungary, you understood well the trials and sufferings of a widow. You lost your beloved husband at a young age and raised four children alone. You truly knew what it meant to trust in God's providence and believe that God would always provide. You adapted to new conditions and became a humble blessing to those around you. Look with compassion upon all who are widowed, especially (*name person*). Present their needs to God and plead their cases before Him. Ask that He bless them with peace, patience, courage, wisdom, hope and renewed faith. Plead with Him to bring their faithfully departed spouses into the light of His presence and grant them eternal peace and joy. Thank you, St. Elizabeth for your prayers and intercession.   Amen.

Prayer to St. Eulalia (runaways and missing children)
(Ann Fitch)

    Blessed martyr St. Eulalia, I come before you seeking your intercession on behalf of (*name youth*) who has run away or is missing. Pray a spirit of protection over him/her and pray that his/her parents be freed from fear and anxiety. Ask God to deeply bless (*name youth*) at this moment and fill him/her to overflowing with peace and the knowledge that he/she is loved beyond all measure. Plead before the Holy Trinity asking that this child's whereabouts be made known and that this child be brought safely back to his/her loving family. St. Eulalia, I have confidence in your intercession and trust in a favorable outcome. Amen.

Prayer to St. Filippo Smaldone (deaf/ear ailments)
(Ann Fitch)

O holy and charitable St. Filippo Smaldone, patron saint of the deaf and those with ear ailments, I come to you seeking your intercession for (*name person*) and all who suffer with ear problems. I know you spent your life dedicated to those who could not hear - to their needs and their welfare. Confident in your advocacy I place (*name person*) in your loving arms and ask you to present him/her to the Holy Trinity. Beg that if it is God's will that (*name person*) be healed completely. If ear problems are to remain I ask you to continue to pray that (*name person*) be profoundly blessed by God with every gift and grace needed to live his/her life to the fullest. Amen.

Prayer to St. Florian (firefighters)
(Ann Fitch)

St. Florian, patron of firefighters I present to you all firefighters, especially (*name person*). I ask that you pray for their protection. Ask the Lord to keep them safe from all harm and to bless them with courage and wisdom as they serve their communities. Pray that they remain dedicated to their work and that they can efficiently and effectively help those in need. Amen.

Prayer to St. Gabriel Possenti (college students)
(Ann Fitch)

St. Gabriel Possenti, great student who loved learning, I ask you to look after (*name student*) and all students who are studying in college. I ask you to place them at the feet of the Father and pray that they are surrounded with good friends who lead them ever closer to Him, excellent teachers who give wise counsel, the ability to concentrate in class, the discipline to complete all work that is due, the understanding necessary to succeed in their studies, and the determination to remain focused on their education and committed to their goals. You, St. Gabriel Possenti, know well what is required of a student, please pray that (*name student*) is successful in all his/her endeavors at school. Thank you for your care and intercession. Amen.

Prayer to St. Gemma Galgani (back problems)
(Ann Fitch)

Oh glorious St. Gemma Galgani you suffered excruciating back pain for years. You know how painful it is to have doctors cauterize your back and how restricting it is to wear an iron brace. You know well what people with back pain suffer. Teach (*name person*) through your perfect example how to suffer out of love for Christ for the salvation of souls. O holy saint, you embraced suffering and sacrifice with tranquility and deep joy. So St. Gemma, we offer to you (*name person*) and all who suffer with back issues. Plead with the Holy Spirit to fill them with every grace needed to endure their suffering with humble resignation, peace and joy. Please take (*name person*) in your holy arms and carry him/her to your beloved Spouse fervently praying that He take (*name person*) in His arms and place him/her with in His Sacred Heart and heal him/her if that be His holy will. Thank you St. Gemma for interceding for (*name person*) and for pleading his/her case before the Lord. I look forward to a favorable outcome through your intercession. Amen.

Prayer to St. Gerard Majella (pregnant women)
(Ann Fitch)

Dear St. Gerard, patron saint of pregnant women, I ask you to lovingly place (*name person*) and her unborn child(ren) in the Blessed Mother's arms. Ask her, as a mother, to plead for their health and safety, before the Holy Trinity with you. Pray that (*name person*) will be patient and trusting during her pregnancy and delivery and that she will have no fears. I thank you for your continued prayers for (*name person*) and her unborn child(ren) and for your constant intercession on their behalf. Amen.

Prayer to St. Germaine Cousin (victims of abuse)
(Ann Fitch)

Blessed St. Germaine, I come before you asking for your intersession for all those who have suffered abuse, especially (*name person*). Present each one to the Holy Trinity asking that they be healed in body, mind, heart, and soul. Plead with God to empower them with courage and strength and to renew their hope and fill them with joy. Pray that they find peace through forgiveness and that they be blessed with every grace they need to live full and happy lives. Amen.

Prayer to St. Gertrude of Nivelles (cats)
(Ann Fitch)

O holy St. Gertrude of Nivelles, patron saint of cats, I ask you to pray that my sweet kitty(ies) always be content, energetic, curious, playful, and good-natured. I pray my cat(s) will be a joy to me and those I love. Carry my cat(s) to the throne of the Father and ask Him to bless my cat(s) with long life and great happiness. Pray dear saint that my cat(s) stay free from illness and that my cat(s) always feel safe, protected, and loved. Thank you for asking blessings upon my cat(s). Ask the Lord to pour out special graces upon all cats and cat owners. May they bring great love to one another and live companionably in peace. Amen.

Prayer to St. Gianna Beretta Molla (the unborn)
(Ann Fitch)

Dear St. Gianna, I present to you all the unborn. Pray with their angel guardians before the throne of God that they develop and grow healthy and strong, that they are protected and kept safe from all harm, and that they are born at full term into families who will love, cherish, and nurture them. We thank you for your love for the unborn and trust that you will plead their cause forever in Heaven. Amen.

Prayer to St. Giles (handicapped)
(Ann Fitch)

St. Giles, you lived your life with a wound that crippled your leg. I come to you asking your prayers on behalf of (*name person*) and all who live with handicaps that cause them to struggle, suffer, or be treated in ways that are discriminatory or unkind. Pray that their bodies are strengthened, that their hearts are healed, and that their minds are blessed with wisdom and understanding. Plead their cases before God and ask Him to bless them with His love and comfort, fill them with His peace and joy, and grant them the graces they need to grow in every virtue. St. Giles, understanding of the needs of those who are handicapped, I trust that you will intercede for (*name person*) and that you will keep him/her in your prayers. Amen.

Prayer to St. Helen (divorcees)
(Ann Fitch)

O holy and blessed St. Helen, you know well what it's like to be a divorcee. You felt the pain of betrayal and rejection, sadness over your marriage ending, anxiety for your children's welfare and stability, and hurt that another woman replaced you. You know what it's like to rebuild your life alone and to co-parent children. Please pray for (*name person*) and all who are divorced or are going through divorce.

Pray, dear saint, that they can let go of all resentment, anger, guilt and fear and trust in the Lord as you did and find peace for their weary hearts, minds and souls. Pray also that they can forgive and have the grace, courage, and strength to move forward with their lives in ways that are healthy, positive and life giving. Thank you, St. Helen, for your prayers and intercession for (name person) and all struggling with divorce and its effects. I truly believe that you are with them, praying for them, and asking God's choicest blessings upon them. Amen.

Prayer to St. Isidore (farmers)
(Ann Fitch)

O St. Isidore, patron saint of farmers, I come to you now asking your intercession on behalf of (name person) and all whose livelihood is based in farming. I ask you to pray that their crops have sufficient water and minerals to grow to fruition and that they are abundant at harvest. Please pray that their crops are protected from strong winds, flooding, hail, rust, and every blight of worm and insect. St. Isidore, please pray that God in His infinite love and wisdom will bless their labors so that they may reap the rewards of work well done here on Earth and in Heaven. Amen.

Prayer to St. James the Greater (arthritis sufferers)
(Ann Fitch)

O St. James, patron saint of those who suffer from the crippling effects of arthritis, I ask that you place every person suffering from this disease, especially (name person), at the feet of God. Ask that He bless them with courage, strength and patience and if it is His holy will that He alleviate all their suffering and restore them to health. I ask all this in Jesus' Name. Amen.

Prayer to St. Joan of Arc (armed forces)
(Ann Fitch)

O most blessed St. Joan of Arc, patroness of the armed forces, I ask that you pray for all military men and women, especially (*name person*), who are defending the freedoms of the country I love both here and abroad. Ask God to bless them, strengthen them, encourage them, and keep them from all harm. If they are wounded or suffering in any way pray that He heal them and restore them to fullness of health quickly and without complications. Thank you St. Joan of Arc for your intercession. Amen.

Prayer to St. John Baptiste de la Salle (teachers)
(Ann Fitch)

O St. John Baptiste de la Salle, teacher of teachers, and helper of those who educate others, I come to you asking your intercession for (*name person*) and all who teach. Pray dear saint that they be caring, compassionate, dedicated, empathetic, generous, kind, joyful, patient, engaging, inspirational, understanding, and above all loving. Intercede for them so that like you they instill in others joy for learning and the desire to become life-long learners. Pray that they are always inspired by the wisdom of the Holy Spirit and that they allow the Holy Spirit to lead them and guide them as they help others pursue truth and knowledge. O holy teacher, pray that all who teach be blessed and fulfilled in knowing they are helping others to grow and become knowledgeable. Amen.

Prayer to St. John of God (heart patients)
(Ann Fitch)

Dearest St. John of God, I come before you on behalf of those suffering from diseases of the heart, especially (*name person*). I ask that you fervently pray that if it is God's will that their hearts be healed of every ailment and that they enjoy fullness of health. If it is not, please pray that they have the grace and strength to bear their sickness with patience and dignity and ask God to bless them with caretakers who are wise and who can alleviate their suffering. Thank you St. John for your love and intercession.   Amen.

Prayer to St. John the Baptist (converts)
(Ann Fitch)

O holy martyr, St. John the Baptist, you worked tirelessly during your life for the conversion of others. Inspired by your success, I turn to you for prayers for all those in need of conversion, especially, (*name person*). Present him/her to the Lord and ask that He in His infinite mercy pour forth His Holy Spirit upon him/her and bless him/her with the gift of true faith. I ask you to pray that (*name person*) enters into full union with the Church and finds eternal peace and joy for his/her soul.   Amen.

Prayer to St. John Vianney (priests)
(Ann Fitch)

O venerable St. John Vianney, I come to you asking for your intercession for all priests, especially (*name person*). Pray that the Holy Spirit fill them to overflowing with every gift and grace they need to serve God and His Church faithfully, lovingly, and obediently. Ask that their hearts be enflamed with the fire of divine love and that their words and actions always lead others to the love of God. With Mary, the Blessed Mother of God, always pray that they have a burning desire for the salvation of souls and intense love for God in the Holy Eucharist.   Amen.

Prayer to St. Joseph (fathers)
(Ann Fitch)

O blessed St. Joseph, loving foster father of Jesus and most chaste spouse of the Blessed Virgin Mary, I ask your intercession on behalf of all fathers, especially (*name person*). Pray that like yours, their actions be loving, understanding, and wise. Implore your beloved Son to instill in them every grace they need to be the best fathers they can be. Pray that like you their hearts will be blessed with ever-increasing love for their children and that they have the fortitude to faithfully care for and provide for their needs. And dear St. Joseph, when their earthly life is complete may they enjoy the beauty of everlasting life in union with you and all the angels and saints.   Amen.

Prayer to St. Joseph (workers)
(Ann Fitch)

O blessed St. Joseph, patron saint of workers, I turn to you asking your powerful intercession on behalf of (*name person*) who is seeking employment. With Mary your most chaste spouse and Jesus your foster son, please go before the Father asking him to help (*name person*) find a job that: utilizes his/her gifts and talents; allows for him/her to be valued and respected by his/her peers; and, provides financially for his/her needs. Pray dear St. Joseph that God opens the door to gainful employment for him/her. Thank you, for presenting this need to God and for praying for its fulfillment.   Amen.

Prayer to St. Joseph of Cupertino (air travelers)
(Ann Fitch)

St. Joseph of Cupertino, I ask your intercession on behalf of all pilots, flight attendants and air travelers, especially (*name person*). Go before the Lord with all the holy angels and humbly ask: that the plane they are travelling in be in excellent working condition; that while in flight He uphold the plane with His almighty hands; that the flight be swift and without incident; and, that He allow them to arrive at their destination safely. Thank you, dear saint, for your constant intercession.   Amen.

Prayer to St. Jude (hopeless cases)
(Ann Fitch)

Dearest St. Jude, glorious apostle, faithful servant and friend of Jesus, patron saint of hopeless cases; I come to you seeking your assistance with (*state your intention*). Despise not my request, but instead carry it to the throne of God and place it at His feet, imploring that He hear and answer favorably. I trust in your assistance and humbly believe that you will continue to pray for my needs and ask God's choicest blessings upon me and those I love. Thank you, St. Jude for your intercession. Amen.

Prayer to St. Juliana (chronic illness)
(Ann Fitch)

Most loving St. Juliana, patroness of the chronically ill, I humbly come before you asking your intercession on behalf of all those who suffer with chronic illness, especially (*name person*). Carry them to the Lord's feet and beg that He bless them with the patience and courage needed to endure their illness and for relief from their pain and suffering. Plead their cause and ask that if it be God's holy will that they be restored to health. Amen.

Prayer to St. Lucy (blind/eye ailments)
(Ann Fitch)

O blessed St. Lucy, patron saint of the blind and those with eye ailments, I come before you seeking your prayers for (*name person*) and all who have eye problems. Confident in your advocacy, I place them all at your feet so that you can carry them to the throne of God and present them to Him for His blessing. Pray dear saint that if it is His holy will that He heal them completely and restore their eyes to full health. If it is not, pray they are filled with peace and that they can courageously face every day with hope and joy in their hearts. Thank you, St. Lucy for your prayers. I trust in your patronage. Amen.

Prayer to St. Luke (doctors)
(Ann Fitch)

O holy apostle, St. Luke, I ask your intercession on behalf of all doctors, especially (*name person*). Humbly lay them at the Divine Physician's feet asking that they have: the wisdom and knowledge necessary to treat their patients effectively and restore them to physical and mental health; the compassion and empathy necessary to be of comfort to those who are suffering; and the strength and grace to fulfill their duties as doctors. I also ask that you pray they are kept safe from all harm and that they never succumb to the illnesses they are treating. O blessed St. Luke, we thank you for your prayers and assistance. Amen.

Prayer to St. Martin de Porres (racial injustice, prejudice)
(Ann Fitch)

O Blessed St. Martin de Porres, you understand well what it is to suffer racial injustice and prejudice. I humbly come to you seeking prayers for (*name person*) and all who are experiencing racial injustice or discrimination in their lives. Ask the Lord to bless them with loving and forgiving hearts, to fill them with healing and peace, and to bless them with the ability to be tolerant of other's narrow-mindedness. Pray, dear saint, that they be kind, gentle and giving as you were, and that they are able to pray for those who mistreat them. Thank you, St. Martin de Porres for your prayers and intercession. Amen.

Prayer to St. Maximillian Kolbe (addicts)
(Ann Fitch)

St. Maximillian Kolbe, patron saint of the addicted, I come before you seeking your assistance and prayers for all those with addictions, especially (*name person*). Pray that God will help him/her break the chains of addiction that hold him/her bound and set him/her free to live a life of health, happiness, and hope. Ask the Lord to look with compassion upon him/her and in His infinite mercy to fill his/her life with people who will hold him/her accountable for his/her actions and help him/her stay away from that which held him/her bound. I ask all this in Jesus' Name. Amen.

Prayer to St. Medard (bad weather)
(Ann Fitch)

St. Medard, I ask you to intercede for all who are in need of protection from bad weather. Ask the Lord to keep His people safe from hurricanes, tornadoes, snowstorms, hail storms, thunderstorms, lightning and any other type of damaging weather. Intercede for all who are affected by power outages, food shortages, unsafe water, and flooding. Please ask the Lord to bless them with His comfort and peace. Pray they have the strength and courage they need to move forward and that they swiftly receive the help and supplies they need. St. Medard, please keep them in your prayers. Amen.

Prayer to St. Michael (police officers)
(Ann Fitch)

O holy Archangel St. Michael, I ask your special protection and prayers for all police men and women, especially (*name person*). Go with all the angels and saints before the throne of God and ask Him to keep them safe from harm, dedicated to serving and protecting their communities, and full of empathy and compassion for their fellow man. O glorious prince of the Heavenly hosts, I thank you for your intercession and protection. Amen.

Prayer to St. Monica (mothers)
(Ann Fitch)

O glorious St Monica, patron saint of mothers, I come before you seeking your prayers for my children, especially (*name person*). You know well the anxieties of a mother and desires of a mother's heart so I ask you to plead for the souls and safety of my children before the Lord. Ask Him to bless them with the graces they need to know love and serve Him with humility, faithfulness and love. I also ask that you pray that I be an example of God's love for my children and that through my prayers and example they will desire a deep, abiding relationship with God. O blessed St. Monica, never cease interceding for my children. Thank you for your patronage. Amen.

Prayer to St. Pauline (diabetics)
(Ann Fitch)

O gracious St. Pauline of the Agonizing Heart of Jesus, I turn to you seeking your prayers on behalf of all those who suffer with diabetes, especially (*name person*). Go before the Lord and ask that He grant them the ability to manage their diabetes, and if it is His holy will, that He heal them of it completely. You know well the progression of this disease. Pray that those who have it pay close attention to their blood sugar levels, their diet and their exercise routines. Intercede for them that they live long, full and healthful lives without the complications that can come from diabetes. Thank you, St. Pauline for your prayers and intercession. Amen.

Prayer to St. Peregrine (cancer patients)
(Ann Fitch)

O blessed St. Peregrine, who was miraculously cured of an incurable cancer, I come before you on behalf of all those who suffer with cancer, especially (*name person*). I ask that you plead for them, asking God to bless their doctors with the wisdom and knowledge needed to bring their cancer into full remission or cure them of it completely. As they are being treated, ask the Lord to grant them the grace and strength to bear their illness with courage, patience and dignity. St. Peregrine, wonder-worker, I am confident in your help for all those afflicted with cancer, especially (*name person*). Amen.

Prayer to St. Peter Damian (insomniacs)
(Ann Fitch)

St. Peter Damian, you were an insomniac for a long period of time. You understand how difficult it is to function after a sleepless night, how hard it is to be kind, understanding and loving when you are exhausted, how frustrating it is to be tired and unable to do your best. Please intercede for (*name person*) before the throne of God and ask that if it be God's will that (*name person*) be able to rest peacefully at night and no longer suffer with insomnia. If it is not

God's will at this time I ask for (*name person*) to have the grace to use any sleepless hours as a time of prayer, offering that sleeplessness for the souls who most need God's love and mercy. St. Peter Damian, thank you for your prayers.   Amen.

Prayer to St. Philomena (infertility)
(Ann Fitch)

O St. Philomena, powerful with God, I come to you asking your intercession for all those suffering through infertility, especially (*name people*). I confidently approach you for prayers on their behalf. I ask you to plead their cause before God asking that if it is His holy will that they conceive and give birth to a healthy, happy baby. If not, pray that God blesses them with humble submission to His will and they accept life without children or that He open the door for them to become parents through adoption. St. Philomena, I know God hears your prayers and answers them, so I trust in your patronage and await a favorable answer to prayer.   Amen.

Prayer to St. Raphael (travelers)
(Ann Fitch)

O holy Archangel St. Raphael, I come to you seeking prayers and protection for all travelers, especially (*name person*). Whether traveling by land, sea or air I entrust them to your protection. Along with all the angels and saints I ask that you intercede on their behalf asking that their travels be free from incident and that they return home safe and sound. O great prince of the heavenly court I thank you for your intercession.   Amen.

Prayer to St. Rita of Cascia (difficult marriages)
(Ann Fitch)

O glorious St. Rita, full of confidence in your intercession, I deign to come before you seeking your prayers for all those in troubled marriages, especially (*name people*). You suffered in your marriage and you know well the needs of those who are struggling within their marriages. I beg you to plead before God on their behalf asking for resolution to their problems, forgiveness of one another for their grievances, healing of their hearts and a renewed trust in one another. Confident in your advocacy in impossible cases I place this case in your capable hands and pray the Lord will bring about a miracle of love. Amen.

Prayer to St. Roch (contagious diseases)
(Ann Fitch)

St. Roch, you helped countless people who suffered from contagious diseases. Intercede on behalf of (*name person*) who is caring for ill people and ask the Lord to protect him/her from contracting any illnesses he/she is helping to treat. Pray the Lord bless (*name person*) with a loving and generous heart and the wisdom and supplies he/she needs to help alleviate pain and suffering and restore ill people back to health.

Pray also, dear saint, that all I know and love are protected from becoming ill with any contagious diseases and that those who are ill with contagious diseases receive the best care available to them so that they can heal and recover fully.

Dear St. Roch, pray for the repose of the souls of those who die from complications due to contagious diseases and ask that their angels carry them into Heaven where they can rest in peace for all eternity. Thank you, St. Roch for your intercession. Amen.

Prayer to St. Roch (dogs)
(Ann Fitch)

O blessed St. Roch, patron saint of dogs, I ask you to pour out your love upon my dog(s). May my sweet dog(s) always be loving and loyal and be a joy to me and those I love. Carry my dog(s) to the throne of the Father and ask Him to bless my dog(s) with long life and great happiness. Pray dear saint that my dog(s) stay free from illness and that my dog(s) always comfort me as your beloved dog comforted and cared for you. Thank you for asking the Lord to bless my dog(s) and for begging Him to pour out special graces upon all dogs and dog owners. May they bring great love to one another and live companionably in peace.   Amen.

Prayer to St. Scholastica (sisters/nuns)
(Ann Fitch)

O gracious St. Scholastica, bride of Christ, I ask your intercession for all religious, especially (*name person*). Please go to your Spouse and ask Him to bless them with every gift and grace they need to live out their calling with joy and a burning love for God and His Church. Ask Him to fortify them and inspire them to be living signs of His presence on Earth and to bless them with steadfast faith, true humility, firm hope, and a burning zeal for the salvation of souls. Amen.

Prayer to St. Stephen (deacons)
(Ann Fitch)

O holy martyr and deacon St. Stephen, I come before you on behalf of (*name person*) and all deacons who faithfully serve the Church. I pray that you ask the Lord to fill their hearts with compassion, their minds with the wisdom of the Holy Spirit, their hearts with zeal and a deep desire for the salvation of souls. I ask you to pray that their families are supportive, understanding, and willing to allow them to serve the Church whenever the need arises. O dear St. Stephen, thank you for your intercession.   Amen.

Prayer to St. Teresa of Avila (headache sufferers)
(Ann Fitch)

O blessed St. Teresa of Avila, patron saint of headache sufferers, look kindly upon (*name person*) and all who suffer and endure pain in the head. Pray for them before your beloved and plead with Him to take away their pain if that be His holy will. If not, along with you, may they join their pain to His own for the salvation of souls.   Amen.

Prayer to St. Thomas Aquinas (students)
(Ann Fitch)

Dear St. Thomas Aquinas, patron saint of students, I come before you on behalf of (*name student(s)*) and all who are in school. Pray, dear saint, along with the Blessed Virgin Mary, that he/she/they be open to learning and that he/she/they be dedicated to his/her/their studies so that he/she/they can grow in knowledge, understanding and wisdom. Pray that (*name student(s)*) will absorb all that needs to be learned, recall facts when necessary and be able to convey what he/she/they studied clearly and concisely when called upon to do so. Thank you, St. Thomas Aquinas for your help and intercession. Amen.

Prayer to St. Thomas More (widowers)
(Ann Fitch)

O holy martyr, St. Thomas More, patron saint of widowers, hear my prayers for (*name person*) and all those whose wives have entered into eternal life. Intercede on their behalf, presenting them at the feet of God asking His blessing of infinite love and mercy upon them. Take up their causes and plead before God's throne for them with the same fervor and zeal that marked your career on Earth. Pray that they bear suffering with joy, loneliness with patience, and despair with renewed hope. If it be God's will, ask that their wives be brought into joyful union with Him and that they have eternal rest granted unto them. Thank you for your patronage and intercession. Amen.

Prayer to St. Timothy (stomach ailments)
(Ann Fitch)

O Blessed St. Timothy, martyr and bishop, we turn to you seeking your prayers for (*name person*) and all who are suffering with stomach ailments. Inspired by your zeal and with complete confidence in your intercession we place him/her in your competent hands trusting that you will carry (*name person*) to the Holy Trinity begging on his/her behalf for relief and healing if that be God's will for him/her. Thank you, St. Timothy for your continued prayers for (*name person*). We trust in your patronage and await a favorable answer to your prayers.   Amen.

Prayer to St. Vincent Ferrer (construction workers)
(Ann Fitch)

O blessed St. Vincent Ferrer, I come to you asking your intercession on behalf of (*name person*) and all who work in construction. Pray dear saint that they be kept safe from harm and that they always have the tools and materials needed to do their job well. Ask the Lord to bless them with the skills they need to complete their work and advance in their field of construction. Pray that the Lord allow them to have steady work so they can provide for their loved ones. Thank you, St. Vincent for your prayers for (*name person*) and all who work in construction.   Amen.

Ann Fitch

PRAYERS BEFORE AND AFTER COMMUNION

Years ago it seemed that everyone had prayer books they used during Mass, especially with prayers before and after Communion. I felt strongly that I needed to include a section of prayers that anyone could pray in order to prepare themselves to receive the King of Kings in Holy Communion and to pray in thanksgiving and petition after receiving Jesus in the Holy Eucharist. I hope what has been included helps you to praise and adore the Lord, enriches your life, and blesses you deeply.

"Persevere in prayer, being watchful in it with thanksgiving."
(Colossians 4:2)

At Elevation of the Host

Praise to You, my Lord and my God.

At Elevation of the Chalice

My Lord and My God, may Your Precious Blood fall upon the souls in most need of Your mercy.

At the Elevation of the Chalice
(St. Padre Pio)

Most Precious Blood, flow on my soul and sanctify it! May the love through which You were shed for me be enkindled in my heart, and purify it! Amen.

Offering of the Precious Blood
(Raccolta)

Eternal Father, I offer You the Most Precious Blood of Jesus Christ in atonement for my sins, and in supplication for the holy souls in Purgatory and for the needs of the holy Church.   Amen.

Act of Desire Before Communion

Jesus, my God and my all, my soul longs for You. My heart yearns to receive You in Holy Communion. Come, Bread of Heaven and Food of Angels, to nourish my soul and rejoice in my heart. Come, most lovable friend of my soul, to inflame me with such love that I may never again be separated from You.   Amen.

Act of Love Before Communion

O God, all that I am and all that I have is from You. You have given me my life. You have numbered me among Your favored children. You have showered me with countless graces and blessings. From all eternity You have known me and loved me. How shall I ever love You in return?

And now in Your merciful goodness You are coming into my soul to knit Yourself most intimately with me through Holy Communion. You came into the world for love of man, but now You are coming from the altar of love for me. You are coming to fill my body, heart, and soul with Your holy love and presence, my Creator, my Redeemer, my Sanctifier, my God.

O Jesus, I want to return Your love. I want to love You with all the powers of my soul. I want to belong only to You, to consecrate myself to You alone. Jesus, let me live for You; let me die for You. May I always be Yours.   Amen.

Act of Love

O my divine Jesus, how shall I return You thanks for the goodness in giving Yourself to me? The only way I can repay Your love is by loving You in return. Yes, my Lord, I love You, and I desire to love You all my life. My Jesus, You alone are sufficient for me. Whom shall I love, if I love not You, my Jesus? You love those who love You. I love You. Oh, how You also love me. If I love You but little, give me the love which You require of me. Amen.

Prayer for Healing at Communion
(Ann Fitch)

Lord Jesus, as I receive You in Holy Eucharist I ask that You bless me and heal me emotionally, psychologically, relationally, spiritually and physically. As Your Body, Blood, Soul, and Divinity penetrates my body and soul cleanse me of anything that separates me from You. My only desire is to walk in complete union with You. Please transform me, Lord. As Your Precious Blood flows through my veins allow me to feel the fire of Your divine love consuming me and allow me to rest in the knowledge that You are healing every fiber of my being. Lord consume me completely and restore me to fullness of health. Thank You, Lord Jesus for humbling Yourself and coming to me in Holy Eucharist, for loving me so completely, and for restoring me to full health me. Amen.

Act of Love After Communion

Dear Jesus, I love You with my whole heart, my whole soul, and with all my strength. May the love of Your own Sacred Heart fill my soul and purify it so that I may die to the world for love of You, as You died on the Cross for love of me. My God, through this Communion You are all mine and I am all Yours; grant that I may be all Yours for all eternity. Amen.

Act of Faith After Communion

Lord Jesus, I believe that You are the Christ, the Son of the living God. I firmly believe that through this Communion You are present within me as God and man, body, blood, soul and divinity. I believe that You enrich my soul with graces and fill my heart with the fullness of Your love. Amen.

Act of Offering After Communion

Lord Jesus, You have given Yourself to me, now let me give myself to You; I give You my body, that it may be chaste and pure. I give You my soul, that it may be free from sin. I give You my heart, that it may always love You. I give You every thought, word, and deed of my life, I consecrate myself entirely to You. Amen.

Come and Reign
(St. Peter Julian Eymard)

Oh! Yes, Lord Jesus, come and reign! Let my body be Your temple, my heart Your throne, my will Your devoted servant; let me be Yours forever, living only in You and for You! Amen.

Communion in the Blood of Christ

We praise and thank You, Lord Jesus, for giving Your redeemed people Your own Body, broken for us, as food, and Your own Blood, poured out for us, as drink.

Through Your Saving Blood, free us from sin and reconcile us in love. Break down every wall of division that separates us from one another and from You. May we be reunited in Your body the Church, born from Your pierced Heart on the cross.

When we partake of Your Precious Blood, communicate to us Your Holy Spirit so that we may be empowered to love others as You have loved us. May our Communion in Your Body and Blood be a source of renewal for Your Church; may it fill us with holy joy and bring us to eternal life.   Amen.

Prayer of the Handmaids of the Eucharist
(Akita, Japan)

Most Sacred Heart of Jesus, truly present in the Holy Eucharist, I consecrate my body and soul to be entirely one with Your Heart, being sacrificed at every instant, on the altars of the world, giving praise to the Father and pleading for the coming of His kingdom. Please receive this humble offering of myself. Use me as You will for the glory of the Father and the salvation of souls. Most holy Mother of God, never let me be separated from Your Divine Son. Please defend and protect me as Your special child.   Amen.

Prayer After Communion
(St. Padre Pio)

Stay with me, Lord, for it is necessary to have You present so that I do not forget You. You know how easily I abandon You.

Stay with me, Lord, because I am weak and I need Your strength, that I may not fall so often.

Stay with me, Lord, for You are my life, and without You, I am without fervor.

Stay with me, Lord, for You are my light, and without You, I am in darkness.

Stay with me Lord, to show me Your will.

Stay with me, Lord, so that I hear Your voice and follow You.

Stay with me, Lord, for I desire to love You very much, and always to be in Your company.

Stay with me, Lord, if You wish me to be faithful to You.

Stay with me, Lord, for as poor as my soul is, I wish it to be a place of consolation for You, a nest of love.

Stay with me, Jesus, for it is getting late and the day is coming to a close, and life passes, death, judgment, eternity approaches. It is necessary to renew my strength, so that I will not stop along the way and for that, I need You. It is getting late and death approaches. I fear the darkness, the temptations, the dryness, the cross, the sorrows. O how I need You, my Jesus, in this night of exile!

Stay with me tonight, Jesus, in life with all its dangers, I need You. Let me recognize You as Your disciples did at the breaking of the bread, so that the Eucharistic Communion be the light which disperses the darkness, the force which sustains me, the unique joy of my heart.

Stay with me, Lord, because at the hour of my death, I want to remain united to You, if not by Communion, at least by grace and love.

Stay with me, Jesus, I do not ask for divine consolation, because I do not merit it, but, the gift of Your Presence, oh yes, I ask this of You!

Stay with me, Lord for it is You alone I look for. Your love, Your grace, Your will, Your Heart, Your Spirit, because I love You and ask no other reward but to love You more and more. With a firm love, I will love You with all my heart while on Earth and continue to love You perfectly during all eternity.   Amen.

Litany Before or After Holy Communion

Lord, have mercy on us. *Lord, have mercy on us.*
Christ, have mercy on us. *Christ, have mercy on us.*
Lord, have mercy on us. *Lord, have mercy on us.*
Christ, hear us. *Christ, graciously hear us.*

God, the Father of Heaven, *have mercy on us.*
God, the Son, Redeemer of the World, *have mercy on us.*
God, the Holy Ghost, *have mercy on us.*
Holy Trinity, one God, *have mercy on us.*

Jesus, Living Bread which came down from Heaven, *have mercy on us.*

Jesus, Bread from Heaven giving life to the world, *have mercy on us.*

Hidden God and Savior, *have mercy on us.*

My Lord and my God, *have mercy on us.*

Who has loved us with an everlasting love, *have mercy on us.*

Whose delights are to be with the children of men, *have mercy on us.*

Who has given Your flesh for the life of the world, *have mercy on us.*

Who invites all to come to You, *have mercy on us.*

Who promises eternal life to those who receive You, *have mercy on us.*

Who had desire to eat the Pasch with us, *have mercy on us.*

Who are ever ready to receive and welcome us, *have mercy on us.*

Who stands at our door knocking, *have mercy on us.*

Who has said that if we will open to You the door, You will come in and sup with us, *have mercy on us.*

Who receives us into Your arms and blesses us with the little children, *have mercy on us.*

Who suffers us to sit at Your feet with Magdalen, *have mercy on us.*

Who invites us to lean on Your bosom with the beloved disciple, *have mercy on us.*

Who has not left us orphans, *have mercy on us.*

Most dear Sacrament, *have mercy on us.*

Sacrament of love, *have mercy on us.*

Sacrament of sweetness, *have mercy on us.*

Life-giving Sacrament, *have mercy on us.*

Sacrament of strength, *have mercy on us.*

My God, and my all, *have mercy on us.*

That our hearts may pant after You as the heart after the fountains of water, *we beseech You, hear us.*

That You would manifest Yourself to us as to the two disciples in the breaking of bread, *we beseech You, hear us.*

That we may know Your voice like Magdalen, *we beseech You, hear us.*

That with a lively faith we may confess with the beloved disciple: It is the Lord, *we beseech You, hear us.*

That You would bless us who have not seen and have believed, *we beseech You, hear us.*

That we may love You in the Blessed Sacrament with our whole heart, with our whole soul, with all our mind, and with all our strength, *we beseech You, hear us.*

That the fruit of each Communion may be fresh love, *we beseech You, hear us.*

That our one desire may be to love You and to do Your will, *we beseech You, hear us.*

That we may ever remain in Your love, *we beseech You, hear us.*

That You would teach us how to receive and welcome You, *we beseech You, hear us.*

That You would teach us to pray, and Yourself pray within us, *we beseech You, hear us.*

That with You every virtue may come into our souls, *we beseech You, hear us.*

That throughout this day You would keep us closely united to You, *we beseech You, hear us.*

That You would give us grace to persevere to the end, *we beseech You, hear us.*

That You would then be our support and Viaticum, *we beseech You, hear us.*

That with You and leaning on You we may safely pass through all
dangers, *we beseech You, hear us.*

That our last act may be one of perfect love, and our last breath a
long deep sigh to be in our Father's house, *we beseech You, hear us.*

That Your sweet face may smile upon us when we appear before You,
we beseech You, hear us.

That our banishment from You, dearest Lord, may not be very long,
we beseech You, hear us.

That when the time is come, we may fly up from our prison to You
and in Your Sacred Heart find our rest forever, *we beseech You,
hear us.*

Lamb of God, Who takes away the sins of the world. *Spare us, O
Lord.*

Lamb of God, Who takes away the sins of the world. *Graciously hear
us.*

Lamb of God, Who takes away the sins of the world. *Have mercy on
us.*

We come to You, dear Lord, with the Apostles, saying: Increase
our faith. Give us a strong and lively faith in the mystery of Your Real
Presence in the midst of us. Give us the splendid faith of the
centurion, which drew from You such praise. Give us the faith of the
beloved disciple, to know You in the dark and say, *"It is the Lord."* Give
us the faith of Martha to confess, *"You are Christ the Son of the Living
God."* Give us the faith of Magdalen to fall at Your feet crying,
"Rabboni, Master!" Give us the faith of all Your saints, to whom the
Blessed Sacrament has been Heaven begun on Earth. In every
Communion increase our faith; for with faith, love and humility and
reverence and all good will come into our souls. Dearest Lord,
increase our faith.   Amen.

Prayer of Thanksgiving
(Ann Fitch)

Thank You Lord for humbling Yourself and coming to me in Holy Communion. Thank You for filling me with Your loving presence. Thank You for Your Precious Blood that courses through my veins touching, blessing, healing and transforming me. Thank You for communing with me and permeating every fiber of my being. I adore You, Lord, and will always sing Your praises.   Amen.

PRAYERS BEFORE THE BLESSED SACRAMENT

Spending time before Jesus in the Blessed Sacrament is a wonderful way to bring blessings into your life and the lives of your loved ones. As Catholics, we believe that Jesus is truly, substantially, supernaturally present in the Consecrated Host. He is there, Body, Blood, Soul and Divinity, waiting for us to visit with Him. He longs for us to spend time with Him hidden in the tabernacle or exposed in a monstrance. He wants us to visit with Him and just be with Him, even if for only a few minutes. He is there – waiting to love us. He is present tangibly, really, sacramentally. He patiently waits for us to come and keep Him company.

Having a group of prayers that can be prayed all at once for a more lengthy visit or chosen one here and there for a shorter visit can be very helpful. Jesus said, *"Come to me, all you who labor and are burdened, and I will give you rest."* (Matthew 11:28) I hope the prayers I have included here will deepen your love for Jesus in Holy Eucharist, help you delve more deeply into your relationship with Him, and bring rest to your body, mind, heart and soul.

"Have no anxiety at all, but in everything, by prayer and petition, with thanksgiving, make your requests known to God. Then the peace of God that surpasses all understanding will guard your hearts and minds in Christ Jesus." (Philippians 4:6-7)

Act of Spiritual Communion
(St. Alphonsus Liguori)

My Jesus, I believe that You are in the Blessed Sacrament. I love You above all things, and long for You in my soul. Since I cannot now receive You sacramentally, come at least spiritually into my heart. As though You have already come, I embrace You and unite myself entirely to You; never permit me to be separated from You. Amen.

O Sacrament I Love
(St. Thérèse of Lisieux)

Come into my heart, O Sacrament that I love. Come into my heart; for my soul hungers for You alone. O living Bread, Bread of Heaven, divine Eucharist! O touching mystery that divine love has instituted! Come dwell in my heart. Amen.

Act of Faith

Lord, Jesus Christ, I firmly believe that You are present in this Blessed Sacrament as true God and true man, with Your Body and Blood, Soul and Divinity. My Redeemer and my judge, I adore Your divine majesty in union with the angels and saints. I believe, O Lord; increase my faith. Amen.

Act of Hope

Good Jesus, in You alone I place all my hope. You are my salvation and my strength, the source of all good. Through Your mercy, through Your passion and death, I hope to obtain the pardon of my sins, the grace of final perseverance, and a happy eternity. Amen.

Act of Love

Jesus, my God, I love You with my whole heart and above all things, because You are the one supreme good and infinitely perfect Being. You have given Your life for me, a poor sinner, and in Your mercy You have even offered Yourself as food for my soul. My God, I love You. Inflame my heart so that I may love You more.   Amen.

Prayer to Jesus in the Blessed Sacrament

O my God, I firmly believe that You are really and corporally present in the Blessed Sacrament of the altar. I adore You here present from the very depths of my heart, and I worship Your sacred presence with all possible humility.

O my soul, what joy to have Jesus Christ always with us, and to be able to speak to Him heart to heart with all confidence.

Grant, O Lord, that I, having adored Your divine Majesty here on Earth in this wonderful Sacrament, may be able to adore It eternally in Heaven.   Amen.

Prayer of Adoration
(St. John Vianney)

I love You, O my God, and my only desire is to love You until the last breath of my life. I love You, O my infinitely lovable God, and I would rather die loving You, than live without loving You. I love You, Lord and the only grace I ask is to love You eternally. My God, if my tongue cannot say in every moment that I love You, I want my heart to repeat it to You as often as I draw breath.   Amen.

Prayer of Adoration
(St. Teresa of Kolkata)

O God, we believe You are here. We adore You and love You with our whole heart and soul because You are most worthy of all our love. We desire to love You as the blessed do in Heaven. Flood our souls with Your Spirit and life. Penetrate and possess our whole being utterly, that our lives may only be a radiance of Yours. Shine through us, and be so in us, that every soul we come in contact with may feel Your presence in our soul. Let them look up and see no longer us, but only Jesus!   Amen.

243

Adoration Prayer
(St. Teresa of Kolkata)

My Lord Jesus Christ, I believe that You are really here in this Sacrament. Night and day You remain here compassionate and loving. You call, You wait for, You welcome everyone who comes to visit You. I thank You, Jesus my Divine Redeemer for coming upon the Earth for our sake and for instituting the Adorable Sacrament of the Holy Eucharist in order to remain with us until the end of the world. I thank You for hiding beneath the Eucharistic species Your infinite majesty and beauty, which Your angels delight to behold, so that I might have courage to approach the throne of Your mercy. I thank You dear Jesus, for having become the priceless Victim, to merit for me the fullness of heavenly favors. Awaken in me such confidence in You that their fullness may descend ever more fruitfully upon my soul. I thank You for offering Yourself in thanksgiving to God for all His benefits, spiritual and temporal which He has bestowed on me. Grant me grace and perseverance in Your faithful service. Amen.

Eucharistic Prayer
(Angel at Fatima)

Most Holy Trinity, I adore You! My God, my God, I love You in the Most Blessed Sacrament. Amen.

Opening Prayer to the Blessed Sacrament
(St. Alphonsus Liguori)

O Jesus in the Blessed Sacrament, inviting, and welcoming all who visit You day and night in this Sacrament, full of pity and love, expecting, inviting, and welcoming all who visit You. I believe that You are really present in the Sacrament of the Altar. From the depth of my nothingness, I adore You; and I thank You for the many graces You have given me, especially for the gift of Yourself in this Sacrament, for the gift of Your most holy Mother as my intercessor, and for the privilege of visiting You in this church.

I now speak to Your most loving Heart with a three-fold intention: to thank You for the great gift of Yourself; to atone for all the insults which Your enemies heap upon You in this Sacrament; and to adore You wherever Your Eucharistic Presence is dishonored or forgotten.

My Jesus, I love You with my whole heart. I am very sorry for my ingratitude to Your infinite goodness. I now resolve, with the help of Your grace, never to offend You again. And, sinful as I am, I consecrate to You my entire self, my whole will, my affections, my desires, and all that I have. From now on, do with me and mine as You please. I ask for and desire only Your love, final perseverance, and the grace always to do Your holy will.

I intercede with You for the souls in Purgatory, especially for those who were most devoted to the Blessed Sacrament, and to Your most holy Mother. I recommend to You also, all poor sinners. And lastly, my dear Savior, I unite all my desires with the desires of Your most loving Heart. Thus united, I present them to Your Eternal Father, and beg Him in Your Name and for love of You, to hear and answer them. Amen.

Lord, Jesus, I Adore You

Lord, Jesus Christ, God made flesh, and Son of the living God, I adore, bless, praise, glorify and magnify You with all my heart. I confess and believe with a sincere and lively faith that You are in this Most Divine Sacrament, true God and true man, present in the greatest and most marvelous way.

I adore You, all-powerful God, with that adoration that is due Your infinite majesty.

I adore You, Living Bread, that came down from Heaven to give life to the world.

I adore You, venerable Sacrament, Who are the treasury of all virtues and graces.

I adore You, most holy of all sacrifices, which You offer to the Father to sanctify souls.

I adore You, with my whole soul, true Body and Blood of my Lord Jesus Christ born of the immaculate womb of the Virgin Mary.

I adore You, Lamb of God, Who takes away the sins of the world.

I adore You, marvelous Sacrament of love, Who are the life of souls and the food of angels.

I adore You, the highest mystery of the Catholic faith.

I adore You, hidden God and Savior of the world.

I adore You, Sacred Host and Chalice of Blessing.

I adore You, precious price of our redemption.

I adore You, most astonishing of all miracles.

I adore You, Divine Viaticum of the sick, Who are the immortal healer.

I adore You, Jesus the reflection of the Father's glory.

I adore You, Divine Word and Eternal Wisdom.

I adore You, most sumptuous banquet of God, at which the angels minister.

I adore You, divine sustenance, by which the sons of men become the sons of God.

I adore You, living and nourishing bread, by which the Creator is united to the creature and mortal man is transformed by God.

I adore You, my God, concealed here in faith but in Heaven revealed clearly to the saints and angels.

I adore You, perennial wellspring of heavenly delights.

I adore You, spiritual nourishment of devout souls.

I adore You, Sacrament of piety and spiritual bond between God and men.

I adore You, Sacred Manna Who strengthens hearts and gives joy to the souls which consume You.

I adore You, most Divine Sacrament, Who are the life of our souls, the balm for our wounds, consolation in our struggles, Whom the angels and saints of Heaven praise, adore and magnify for all eternity.   Amen.

Act of Adoration
(St. Francis of Assisi)

I adore You, O Jesus, true God and true Man, here present in the Holy Eucharist, humbly kneeling before You and united in spirit with all the faithful on Earth and all the blessed in Heaven. In deepest gratitude for so great a blessing, I love You, my Jesus, with my whole heart, for You are all perfect and all worthy of love.

Give me grace nevermore in any way to offend You, and grant that I, being refreshed by Your Eucharistic presence here on Earth, may be found worthy to come to the enjoyment with Mary of Your eternal and ever blessed presence in Heaven.

I believe that You, O Jesus, are in the Most Blessed Sacrament! I love You and desire You! Come into my heart. I embrace You. O never leave me! May the burning and most sweet power of Your love, O Lord Jesus Christ, absorb my mind, that I may die through love of Your love, Who was pleased to die through love of my love. Amen.

Jesus, Our God
(Sandy Rongish)

Jesus, our God, Living Bread of Heaven, I adore You.

Jesus, our God, life and heart of the Church, I adore You.

Jesus, our God, radiant mystery of faith, I adore You.

Jesus, our God, mystery of mercy for all mankind, I adore You.

Jesus, our God, center and summit of the Church's life, I adore You.

Jesus, our God, source of charity, I adore You.

Jesus, our God, nourishment of the faithful, I adore You.

Jesus, our God, priceless treasure of all who receive You, I adore You.

Jesus, our God, love of the Father, I adore You.

Jesus, our God, Good Shepherd, Bread Divine, I adore You.

Jesus, our God, Divine One who opens our eyes to light and our hearts to new hope, I adore You.

Jesus, our God, source of holiness, I adore You.

Jesus, our God, poured out for us, I adore You.

Jesus, our God, Who was obedient unto death, I adore You.

Jesus, our God, helper of all who come to You, I adore You.

Jesus, our God, foretaste of the joy of Heaven, I adore You.

Jesus, our God, bread of angels and of pilgrims, I adore You.

Jesus, our God, I adore You for all time, past, present, and future, for every soul that ever was, is, or shall be created. Grant me the grace to comfort You. Jesus, I live for You; Jesus, I die for You; Jesus, I am Yours in life and in death.   Amen.

Invocations to the Heart of Jesus

Heart of Jesus in the Eucharist, I adore You.

Sweet Companion of our exile, I adore You.

Eucharistic Heart of Jesus, I adore You.

Heart solitary, Heart humiliated, I adore You.

Heart abandoned, Heart forgotten, I adore You.

Heart despised, Heart outraged, I adore You.

Heart ignored by men, I adore You.

Heart, lover of our hearts, I adore You.

Heart pleading for love, I adore You.

Heart patient in waiting for us, I adore You.

Heart eager to hear our prayers, I adore You.

Heart desiring that we should pray to You, I adore You.

Heart, source of fresh graces, I adore You.

Heart silent, desiring to speak to souls, I adore You.

Heart, sweet refuge of the hidden life, I adore You.

Heart, teacher of the secrets of union with God, I adore You.
Heart of Him Who sleeps, yet ever watches, I adore You.
Eucharistic Heart of Jesus, have mercy on us.

Jesus Victim, I wish to comfort You; I unite myself to You; I offer myself in union with You. I count myself as nothing before You; I desire to forget myself in order to think of You, to be forgotten and despised for love of You, not to be understood, not to be loved, except by You. I will hold my peace that I may listen to You; I will forsake myself that I may lose myself in You.

Grant that I may quench Your thirst for my salvation, Your burning thirst for my sanctification, and that, being purified, I may bestow on You a pure and true love. I would no longer weary Your expectations; take me, I give myself to You. I entrust to You all my actions - my mind that You may enlighten it, my heart that You may direct it, my will that You may establish it, my misery that You may relieve it, my soul and my body that You may feed them.

Eucharistic Heart of my Jesus, Whose Blood is the life of my soul, may it be no longer I who live, but You alone Who lives in me.   Amen.

The Anima Christi
(St. Elizabeth Ann Seton)

Soul of Jesus, sanctify me.
Blood of Jesus, wash me.
Passion of Jesus, comfort me.
Wounds of Jesus, hide me.
Heart of Jesus, receive me.
Spirit of Jesus, enliven me.
Goodness of Jesus, pardon me.
Beauty of Jesus, draw me.
Humility of Jesus, humble me.
Peace of Jesus, pacify me.
Love of Jesus, inflame me.

Kingdom of Jesus, come to me.

Grace of Jesus, replenish me.

Mercy of Jesus, pity me.

Sanctity of Jesus, sanctify me.

Purity of Jesus, purify me.

Cross of Jesus, support me.

Nails of Jesus, hold me.

Mouth of Jesus, bless me in life, in death, in time and eternity.

Mouth of Jesus, defend me in the hour of death.

Mouth of Jesus, call me to come to You.

Mouth of Jesus, receive me with Your saints in glory evermore.

Let us pray:

Unite me to Yourself, O adorable Victim. Life-giving Heavenly Bread, feed me, sanctify me, reign in me, transform me to Yourself. Live in me; let me live in You; let me adore You in Your life-giving Sacrament as my God, listen to You as my master, obey You as my king, imitate You as my model, follow You as my shepherd, love You as my Father, seek You as my physician Who will heal all the maladies of my soul. Be indeed my way, truth and life; sustain me, O Heavenly Manna, through the desert of this world, until I behold You unveiled in Your glory. Amen

The Angel's Prayer
(Angel at Fatima)

O most Holy Trinity, Father, Son, and Holy Spirit, I adore You profoundly. I offer You the most precious Body, Blood, Soul and Divinity of Jesus Christ, present in all the tabernacles of the world, in reparation for the outrages, sacrileges and indifferences by which He is offended. By the infinite merits of the Sacred Heart of Jesus and the Immaculate Heart of Mary, I beg the conversion of sinners. Amen.

Thirty-Three Petitions in Honor of the Sacred Humanity

O good Jesus, Word of the eternal Father, convert me.

O good Jesus, son of Mary, make me her child.

O good Jesus, my master, teach me.

O good Jesus, Prince of Peace, give me peace.

O good Jesus, my refuge, receive me.

O good Jesus, my pastor, feed my soul.

O good Jesus, model of patience, comfort me.

O good Jesus, meek and humble of heart, make my heart like unto Yours.

O good Jesus, my redeemer, save me.

O good Jesus, my God and my all, possess me.

O good Jesus, the true way, direct me.

O good Jesus, eternal truth, instruct me.

O good Jesus, life of the blessed, make me live in You.

O good Jesus, my support, strengthen me.

O good Jesus, my justice, justify me.

O good Jesus, my mediator, reconcile me to Your Father.

O good Jesus, physician of my soul, heal me.

O good Jesus, my judge, absolve me.

O good Jesus, my king, govern me.

O good Jesus, my sanctification, sanctify me.

O good Jesus, abyss of goodness, pardon me.

O good Jesus, Living Bread from Heaven, satiate me.

O good Jesus, the father of the prodigal, receive me.

O good Jesus, joy of my soul, refresh me.

O good Jesus, my helper, assist me.

O good Jesus, magnet of love, attract me.

O good Jesus, my protector, defend me.

O good Jesus, my hope, sustain me.

O good Jesus, object of my love, make me love You.

O good Jesus, fountain of life, cleanse me.

O good Jesus, my propitiation, purify me.

O good Jesus, my last end, let me obtain You.

O good Jesus, my glory, glorify me.   Amen.

Jesus, hear my prayer. Jesus, graciously hear me.

Let Us Pray:

O Lord Jesus Christ, Who has said, "*Ask and you shall receive, seek and you shall find, knock and it shall be opened unto you,*" mercifully attend to our supplications, and grant us the gift of Your divine charity, that we may ever love You with our whole hearts, and may never cease from praising You, Who lives and reigns world without end.   Amen.

Aspirations

My Lord and my God.

O Sacrament Most Holy, O Sacrament Divine, all praise and all
   thanksgiving be every moment Thine!

Blessed be Jesus in the Most Holy Sacrament of the Altar.

Blessed be God.

Glory to You O Lord.

O Lord, I love You. May all hearts burn with love for You.

Lord consume me with the fire of Your love.

Eucharistic Heart of Jesus, burning with love for me, may I love You
   more and more.

Come, O Lord, into my heart and set it aflame.

Lord Jesus, grant that I may love You ever more.

With all that I am, I love You, my God.

Jesus, You alone are sufficient for me.

My Lord and my all.

My Lord and my God, I love You above all things.

Jesus, my God, I love You above all things!

O Lord, may You be praised, honored and glorified in all the monstrances of the world.

Here I am Lord, I come to do Your will.

I desire only to please You, O my God.

Lord, Jesus Christ, Son of God, have mercy on me, a sinner.

In You, O Lord I take refuge.

Lord, grant me Your peace.

My Jesus, mercy.

Jesus, I trust in You.

Pardon Prayer
(by Angel of Fatima)

My God, I believe, I adore, I hope, and I love You! I ask pardon for those who do not believe, do not adore, do not hope, and do not love You. Amen.

Each Time I Look

Jesus, each time I look at the sacred Host, sanctify my eyes, that they may close to that which is earthly and open to that which is Your holy will.

Jesus, each time I look at the sacred Host, send a ray of divine light into my soul that I may better know You and serve You.

Jesus, each time I look at the sacred Host, send a flame of divine love into my heart to consume everything in it that is displeasing to You and set it aflame with love for You.

Jesus, each time I look at the sacred Host, bless my mind with the clarity of Your wisdom that I may rest immersed in Your divine mercy.

Jesus, each time I look at the sacred Host, may I be filled with joyful thanksgiving and sing Your praises. Amen.

The Blessing

O my Jesus, fountain of inexhaustible blessings, Who did bless Your
apostles before ascending into Heaven, bless me also and with Your
presence sanctify me.

Bless my memory, that it may ever call You to mind.

Bless my understanding, that it may always think of You.

Bless my will, that it may never seek or desire anything which may be
displeasing to You.

Bless my body and all its actions.

Bless my heart with all its affections.

Bless me in life and at the hour of my death.

Bless me in time and in eternity; and grant that Your blessing may be
to me a pledge of eternal happiness.

Bless all the faithful.

Bless all my loved ones.

Bless everyone to whom I owe any gratitude, and bring us all to rest
in Your Sacred Heart forever.   Amen.

Jesus, Help Me

In every need let me come to You with humble trust, saying: *Jesus,
help me.*

In all my doubts, temptations, and troubles of mind, *Jesus, help me.*

When I am lonely or tired, *Jesus, help me.*

When my plans have failed, and I am disappointed, *Jesus, help me.*

When others let me down, and my heart is filled with sorrow, *Jesus,
help me.*

When I am filled with concern for those I love, *Jesus, help me.*

When I feel impatient, and my cross is hard to carry, *Jesus, help me.*

When I sin and need to seek Your mercy and forgiveness, *Jesus, help
me.*

Always, in every way, *Jesus, help me, and never leave me.*   Amen.

Blood of Jesus, Help Me!

In every need let me come to You with humble trust saying, Blood of Jesus, help me!

In all my doubts, perplexities, and temptations, Blood of Jesus, help me!

In hours of loneliness, weariness and trials, Blood of Jesus, help me!

In the failure of my plans and hopes, in disappointments, troubles and sorrows, Blood of Jesus, help me!

When my heart is cast down by failure, at seeing no good come from my efforts, Blood of Jesus, help me!

When others fail me, and Your grace alone can assist me, Blood of Jesus, help me!

When I throw myself on Your tender love as my Father and Savior, Blood of Jesus, help me!

When I feel impatient, and my cross irritates me, Blood of Jesus, help me!

When I am ill, Blood of Jesus, help me!

Always, always in spite of weakness, falls and shortcomings, of every kind, Blood of Jesus, help me and never forsake me.   Amen.

Prayer When Burdened
(Ann Fitch)

Lord Jesus, I come before You, weighed down by the crosses I carry. You have told us Your yoke is easy and Your burden light and that we must pick up our cross and follow You. Trusting in You, I give you all that burdens me. I ask You to renew my strength and bless me with the courage I need to continue bearing my crosses lovingly and without complaint.

As I rest here in Your presence, fill me to overflowing with Your love and encouragement. O Lord, in Your compassion, bless me with hope and grace. As I join my suffering to Yours for the salvation of souls fill my heart and soul with joy and peace. Thank You, Lord for easing my burdens and blessing me with Your merciful love. Amen.

Dear Jesus
(Ann Fitch)

Dear Jesus, so often I have come before You asking for things. Encouraged by Your constant assistance, I ask this very special favor (*mention request*). Take it dear Jesus and place it within Your Sacred Heart, where Our Father sees it. Then, it will become Your request before Him not mine. Grant that it will be granted if it is Your holy will. Thank You, Jesus. Amen.

Prayer for All
(Ann Fitch)

Lord Jesus, I recommend to You everyone who is dear to me. Bless each one with Your love and keep them in Your care.

Lord Jesus, I offer to You all who are sick, suffering, hungry or homeless. Bless them with comfort, healing and strength.

Lord Jesus, I pray for all the souls of the departed, especially those in Purgatory. Bless them with Your mercy and grant them eternal rest in union with You.

Lord Jesus, I pray for all people of faith that they will walk in truth and love. Bless those who have no faith that they may be blessed with the gift of faith.

Lord Jesus, bless our Holy Father the Pope, the bishops and clergy, and all religious men and women. May they be Your presence to all they encounter.

Lord Jesus, strengthen the heavily burdened, revive hope in the despairing, and grant liberty to victims of injustice and persecution.

Lord Jesus, impart wisdom to judges, civil servants, and all who hold positions of leadership. May they never abuse their positions of power.

Lord Jesus, You know every human need. In Your infinite compassion and mercy meet every need and bless every person. Amen.

Prayer for 1,000 Souls to be Released from Purgatory
(St. Gertrude)

Eternal Father, I offer You the most Precious Blood of Your Divine Son, Jesus, in union with the Masses said throughout the world today, for all the holy souls in Purgatory, for sinners everywhere, for sinners in the universal Church, those in my own home and within my family. Amen.

Prayer to the Heart of Jesus for the Souls in Purgatory

O gentle Heart of Jesus, ever present in the Blessed Sacrament, ever consumed with burning love for the poor captive souls in Purgatory, have mercy on them. Be not severe in Your judgments, but let some drops of Your Precious Blood fall upon the devouring flames. And, merciful Savior, send Your angels to conduct them to a place of refreshment, light, and peace when their souls are pure and ready to enter into eternal joy with You. Amen.

Prayer for Conversion

O God, all hearts are in Your hands. You can bend, as it pleases You, the most stubborn, and soften the most obdurate. I beseech You, by the Holy Name, the Most Precious Blood, the merits, wounds and Divine Heart, of Jesus, Your beloved Son, to grant the conversion of (*name the person/people*). Amen.

Chaplet of the Adorable Sacrament

This chaplet is prayed using an ordinary rosary.

Begin by holding the crucifix and making the **Sign of the Cross**.

Say an **Our Father**, a **Hail Mary**, and the **Glory Be** for the intentions of the Holy Father.

On the single beads say:

Lord Jesus, I offer You my sorrow for the many sacrileges committed against You and the indifference shown You in the Holy Sacrament of the Altar.

On the sets of 10 beads say:

Jesus, I adore You in the most Blessed Sacrament.

To conclude, pray the following:

Holy Mother Mary, please present this prayer to your Son, Jesus, and bring consolation to His Sacred Heart. Please give Him my thanks for His divine presence in the Blessed Sacrament. He has treated us with mercy and love by staying with us. May my life be my thanksgiving prayer to Him. Jesus, I trust in You. Amen.

Litany of the Love of God

Lord, have mercy on us. *Christ, have mercy on us.*
Lord, have mercy on us. Christ, hear us. *Christ, graciously hear us.*
God the Father of Heaven, *have mercy on us.*
God the Son, Redeemer of the World, *have mercy on us.*
God the Holy Ghost, *have mercy on us.*
Holy Trinity, One God, *have mercy on us.*

You Who are Infinite Love, *I love You, O my God.*
You Who did first love me, *I love You, O my God.*
You Who commands me to love You, *I love You, O my God.*
With all my heart, *I love You, O my God.*
With all my soul, *I love You, O my God.*
With all my mind, *I love You, O my God.*
With all my strength, *I love You, O my God.*
Above all possessions and honor, *I love You, O my God.*
Above all pleasures and enjoyments, *I love You, O my God.*
More than myself and all that belongs to me, *I love You, O my God.*

More than all my relatives and friends, *I love You, O my God.*

More than all men and angels, *I love You, O my God.*

Above all created things in Heaven or on Earth, *I love You, O my God.*

Only for Yourself, *I love You, O my God.*

Because You are the sovereign good, *I love You, O my God.*

Because You are infinitely worthy of being loved, *I love You, O my God.*

Because You are infinitely perfect, *I love You, O my God.*

Even had You not promised me Heaven, *I love You, O my God.*

Even had You not menaced me with Hell, *I love You, O my God.*

Even should You try me by want and misfortune, *I love You, O my God.*

In wealth and in poverty, *I love You, O my God.*

In prosperity and in adversity, *I love You, O my God.*

In health and in sickness, *I love You, O my God.*

In life and in death, *I love You, O my God.*

In time and in eternity, *I love You, O my God.*

In union with that love wherewith all the saints and all the angels love You in Heaven, *I love You, O my God.*

In union with that love wherewith the Blessed Virgin Mary loves You, *I love You, O my God.*

In union with that infinite love wherewith You love Yourself eternally, *I love You, O my God.*

My God, Who possesses in incomprehensible abundance all that is perfect and worthy of love, annihilate in me all guilty, sensual and undue love for creatures; kindle in my heart the pure flame of Your love, so that I may love nothing but You or in You, until being entirely consumed by holy love of You, I may go to love You eternally with the elect in Heaven, the country of pure love.   Amen.

Litany of the Most Blessed Sacrament

Lord, have mercy. *Lord, have mercy.*

Christ, have mercy. *Christ, have mercy.*

Lord, have mercy. *Lord, have mercy.*

Christ, hear us. *Christ, graciously hear us.*

God the Father of Heaven, *have mercy on us.*

God the Son, Redeemer of the World, *have mercy on us.*

God, the Holy Spirit, *have mercy on us.*

Holy Trinity, One God, *have mercy on us.*

O Living Bread, Who from Heaven descended, *have mercy on us.*

Hidden God and Savior, *have mercy on us.*

Perpetual sacrifice, *have mercy on us.*

Lamb without spot, *have mercy on us.*

Most pure feast, *have mercy on us.*

Food of angels, *have mercy on us.*

Hidden manna, *have mercy on us.*

Memorial of God's wonders, *have mercy on us.*

Super substantial Bread, *have mercy on us.*

Word made flesh, dwelling in us, *have mercy on us.*

Holy Victim, *have mercy on us.*

O Cup of Blessing, *have mercy on us.*

O Mystery of Faith, *have mercy on us.*

O most high and venerable Sacrament, *have mercy on us.*

O most holy of all sacrifices, *have mercy on us.*

O true propitiatory sacrifice for the living and the dead, *have mercy on us.*

O heavenly antidote, by which we are preserved from sin, *have mercy on us.*

O stupendous miracle above all others, *have mercy on us.*

O most holy commemoration of the passion of Christ, *have mercy on us.*

O gift transcending all gifts, *have mercy on us.*

O extraordinary memorial of divine love, *have mercy on us.*

Medicine of immortality, *have mercy on us.*

Awesome and life-giving Sacrament, *have mercy on us.*

Unbloody Sacrifice, *have mercy on us.*

Sweetest banquet at which the angels serve, *have mercy on us.*

Bond of love, *have mercy on us.*

Offering and oblation, *have mercy on us.*

Refreshment of holy souls, *have mercy on us.*

Viaticum of those dying in the Lord, *have mercy on us.*

Pledge of future glory, *have mercy on us.*

Be merciful, spare us, O Lord. *Be merciful, graciously hear us, O Lord.*

From the unworthy reception of Your Body and Blood, *deliver us, O Lord.*

From passions of the flesh, *deliver us, O Lord.*

From pride, *deliver us, O Lord.*

From every occasion of sin, *deliver us, O Lord.*

Through that most ardent love, with which You instituted this Divine Sacrament, *deliver us, O Lord.*

Through the most Precious Blood, which You have left for us upon the altar, *deliver us, O Lord.*

Through those five wounds of Your most holy body, which was given up for us, *deliver us, O Lord.*

Sinners we are, *we beseech You, hear us.*

That You would graciously preserve and augment the faith, reverence, and devotion in us towards this admirable Sacrament, *we beseech You, hear us.*

That You would graciously lead us through the true confession of our sins to a frequent reception of the Eucharist, *we beseech You, hear us.*

That You would graciously free us from every heresy, falsehood, and blindness of the heart, *we beseech You, hear us.*

That You would graciously impart to us the heavenly and precious fruits of this most Holy Sacrament, *we beseech You, hear us.*

That You would graciously protect and strengthen us in our hour of death with this heavenly Viaticum, *we beseech You, hear us.*

O Son of God, *we beseech You, hear us.*

Lamb of God, Who takes away the sins of the world, *spare us, O Lord.*

Lamb of God, Who takes away the sins of the world, *graciously hear us, O Lord.*

Lamb of God, Who takes away the sins of the world, *have mercy on us, O Lord.*

Christ, hear us. *Christ, hear us.*

Christ, graciously hear us. *Christ, graciously hear us.*

Lord, have mercy. *Lord, have mercy.*

Christ, have mercy. *Christ, have mercy.*

Lord, have mercy. *Lord, have mercy.*

O God, Who under a marvelous Sacrament has left us a memorial of Your passion; grant us; we beseech You; so to venerate the sacred mysteries of Your Body and Blood, that we may ever perceive within us the fruit of Your redemption. You, Who lives and reigns forever and ever. Amen.

Litany of the Precious Blood

Lord, have mercy on us. *Christ, have mercy on us.*

Lord, have mercy on us. Christ, hear us. *Christ, graciously hear us.*

God, the Father of Heaven, *have mercy on us.*

God the Son, Redeemer of the World, *have mercy on us.*

God, the Holy Ghost, *have mercy on us.*

Holy Trinity, One God, *have mercy on us.*

Blood of Jesus, the Son of the Eternal Father, *cleanse us, O Precious Blood!*

Blood of Jesus, formed by the Holy Ghost in the heart of the Virgin Mother, *cleanse us, O Precious Blood!*

Blood of Jesus, substantially united to the Word of God, *cleanse us, O Precious Blood!*

Blood of Jesus, of infinite majesty, *cleanse us, O Precious Blood!*

Blood of Jesus, of infinite worth, *cleanse us, O Precious Blood!*

Blood of Jesus, shed in the circumcision, *cleanse us, O Precious Blood!*

Blood of Jesus, shed in the agony on Mount Olivet, *cleanse us, O Precious Blood!*

Blood of Jesus, shed in the crowning of thorns, *cleanse us, O Precious Blood!*

Blood of Jesus, shed in the scourging, *cleanse us, O Precious Blood!*

Blood of Jesus, shed on the Way of the Cross, *cleanse us, O Precious Blood!*

Blood of Jesus, shed at the crucifixion, *cleanse us, O Precious Blood!*

Blood of Jesus, shed at the opening of Your sacred side, *cleanse us, O Precious Blood!*

Blood of Jesus, shed in love for mankind, *cleanse us, O Precious Blood!*

Blood of Jesus, shed in obedience to the Father, *cleanse us, O Precious Blood!*

Blood of Jesus, sacrifice to divine justice, *cleanse us, O Precious Blood!*

Blood of Jesus, memorial of the bitter passion, *cleanse us, O Precious Blood!*

Blood of Jesus, seal of the new and eternal testament, *cleanse us, O Precious Blood!*

Blood of Jesus, which formed the Church, our Mother, *cleanse us, O Precious Blood!*

Blood of Jesus, which ransomed us from the slavery of Satan, *cleanse us, O Precious Blood!*

Blood of Jesus, which reopened Heaven for us, *cleanse us, O Precious Blood!*

Blood of Jesus, which cries more loudly than the blood of Abel, *cleanse us, O Precious Blood!*

Blood of Jesus, which pacifies the wrath of the Father, *cleanse us, O Precious Blood!*

Blood of Jesus, which mitigates or averts punishments, *cleanse us, O Precious Blood!*

Blood of Jesus, propitiation for our sins, *cleanse us, O Precious Blood!*

Blood of Jesus, cleansing bath for the sinful soul, *cleanse us, O Precious Blood!*

Blood of Jesus, balsam for the wounds of the soul, *cleanse us, O Precious Blood!*

Blood of Jesus, source of peace and reconciliation, *cleanse us, O Precious Blood!*

Blood of Jesus, flowing in the Eucharistic Heart, *cleanse us, O Precious Blood!*

Blood of Jesus, imploring grace for us, *cleanse us, O Precious Blood!*

Blood of Jesus, flowing mystically in the Holy Sacrifice, *cleanse us, O Precious Blood!*

Blood of Jesus, inebriating drink of the children of God, *cleanse us, O Precious Blood!*

Blood of Jesus, healing drink of the sick and weak, *cleanse us, O Precious Blood!*

Blood of Jesus, refreshing drink of the banished children of Eve, *cleanse us, O Precious Blood!*

Blood of Jesus, love-potion of God-loving souls, *cleanse us, O Precious Blood!*

Blood of Jesus, celestial wine of virgins, *cleanse us, O Precious Blood!*

Blood of Jesus, source of all consolation, *cleanse us, O Precious Blood!*

Blood of Jesus, source of love and mercy, *cleanse us, O Precious Blood!*

Blood of Jesus, source of life and holiness, *cleanse us, O Precious Blood!*

Blood of Jesus, medicine of immortality, *cleanse us, O Precious Blood!*

Blood of Jesus, reviled and despised, *cleanse us, O Precious Blood!*

Blood of Jesus, worthy of all praise, *cleanse us, O Precious Blood!*

Blood of Jesus, comfort of the patriarchs, *cleanse us, O Precious Blood!*

Blood of Jesus, desire of the prophets, *cleanse us, O Precious Blood!*

Blood of Jesus, power and strength of the apostles and martyrs, *cleanse us, O Precious Blood!*

Blood of Jesus, sanctification of virgins and confessors, *cleanse us, O Precious Blood!*

Blood of Jesus, terror of evil spirits, *cleanse us, O Precious Blood!*

Blood of Jesus, salvation of those who trust in You, *cleanse us, O Precious Blood!*

Blood of Jesus, hope of those who die in You, *cleanse us, O Precious Blood!*

Blood of Jesus, consolation and refreshment of the poor souls, *cleanse us, O Precious Blood!*

Blood of Jesus, key of Heaven, *cleanse us, O Precious Blood!*

Blood of Jesus, pledge of eternal blessedness, *cleanse us, O Precious Blood!*

Blood of Jesus, delight of all the saints, *cleanse us, O Precious Blood!*

Blood of Jesus, the Lamb without spot or blemish, *cleanse us, O Precious Blood!*

Lamb of God, Who takes away the sins of the world. *Spare us, O Lord!*

Lamb of God, Who takes away the sins of the world. *Graciously hear us, O Lord!*

Lamb of God, Who takes away the sins of the world. *Have mercy on us, O Lord.*

You have redeemed us, O Lord, in Your Blood, and made us a kingdom to our God.

Let us pray:

Almighty and eternal God, You have given Your only-begotten Son as a Savior to the world, and Who did will to be reconciled by His Blood, grant us, we beseech You, the grace so to honor the price of our salvation, and through its power to be protected against all the evils of the present life, that we may enjoy the fruit thereof forever in Heaven. Through Jesus Christ, Our Lord, Who lives and reigns with You in the unity of the Holy Spirit, God, world without end. Amen.

Prayer of Thanksgiving
(Ann Fitch)

Thank You, Lord Jesus, for humbling Yourself and coming to us under the veil of the Most Holy Eucharist. Thank You for giving Yourself to us in Holy Communion. Thank You for being here for us to adore, praise and glorify. Thank You for Your love, compassion, forgiveness and mercy. May we always come to visit You in the Blessed Sacrament and offer You all of whom we are. Amen.

LITANIES

Litanies have long been a beloved form of prayer in the holy Catholic Church. The word litany comes from the Greek word "litê" meaning supplication or to entreat. While litanies can vary in length, subject, and responses they all share a common form of invocation followed with an unvarying response. They are modeled after Psalm 136 in which lines are concluded with, *"for his mercy endures forever."*

The litany most familiar to Catholics is The Litany of the Saints, which can be traced back to the 3rd and 4th centuries. There are six litanies that are approved by the Church for public recitation: The Litany of the Holy Name of Jesus; The Litany of the Sacred Heart of Jesus; The Litany of the Most Precious Blood of Jesus; The Litany of the Blessed Virgin Mary (also known as the Litany of Loreto); The Litany of St. Joseph; and, The Litany of the Saints. All other litanies are for private recitation and devotion.

In this section I have included litanies that I have found to be marvelous in helping me meditate on different aspects of God, the Blessed Virgin Mary and the saints. I pray they will enrich your prayer life and help you grow in your love for God, Mary and the saints.

"Let the words of my mouth be acceptable, the thoughts of my heart before you, Lord." (Psalm 19:14)

Litany to the Most Holy Trinity

Blessed be the Holy Trinity and undivided Unity; we will give glory to Him, because He has shown His mercy to us.

O Lord our Lord, how wonderful is Your Name in all the Earth!
O the depth of the riches of the wisdom and of the knowledge of
  God!

Lord, have mercy. *Lord, have mercy.*
Christ, have mercy. *Christ, have mercy.*
Lord, have mercy. *Lord, have mercy.*
Blessed Trinity, hear us. *Adorable Unity, graciously hear us.*

God the Father of Heaven, *have mercy on us.*
God the Son, Redeemer of the World, *have mercy on us.*
God the Holy Ghost, *have mercy on us.*
Holy Trinity, One God, *have mercy on us.*
Father from Whom are all things, *have mercy on us.*
Son through Whom are all things, *have mercy on us.*
Holy Ghost in Whom are all things, *have mercy on us.*
Holy and undivided Trinity, *have mercy on us.*
Father everlasting, *have mercy on us.*
Only-begotten Son of the Father, *have mercy on us.*
Spirit Who proceeds from the Father and the Son, *have mercy on us.*
Co-eternal Majesty of Three Divine Persons, *have mercy on us.*
Father, the Creator, *have mercy on us.*
Son, the Redeemer, *have mercy on us.*
Holy Ghost, the Comforter, *have mercy on us.*
Holy, holy, holy, Lord God of hosts, *have mercy on us.*
Who is, Who was, and Who is to come, *have mercy on us.*
God Most High, Who inhabits eternity, *have mercy on us.*
To Whom alone are due all honor and glory, *have mercy on us.*
Who alone does great wonders, *have mercy on us.*
Power infinite, *have mercy on us.*
Wisdom, incomprehensible, *have mercy on us.*
Love unspeakable, *have mercy on us.*

Be merciful, *spare us, O Holy Trinity.*
Be merciful, *graciously hear us, O Holy Trinity.*

From all evil, *deliver us, O Holy Trinity.*
From all sin, *deliver us, O Holy Trinity.*
From all pride, *deliver us, O Holy Trinity.*
From all love of riches, *deliver us, O Holy Trinity.*
From all uncleanness, *deliver us, O Holy Trinity.*
From all sloth, *deliver us, O Holy Trinity.*
From all inordinate affection, *deliver us, O Holy Trinity.*
From all envy and malice, *deliver us, O Holy Trinity.*
From all anger and impatience, *deliver us, O Holy Trinity.*
From every thought, word, and deed contrary to Your holy law,
    deliver us, O Holy Trinity.
From Your everlasting malediction, *deliver us, O Holy Trinity.*
Through Your plenteous loving kindness, *deliver us, O Holy Trinity.*
Through the exceeding treasure of Your goodness and love, *deliver
    us, O Holy Trinity.*
Through the depths of Your wisdom and knowledge, *deliver us, O
    Holy Trinity.*
Through all Your unspeakable perfections, *deliver us, O Holy Trinity.*

We sinners, *we beseech You, hear us.*

That we may ever serve You alone, *we beseech You, hear us.*
That we may worship You in spirit and in truth, *we beseech You, hear
    us.*
That we may love You with all our heart, with all our soul, and with
    all our strength, *we beseech You, hear us.*
That, for Your sake, we may love our neighbor as ourselves, *we
    beseech You, hear us.*

That we may faithfully keep Your holy commandments, *we beseech You, hear us.*

That we may never defile our bodies and souls with sin, *we beseech You, hear us.*

That we may go from grace to grace, and from virtue to virtue, *we beseech You, hear us.*

That we may finally enjoy the sight of You in glory, *we beseech You, hear us.*

That You would vouchsafe to hear us, *we beseech You, hear us.*

O Blessed Trinity, *we beseech You, deliver us.*

O Blessed Trinity, *we beseech You, save us.*

O Blessed Trinity, *have mercy on us.*

Lord, have mercy. Christ, have mercy. Lord, have mercy.

Pray one **Our Father** and one **Hail Mary**.

Blessed are You, O Lord, in the firmament of Heaven, and worthy to be praised, and glorious, and highly exalted forever.

Almighty and everlasting God, Who has granted Your servants in the confession of the true faith, to acknowledge the glory of an eternal Trinity, and in the power of Your majesty to adore a Unity: we beseech You that by the strength of this faith we may be defended from all adversity, through Jesus Christ Our Lord.   Amen.

Litany to God the Son

O Jesus, Who for love of me consented to become man, *I thank You with all my heart.*

O Jesus, Who for love of me passed nine months in the womb of a Virgin, *I thank You with all my heart.*

O Jesus Who for love of me willed to be born in a poor stable, *I thank You with all my heart.*

O Jesus Who for love of me worked in the sweat of Your brow, *I thank You with all my heart.*

O Jesus, Who for love of me suffered a painful passion, *I thank You with all my heart.*

O Jesus, Who for love of me hung on the cross for three hours and died in ignominy on it, *I thank You with all my heart.*

O Jesus, Who from the cross gave me Mary to be my mother, *I thank You with all my heart.*

O Jesus, Who ascended into Heaven, to prepare a place for me and to make Yourself my advocate with the Father, *I thank You with all my heart.*

O Jesus, Who for love of me resides day and night in the tabernacle, *I thank You with all my heart.*

O Jesus, Who for love of me immolates Yourself every morning on the altar, *I thank You with all my heart.*

O Jesus, Who comes so often into my heart by Holy Communion, *I thank You with all my heart.*

O Jesus, Who in the holy tribunal so often washes me in Your Precious Blood, *I thank You with all my heart.*

Litany to Jesus in the Womb of Mary

Jesus, knit so wonderfully in the womb of Mary, *have mercy on us.*

Jesus, conceived by the Holy Spirit in the womb of Mary, *have mercy on us.*

Jesus, uniquely human from the moment of conception in the womb of Mary, *have mercy on us.*

Jesus, present at creation, created in the womb of Mary, *have mercy on us.*

Jesus, word made flesh, taking on a human body in the womb of Mary, *have mercy on us.*

Jesus, subject to human development in the womb of Mary, *have mercy on us.*

Jesus, whose Precious Blood first flowed through tiny arteries and veins in the womb of Mary, *have mercy on us.*

Jesus, hidden nine months in the womb of Mary, *have mercy on us.*

Jesus, begotten by God, nourished by the substance and blood of His Most Holy Mother in the womb of Mary, *have mercy on us.*

Jesus, leaping from eternity into time, in the womb of Mary, *have mercy on us.*

Jesus, revealing with His Father and the Holy Spirit all wisdom and knowledge to His Most Holy Mother, in the womb of Mary, *have mercy on us.*

Jesus, aware of His role as Redeemer in the womb of Mary, *have mercy on us.*

Jesus, sanctifier of His precursor from the womb of Mary, *have mercy on us.*

Jesus, Eternal Word, Divine Child, embraced by the Father, in the womb of Mary, *have mercy on us.*

Jesus, raising His Mother to the heights of sanctification, in the womb of Mary, *have mercy on us.*

Jesus, everlasting delight of Heaven, in the womb of Mary, *have mercy on us.*

Jesus, manifesting His Incarnation to His Holy Mother, in the womb of Mary, *have mercy on us.*

Jesus, adored and contemplated by His Mother in the sanctuary of her womb, *have mercy on us.*

Jesus, before whom the angels prostrated themselves, in the womb of Mary, *have mercy on us.*

Jesus, in whom the very angels beheld the humanity of the infant God and the union of the two natures of the Word in the virginal womb of Mary, *have mercy on us.*

Jesus, whose holy limbs first budded in the womb of Mary, *have mercy on us.*

Jesus, whose Godhead the world cannot contain, weighing only a few grams in the womb of Mary, *have mercy on us.*

Jesus, Divine Immensity, once measuring only tenths of an inch in the womb of Mary, *have mercy on us.*

Jesus, Sacrificial Lamb, Docile Infant in the womb of Mary, *have mercy on us.*

Jesus, who was to suffer the agony and passion of death, accepting the human capacity for pain and grief, in the womb of Mary, *have mercy on us.*

Jesus, Lamb of God in the womb of Mary, spare us, O Lord. *Have mercy on us.*

Jesus, Holy Innocent in the womb of Mary, graciously hear us, O Lord. *Have mercy on us.*

Jesus, Son of God and Messiah in the womb of Mary, have mercy on us, O Lord. *Have mercy on us.*

Let Us Pray:

God, our Creator, You formed us as women and men, equal partners in the stewardship of Your world: joined forever as sisters and brothers, yet within each of us lives a rich diversity of different gifts, different hopes and different limitations. In Jesus, Your Word born fully in our flesh, You have seen and loved in us all that You have made us to be. Though graced, we are limited and often weak. But our weaknesses themselves are no obstacle to Your passion for us. Teach us to see in ourselves what You have seen in each of us from birth. Teach us to know our gifts and limits. Keep us confidently on the path of self-knowledge, fullness of wisdom, and joy in being Your children. We ask this through Christ and the Holy Spirit, with You, One God, forever and ever. Amen.

Litany of the Holy Name of Jesus

Lord, have mercy on us. *Christ, have mercy on us.*
Lord, have mercy on us. *Lord, have mercy on us.*
Jesus, hear us. *Jesus, graciously hear us.*

God the Father of Heaven, *have mercy on us.*
God the Son, Redeemer of the World, *have mercy on us.*
God the Holy Spirit, *have mercy on us.*
Holy Trinity, one God, *have mercy on us.*

Jesus, Son of the Living God, *have mercy on us.*
Jesus, splendor of the Father, *have mercy on us.*
Jesus, brightness of eternal light, *have mercy on us.*
Jesus, King of Glory, *have mercy on us.*
Jesus, Sun of Justice, *have mercy on us.*
Jesus, Son of the Virgin Mary, *have mercy on us.*
Jesus, most amiable, *have mercy on us.*
Jesus, most admirable, *have mercy on us.*
Jesus, mighty God, *have mercy on us.*
Jesus, Father of the world to come, *have mercy on us.*
Jesus, angel of the great counsel, *have mercy on us.*
Jesus, most powerful, *have mercy on us.*
Jesus, most patient, *have mercy on us.*
Jesus, meek and humble of heart, *have mercy on us.*
Jesus, lover of chastity, *have mercy on us.*
Jesus, lover of us, *have mercy on us.*
Jesus, God of peace, *have mercy on us.*
Jesus, author of life, *have mercy on us.*
Jesus, example of virtues, *have mercy on us.*
Jesus, zealous lover of souls, *have mercy on us.*
Jesus, our God, *have mercy on us.*
Jesus, our refuge, *have mercy on us.*

Jesus, father of the poor, *have mercy on us.*

Jesus, treasure of the faithful, *have mercy on us.*

Jesus, good shepherd, *have mercy on us.*

Jesus, true light, *have mercy on us.*

Jesus, eternal wisdom, *have mercy on us.*

Jesus, infinite goodness, *have mercy on us.*

Jesus, our way and our life, *have mercy on us.*

Jesus, joy of angels, *have mercy on us.*

Jesus, king of patriarchs, *have mercy on us.*

Jesus, teacher of the evangelists, *have mercy on us.*

Jesus, strength of martyrs, *have mercy on us.*

Jesus, light of confessors, *have mercy on us.*

Jesus, purity of virgins, *have mercy on us.*

Jesus, crown of all saints, *have mercy on us.*

Be merciful unto us, *Jesus, spare us.*

Be merciful unto us, *Jesus, hear us.*

From all evil, *Jesus, deliver us.*

From all sin, *Jesus, deliver us.*

From Your wrath, *Jesus, deliver us.*

From the snares of the devil, *Jesus, deliver us.*

From the spirit of uncleanness, *Jesus, deliver us.*

From everlasting death, *Jesus, deliver us.*

From the neglect of the inspirations, *Jesus, deliver us.*

Through the mystery of Your holy incarnation, *Jesus, deliver us.*

Through Your nativity, *Jesus, deliver us.*

Through Your infancy, *Jesus, deliver us.*

Through Your most divine life, *Jesus, deliver us.*

Through Your labors, *Jesus, deliver us.*

Through Your agony and passion, *Jesus, deliver us.*

Through Your cross and dereliction, *Jesus, deliver us.*

Through Your faintness and weariness, *Jesus, deliver us.*

Through Your death and burial, *Jesus, deliver us.*

Through Your resurrection, *Jesus, deliver us.*

Through Your institution of the Most Holy Eucharist, *Jesus, deliver us.*

Through Your joys, *Jesus, deliver us.*

Through Your glory, *Jesus, deliver us.*

Lamb of God Who takes away the sins of the world, *spare us, O Jesus.*

Lamb of God Who takes away the sins of the world, *graciously hear us, O Jesus.*

Lamb of God Who takes away the sins of the world, *have mercy on us, O Jesus.*

Jesus, hear us. *Jesus, graciously hear us.*

O Lord Jesus Christ, Who said: *"Ask and you shall receive, seek and you shall find, knock and it shall be opened unto you;"* grant we beseech You to us Your supplicants, the gift of Your most divine love, that we may love You with our whole heart, in all our words and works, and never cease from praising You. O Lord, give us a perpetual fear as well as love of Your holy Name, for You never cease to govern those You found upon the strength of Your love, Who live and reign world without end.   Amen.

The Litany of the Sacred Heart of Jesus

Lord, have mercy. *Lord, have mercy.*

Christ, have mercy. *Christ, have mercy.*

Lord, have mercy. *Lord, have mercy.*

Christ, hear us. *Christ, graciously hear us.*

God, the Father of Heaven, *have mercy on us.*

God, the Son, Redeemer of the World, *have mercy on us.*

God, the Holy Ghost, *have mercy on us.*

Holy Trinity, one God, *have mercy on us.*

Heart of Jesus, Son of the eternal Father, *have mercy on us.*

Heart of Jesus, formed in the womb of the Virgin Mother by the Holy Spirit, *have mercy on us.*

Heart of Jesus, united substantially with the Word of God, *have mercy on us.*

Heart of Jesus, of infinite majesty, *have mercy on us.*

Heart of Jesus, sacred temple of God, *have mercy on us.*

Heart of Jesus, tabernacle of the Most High, *have mercy on us.*

Heart of Jesus, house of God and gate of Heaven, *have mercy on us.*

Heart of Jesus, burning furnace of charity, *have mercy on us.*

Heart of Jesus, abode of justice and love, *have mercy on us.*

Heart of Jesus, full of goodness and love, *have mercy on us.*

Heart of Jesus, abyss of all virtues, *have mercy on us.*

Heart of Jesus, most worthy of all praise, *have mercy on us.*

Heart of Jesus, King and center of all hearts, *have mercy on us.*

Heart of Jesus, in Whom are all the treasures of wisdom and knowledge, *have mercy on us.*

Heart of Jesus, in Whom dwells all the fullness of the Divinity, *have mercy on us.*

Heart of Jesus, in Whom the Father is well pleased, *have mercy on us.*

Heart of Jesus, of Whose fullness we have all received, *have mercy on us.*

Heart of Jesus, desire of the everlasting hills, *have mercy on us.*

Heart of Jesus, patient and rich in mercy, *have mercy on us.*

Heart of Jesus, enriching to all who invoke You, *have mercy on us.*

Heart of Jesus, fountain of life and holiness, *have mercy on us.*

Heart of Jesus, propitiation for our sins, *have mercy on us.*

Heart of Jesus, saturated with revilings, *have mercy on us.*

Heart of Jesus, bruised for our offenses, *have mercy on us.*

Heart of Jesus, obedient unto death, *have mercy on us.*

Heart of Jesus, pierced with a lance, *have mercy on us.*

Heart of Jesus, source of all consolation, *have mercy on us.*

Heart of Jesus, our life and resurrection, *have mercy on us.*

Heart of Jesus, our peace and reconciliation, *have mercy on us.*

Heart of Jesus, victim for our sins, *have mercy on us.*

Heart of Jesus, salvation of those who trust in You, *have mercy on us.*

Heart of Jesus, hope of those who die in You, *have mercy on us.*

Heart of Jesus, delight of all saints, *have mercy on us.*

Lamb of God, You take away the sins of the world, *spare us, O Lord.*

Lamb of God, You take away the sins of the world, *graciously hear us, O Lord.*

Lamb of God, You takes away the sins of the world, *have mercy on us.*

Jesus, meek and humble of heart, *make our hearts like Yours.*

Almighty and eternal God, look upon the Heart of Your most beloved Son and upon the praises and satisfaction which He offers You in the name of sinners; and to those who implore Your mercy, in Your great goodness, grant forgiveness in the Name of the same Jesus Christ, Your Son, Who lives and reigns with You forever and ever. Amen.

Litany of Jesus Our Redeemer

Lord, have mercy. *Lord, have mercy.*

Christ, have mercy. *Christ, have mercy.*

Lord, have mercy. *Lord, have mercy.*

Christ, hear us. *Christ, graciously hear us.*

Father in Heaven, *have mercy on us.*

Son, Redeemer of the World, *have mercy on us.*

Holy Spirit, the Paraclete, *have mercy on us.*

Holy Trinity, one God, *have mercy on us.*

Jesus, Holy One of God, *give us Your salvation.*
Jesus, the only Just One, *give us Your salvation.*
Jesus, obedient Son, *give us Your salvation.*
Jesus, face of the divine mercy, *give us Your salvation.*
Redeemer of humanity, *give us Your salvation.*
Savior of the world, *give us Your salvation.*
Victor over death, *give us Your salvation.*
Strong and victorious Prince, *give us Your salvation.*
Jesus, servant of the Lord, *give us Your salvation.*
Jesus, man of sorrows, *give us Your salvation.*
Jesus, united with the poor, *give us Your salvation.*
Jesus, kind to sinners, *give us Your salvation.*
Christ, our reconciliation, *give us Your salvation.*
Christ, our life, *give us Your salvation.*
Christ, our hope, *give us Your salvation.*
Christ, our peace and harmony, *give us Your salvation.*
Jesus, Word that saves, *give us Your salvation.*
Jesus, hand stretched out to sinners, *give us Your salvation.*
Jesus, way that leads to peace, *give us Your salvation.*
Jesus, light that conquers the darkness, *give us Your salvation.*
Jesus, sustainer of the weak, *give us Your salvation.*
Jesus, peace of the oppressed, *give us Your salvation.*
Jesus, comfort of the suffering, *give us Your salvation.*
Jesus, mercy of sinners, *give us Your salvation.*
Jesus, defense of the offended, *give us Your salvation.*
Jesus, welcome of the excluded, *give us Your salvation.*
Jesus, justice of the oppressed, *give us Your salvation.*
Jesus, homeland of the exiled, *give us Your salvation.*
Heart of Christ, pierced by a lance, *give us Your salvation.*

Heart of Christ, victim of expiation, *give us Your salvation.*

Heart of Christ, rich in mercy, *give us Your salvation.*

Heart of Christ, fount of holiness, *give us Your salvation.*

Blood of Christ, price of our ransom, *give us Your salvation.*

Blood of Christ, poured out for our sins, *give us Your salvation.*

Blood of Christ, seal of the New Covenant, *give us Your salvation.*

Blood of Christ, drink and purifying bath, *give us Your salvation.*

Jesus, Lamb of God, *give us Your salvation.*

Jesus, Lamb without blemish, *give us Your salvation.*

Jesus, redeeming Lamb, *give us Your salvation.*

Jesus, victorious Lamb, *give us Your salvation.*

Jesus, gate of the city of peace, *give us Your salvation.*

Jesus, firstborn of the new creation, *give us Your salvation.*

Jesus, lamp of the eternal Jerusalem, *give us Your salvation.*

Jesus, guardian of the Book of Life, *give us Your salvation.*

Lord, from You springs forth the water of life, *give us Your salvation.*

Lord, from You flows the redeeming Blood, *give us Your salvation.*

Lord, through You the Holy Spirit is given to us, *give us Your salvation.*

Lord, through You paradise is reopened, *give us Your salvation.*

Lamb of God, You take away the sins of the world; *have mercy on us.*

Lamb of God, You take away the sins of the world; *have mercy on us.*

Lamb of God, You take away the sins of the world; *have mercy on us.*

Litany of the Passion
(John Henry Cardinal Newman)

Lord, have mercy. *Lord, have mercy.*

Christ, have mercy. *Christ, have mercy.*

Lord, have mercy. *Lord, have mercy.*

Christ, hear us. *Christ, graciously hear us.*

God, the Father of Heaven, *have mercy on us.*

God, the Son, Redeemer of the World, *have mercy on us.*

God, the Holy Ghost, *have mercy on us.*

Holy Trinity, one God, *have mercy on us.*

Jesus, the eternal wisdom, *have mercy on us.*

The Word made flesh, *have mercy on us.*

Hated by the world, *have mercy on us.*

Sold for thirty pieces of silver, *have mercy on us.*

Sweating blood in Your agony, *have mercy on us.*

Betrayed by Judas, *have mercy on us.*

Forsaken by Your disciples, *have mercy on us.*

Struck upon the cheek, *have mercy on us.*

Accused by false witnesses, *have mercy on us.*

Spit upon in the face, *have mercy on us.*

Denied by Peter, *have mercy on us.*

Mocked by Herod, *have mercy on us.*

Scourged by Pilate, *have mercy on us.*

Rejected for Barabbas, *have mercy on us.*

Loaded with the cross, *have mercy on us.*

Crowned with thorns, *have mercy on us.*

Stripped of Your garments, *have mercy on us.*

Nailed to the tree, *have mercy on us.*

Reviled by the Jews, *have mercy on us.*

Scoffed at by the malefactor, *have mercy on us.*

Wounded in the side, *have mercy on us.*

Shedding Your last drop of blood, *have mercy on us.*

Forsaken by Your Father, *have mercy on us.*

Dying for our sins, *have mercy on us.*

Taken down from the cross, *have mercy on us.*

Laid in the sepulcher, *have mercy on us.*

Rising gloriously, *have mercy on us.*
Ascending into Heaven, *have mercy on us.*
Sending down the Paraclete, *have mercy on us.*
Jesus our sacrifice, *have mercy on us.*
Jesus our mediator, *have mercy on us.*
Jesus our judge, *have mercy on us.*

Be merciful, *spare us, O Lord.*
Be merciful, *graciously hear us, O Lord.*
From all sin, *Lord Jesus, deliver us.*
From all evil, *Lord Jesus, deliver us.*
From anger and hatred, *Lord Jesus, deliver us.*
From malice and revenge, *Lord Jesus, deliver us.*
From unbelief and hardness of heart, *Lord Jesus, deliver us.*
From blasphemy and sacrilege, *Lord Jesus, deliver us.*
From hypocrisy and covetousness, *Lord Jesus, deliver us.*
From blindness of the understanding, *Lord Jesus, deliver us.*
From contempt of Your warnings, *Lord Jesus, deliver us.*
From relapse after Your judgments, *Lord Jesus, deliver us.*
From danger of soul and body, *Lord Jesus, deliver us.*
From everlasting death, *Lord Jesus, deliver us.*

We sinners, *we beseech You, hear us.*
That You would spare us, *we beseech You, hear us.*
That You would pardon us, *we beseech You, hear us.*
That You would defend Your Church, *we beseech You, hear us.*
That You would bless Your own, *we beseech You, hear us.*
That You would convert Your foes, *we beseech You, hear us.*
That You would spread the truth, *we beseech You, hear us.*
That You destroy error, *we beseech You, hear us.*
That You would break to pieces false gods, *we beseech You, hear us.*
That You would increase Your elect, *we beseech You, hear us.*

That You would let loose the holy souls in prison, *we beseech You, hear us.*

That You would unite us to Your saints above, *we beseech You, hear us.*

Lamb of God, who takes away the sins of the world, *spare us, O Lord.*

Lamb of God, who takes away the sins of the world, *graciously hear us, O Lord.*

Lamb of God, who takes away the sins of the world, *have mercy on us.*

Christ, hear us. *Christ, graciously hear us.*

Lord, have mercy. *Lord, have mercy.*

We adore You, O Christ, and we bless You, *because through Your holy cross You did redeem the world.*

O God, Who for the redemption of the world was pleased to be born; to be circumcised; to be rejected; to be betrayed; to be bound with thongs; to be led to the slaughter; to be shamefully gazed at; to be falsely accused; to be scourged and torn; to be spit upon, and crowned with thorns; to be mocked and reviled; to be buffeted and struck with rods; to be stripped; to be nailed to the cross; to be hoisted up thereon; to be reckoned among thieves; to have gall and vinegar to drink; to be pierced with a lance: through Your most holy passion, which we, Your sinful servants, call to mind, and by Your holy cross and gracious death, deliver us from the pains of Hell, and lead us whither You did lead the thief who was crucified with You, who with the Father and the Holy Ghost lives and reigns, God, world without end. Amen.

The Litany of the Mercy of God

Lord, have mercy on us. *Lord, have mercy on us.*

Christ, have mercy on us. *Christ, have mercy on us.*

Christ, hear us. *Christ, graciously hear us.*

God the Father of Heaven, *have mercy on us.*
God the Son, Redeemer of the World, *have mercy on us.*
God the Holy Spirit, *have mercy on us.*
Holy Trinity, One God, *have mercy on us.*

Mercy of God, supreme attribute of the Creator, *we trust in You.*
Mercy of God, greatest perfection of the Redeemer, *we trust in You.*
Mercy of God, unfathomable love of the Sanctifier, *we trust in You.*
Mercy of God, inconceivable mystery of the Holy Trinity, *we trust in You.*
Mercy of God, expression of the greatest power of the Most High, *we trust in You.*
Mercy of God, revealed in the creation of the heavenly spirits, *we trust in You.*
Mercy of God, summoning us to existence out of nothingness, *we trust in You.*
Mercy of God, embracing the whole universe, *we trust in You.*
Mercy of God, bestowing upon us immortal life, *we trust in You.*
Mercy of God, shielding us from merited punishments, *we trust in You.*
Mercy of God, raising us from the misery of sin, *we trust in You.*
Mercy of God, justifying us in the Word Incarnate, *we trust in You.*
Mercy of God, flowing from the wounds of Christ, *we trust in You.*
Mercy of God, gushing from the Most Sacred Heart of Jesus, *we trust in You.*
Mercy of God, giving to us the Most Blessed Virgin Mary as Mother of Mercy, *we trust in You.*
Mercy of God, shown in the revelation of the divine mysteries, *we trust in You.*
Mercy of God, manifested in the institution of the universal Church, *we trust in You.*

Mercy of God, contained in the institution of the holy Sacraments, *we trust in You.*

Mercy of God, bestowed upon mankind in the Sacraments of Baptism and Penance, *we trust in You.*

Mercy of God, granted in the Sacraments of the Altar and the Priesthood, *we trust in You.*

Mercy of God, shown in calling us to the Holy Faith, *we trust in You.*

Mercy of God, revealed in the conversion of sinners, *we trust in You.*

Mercy of God, manifested in the sanctification of the just, *we trust in You.*

Mercy of God, fulfilled in the perfecting of the saintly, *we trust in You.*

Mercy of God, font of health for the sick and the suffering, *we trust in You.*

Mercy of God, solace of anguished hearts, *we trust in You.*

Mercy of God, hope of souls afflicted with despair, *we trust in You.*

Mercy of God, always and everywhere accompanying all people, *we trust in You.*

Mercy of God, anticipating us with graces, *we trust in You.*

Mercy of God, peace of the dying, *we trust in You.*

Mercy of God, refreshment and relief of the souls in Purgatory, *we trust in You.*

Mercy of God, heavenly delight of the blessed, *we trust in You.*

Mercy of God, crown of all the saints, *we trust in You.*

Mercy of God, inexhaustible source of miracles, *we trust in You.*

Lamb of God, Who showed us Your greatest mercy in redeeming the world on the Cross, *spare us, O Lord.*

Lamb of God, Who mercifully offers Yourself for us in every Holy Mass, *graciously hear us, O Lord.*

285

Lamb of God, Who takes away the sins of the world through Your inexhaustible Mercy, *have mercy on us.*

Lord, have mercy on us.
Christ, have mercy on us.
Lord, have mercy on us.

V. The tender mercies of the Lord are over all His works.
R. The mercies of the Lord I will sing forever.

O God, Whose mercy is infinite and Whose treasures of pity are inexhaustible, graciously look down upon us and increase in us Your mercy so that we may never, even in the greatest trials, give way to despair, but may always trustfully conform ourselves to Your holy will, which is mercy itself. Through Our Lord Jesus Christ, the King of Mercy, Who with You and the Holy Spirit shows us mercy forever and ever.   Amen.

Divine Mercy Litany
(St. Faustina Kowalska)

Divine Mercy, gushing forth from the bosom of the Father, *I trust in You.*
Divine Mercy, greatest attribute of God, *I trust in You.*
Divine Mercy, incomprehensible mystery, *I trust in You.*
Divine Mercy, fountain gushing forth from the mystery of the Most Blessed Trinity, *I trust in You.*
Divine Mercy, unfathomed by any intellect, human or angelic, *I trust in You.*
Divine Mercy, from which wells forth all life and happiness, *I trust in You.*
Divine Mercy, better than the heavens, *I trust in You.*
Divine Mercy, source of miracles and wonders, *I trust in You.*
Divine Mercy, encompassing the whole universe, *I trust in You.*

Divine Mercy, descending to Earth in the Person of the Incarnate Word, *I trust in You.*

Divine Mercy, which flowed out from the open wound of the Heart of Jesus, *I trust in You.*

Divine Mercy, enclosed in the Heart of Jesus for us, and especially for sinners, *I trust in You.*

Divine Mercy, unfathomed in the institution of the Sacred Host, *I trust in You.*

Divine Mercy, in the founding of the Holy Church, *I trust in You.*

Divine Mercy, in the Sacrament of Holy Baptism, *I trust in You.*

Divine Mercy, in our justification through Jesus Christ, *I trust in You.*

Divine Mercy, accompanying us through our whole life, *I trust in You.*

Divine Mercy, embracing us especially at the hour of death, *I trust in You.*

Divine Mercy, endowing us with immortal life, *I trust in You.*

Divine Mercy, accompanying us every moment of our life, *I trust in You.*

Divine Mercy, shielding us from the fires of Hell, *I trust in You.*

Divine Mercy, in the conversion of hardened sinners, *I trust in You.*

Divine Mercy, astonishment for angels, incomprehensible to saints, *I trust in You.*

Divine Mercy, unfathomed in all the mysteries of God, *I trust in You.*

Divine Mercy, lifting us out of every misery, *I trust in You.*

Divine Mercy, source of our happiness and joy, *I trust in You.*

Divine Mercy, in calling us forth from nothingness to existence, *I trust in You.*

Divine Mercy, embracing all the works of His hands, *I trust in You.*

Divine Mercy, crown of all God's handiwork, *I trust in You.*

Divine Mercy, in which we are all immersed, *I trust in You.*

Divine Mercy, sweet relief for anguished hearts, *I trust in You.*

Divine Mercy, only hope of despairing souls, *I trust in You.*

Divine Mercy, repose of hearts, peace amidst fear, *I trust in You.*
Divine Mercy, delight and ecstasy of holy souls, *I trust in You.*
Divine Mercy, inspiring hope against all hope, *I trust in You.*

Eternal God, in Whom mercy is endless and the treasury of compassion inexhaustible, look kindly upon us and increase Your mercy in us, that in difficult moments we might not despair nor become despondent, but with great confidence submit ourselves to Your holy will, which is love and mercy itself.   Amen.

The Litany of Resignation to the Will of God

Lord, have mercy. *Lord, have mercy.*
Christ, have mercy. *Christ, have mercy.*
Lord, have mercy. *Lord, have mercy.*
Christ, hear us. *Christ, graciously hear us.*

God the Father, Who has created me, *hallowed be Your will.*
God the Son, Who has redeemed me, *not my will but Yours be done.*
God the Holy Ghost, Who has offered sanctification, *blessed be the most sweet will of God.*

You Who knows and foresee all things, *have mercy on us.*
You Who governs and rules all things, *have mercy on us.*
You Who, according to Your inscrutable designs effects all things in a wonderful manner, *have mercy on us.*
You Who permits evil in order to derive good for the salvation of the elect, *have mercy on us.*

In all things and in all possible events, *Your holy will be done, O my God.*
In all circumstances and disgraces, *Your holy will be done, O my God.*
In my state and employment, *Your holy will be done, O my God.*
In my affairs and occupations, *Your holy will be done, O my God.*

In all my actions, *Your holy will be done, O my God*.

In my health and strength, *Your holy will be done, O my God*.

In my body and soul, *Your holy will be done, O my God*.

In my life and death, *Your holy will be done, O my God*.

In myself and in those who belong to me, *Your holy will be done, O my God*.

In all men and angels, *Your holy will be done, O my God*.

In all creatures, *Your holy will be done, O my God*.

In all parts of the Earth, *Your holy will be done, O my God*.

At all times, *Your holy will be done, O my God*.

For all eternity, *Your holy will be done, O my God*.

Although weak nature complains, *Your holy will be done, O my God*.

Although it costs much to self-love and sensuality, *Your holy will be done, O my God*.

Solely and only through love for You and Your good pleasure, *Your holy will be done, O my God*.

Because You are my Creator, *Your holy will be done, O my God*.

Because You are the Supreme Lord of all things, *Your holy will be done, O my God*.

Because You are infinite perfection, therefore do I say, *Your holy will be done, O my God*.

With all the saints in Heaven, with the Blessed Virgin Mary, *Your holy will be done, O my God*.

With Jesus in the Garden of Olives, *Your holy will be done, O my God*.

Pray the **Our Father**.

V. May the just, most amiable will of God be done in all things.

R. May it be praised and magnified forever! Amen.

Grant me Your grace, O Father, that perfect resignation to Your holy will may be with me, and labor with me, and continue with me to the end. Grant me always to desire and will that which is most acceptable to You and which pleases You best. Let Your will be mine, and let my will always follow Yours and agree perfectly with it. Let me always will the same as You; let me not be able to will anything except what You will. Amen.

Litany of the Blessed Virgin Mary
(Litany of Loreto)

Lord, have mercy. *Lord, have mercy.*
Christ, have mercy. *Christ, have mercy.*
Lord, have mercy. *Lord, have mercy.*

God, our Father in Heaven, *have mercy on us.*
God, the Son, Redeemer of the World, *have mercy on us.*
God, the Holy Spirit, *have mercy on us.*
Holy Trinity, one God, *have mercy on us.*

Holy Mary, *pray for us.*
Holy Mother of God, *pray for us.*
Holy Virgin of virgins, *pray for us.*
Mother of Christ, *pray for us.*
Mother of divine grace, *pray for us.*
Mother most pure, *pray for us.*
Mother most chaste, *pray for us.*
Mother inviolate, *pray for us.*
Mother undefiled, *pray for us.*
Mother most amiable, *pray for us.*
Mother most admirable, *pray for us.*
Mother of good counsel, *pray for us.*
Mother of our Creator, *pray for us.*
Mother of our Savior, *pray for us.*
Mother of the Church, *pray for us.*
Virgin most prudent, *pray for us.*

Virgin most venerable, *pray for us.*
Virgin most renowned, *pray for us.*
Virgin most powerful, *pray for us.*
Virgin most merciful, *pray for us.*
Virgin most faithful, *pray for us.*
Mirror of justice, *pray for us.*
Seat of wisdom, *pray for us.*
Cause of our joy, *pray for us.*
Spiritual vessel, *pray for us.*
Vessel of honor, *pray for us.*
Singular vessel of devotion, *pray for us.*
Mystical Rose, *pray for us.*
Tower of David, *pray for us.*
Tower of ivory, *pray for us.*
House of gold, *pray for us.*
Ark of the Covenant, *pray for us.*
Gate of Heaven, *pray for us.*
Morning Star, *pray for us.*
Health of the sick, *pray for us.*
Refuge of sinners, *pray for us.*
Comforter of the afflicted, *pray for us.*
Help of Christians, *pray for us.*

Queen of angels, *pray for us.*
Queen of patriarchs, *pray for us.*
Queen of prophets, *pray for us.*
Queen of apostles, *pray for us.*
Queen of martyrs, *pray for us.*
Queen of confessors, *pray for us.*
Queen of virgins, *pray for us.*
Queen of all saints, *pray for us.*

Queen conceived without original sin, *pray for us.*
Queen assumed into Heaven, *pray for us.*
Queen of the Holy Rosary, *pray for us.*
Queen of families, *pray for us.*
Queen of peace, *pray for us.*

Grant, we beg You, O Lord God, that we Your servants may enjoy lasting health of mind and body, and by the glorious intercession of Blessed Mary, ever Virgin, be delivered from present sorrow and enter into the joy of eternal happiness through Christ our Lord. Amen.

Litany of the Sorrowful Mother

Lord, have mercy on us. *Lord, have mercy on us.*
Christ, have mercy on us. *Christ, have mercy on us.*
Lord, have mercy on us. *Lord, have mercy on us.*
Christ, hear us. *Christ, graciously hear us.*

God the Father of Heaven, *have mercy on us.*
God the Son, Redeemer of the World, *have mercy on us.*
God the Holy Ghost, *have mercy on us.*
Holy Trinity, One God, *have mercy on us.*

Holy Mary, conceived without sin, *pray for us.*
Holy Mother of God, *pray for us.*
Mother of Christ, *pray for us.*
Mother of our Savior crucified, *pray for us.*
Mother most sorrowful, *pray for us.*
Mother most tearful, *pray for us.*
Mother most afflicted, *pray for us.*
Mother most lonely, *pray for us.*
Mother most desolate, *pray for us.*
Mother pierced by the sword of sorrow, *pray for us.*
Queen of martyrs, *pray for us.*

Comfort of the sorrowful, *pray for us.*

Help of the needy, *pray for us.*

Protectress of the forsaken, *pray for us.*

Support of widows and orphans, *pray for us.*

Health of the sick, *pray for us.*

Hope of the troubled, *pray for us.*

Haven of the ship-wrecked, *pray for us.*

Refuge of sinners, *pray for us.*

Hope of the despairing, *pray for us.*

Mother of mercy, *pray for us.*

Through your poverty in the stable of Bethlehem, *pray for us.*

Through your sorrow at the prophecy of Simeon, *pray for us.*

Through your sad flight into Egypt, *pray for us.*

Through your anxiety when seeking your lost child, *pray for us.*

Through your grief when seeing your Divine Son persecuted, *pray for us.*

Through your fear and anxiety when Jesus was apprehended, *pray for us.*

Through your pain caused by the treason of Judas and the denial of Peter, *pray for us.*

Through your sad meeting with Jesus on the way of the Cross, *pray for us.*

Through the tortures of your loving heart at the Crucifixion of Jesus, *pray for us.*

Through your agony at the death of Jesus, *pray for us.*

Through the sword of sorrow that pierced your heart when the side of Jesus was transfixed by the lance, *pray for us.*

Through your lamentations over the dead body of your Divine Son lying on your bosom, *pray for us.*

Through your deep mourning at His tomb, *pray for us.*

Through your desolation after the burial of Jesus, *pray for us.*
Through the tears you did shed for your beloved Son, *pray for us.*
Through your wonderful resignation to the will of God in all your
 sufferings, *pray for us.*

O Queen of peace, *pray for us.*
In all our tribulations, *pray for us.*
In our illnesses and pains, *pray for us.*
In our sorrows and afflictions, *pray for us.*
In our need and destitution, *pray for us.*
In our fears and dangers, *pray for us.*
In the hour of our death, *pray for us.*
On the day of judgment, *pray for us.*

Lamb of God, Who takes away the sins of the world, *spare us, O Lord.*
Lamb of God, Who takes away the sins of the world, *graciously hear
 us, O Lord.*
Lamb of God, Who takes away the sins of the world, *have mercy on
 us, O Lord.*

V. Pray for us, O Sorrowful Virgin,
R. That we may be made worthy of the promises of Christ.

We beseech You, O Lord Jesus Christ, let Your mother, the
Blessed Virgin Mary, whose holy soul was pierced by a sword of
sorrow at the hour of Your passion, implore Your mercy for us, both
now and at the hour of our death, Who lives and reigns, world
without end.   Amen.

Litany of St. Joseph

Lord, have mercy. *Lord, have mercy.*
Christ, have mercy. *Christ, have mercy.*
Lord, have mercy. *Lord, have mercy.*

Christ, hear us. *Christ, graciously hear us.*

God, the Father of Heaven, *have mercy on us.*
God the Son, Redeemer of the World, *have mercy on us.*
God the Holy Spirit, *have mercy on us.*
Holy Trinity, One God, *have mercy on us.*

Holy Mary, *pray for us.*
St. Joseph, *pray for us.*
Renowned offspring of David, *pray for us.*
Light of Patriarchs, *pray for us.*
Spouse of the Mother of God, *pray for us.*
Chaste guardian of the Virgin, *pray for us.*
Foster-father of the Son of God, *pray for us.*
Diligent protector of Christ, *pray for us.*
Head of the Holy Family, *pray for us.*
Joseph most just, *pray for us.*
Joseph most chaste, *pray for us.*
Joseph most prudent, *pray for us.*
Joseph most strong, *pray for us.*
Joseph most obedient, *pray for us.*
Joseph most faithful, *pray for us.*
Mirror of patience, *pray for us.*
Lover of poverty, *pray for us.*
Model of artisans, *pray for us.*
Glory of home life, *pray for us.*
Guardian of virgins, *pray for us.*
Pillar of families, *pray for us.*
Solace of the wretched, *pray for us.*
Hope of the sick, *pray for us.*
Patron of the dying, *pray for us.*
Terror of demons, *pray for us.*

Protector of the holy Church, *pray for us.*

Lamb of God, Who takes away the sins of the world, *spare us, O Lord.*
Lamb of God, Who takes away the sins of the world, *graciously hear us, O Lord.*
Lamb of God, Who takes away the sins of the world, *have mercy on us.*

He made him the lord of his house, *and ruler of all His possessions.*

O God, in Your ineffable providence You were pleased to choose Blessed Joseph to be the spouse of your most holy Mother; grant, we beg You, that we may be worthy to have him for our intercessor in Heaven whom on Earth we venerate as our protector: You who live and reign forever and ever.   Amen.

Litany of the Saints

Lord, have mercy on us. *Lord, have mercy on us.*
Christ, have mercy on us. *Christ, have mercy on us.*
Lord, have mercy on us. *Lord, have mercy on us.*
Christ, hear us. *Christ, graciously hear us.*

God, the Father of Heaven, *have mercy on us.*
God the Son, Redeemer of the World, *have mercy on us.*
God the Holy Ghost, *have mercy on us.*
Holy Trinity, one God, *have mercy on us.*

Holy Mary, *pray for us.*
Holy Mother of God, *pray for us.*
Holy Virgin of virgins, *pray for us.*
St. Michael, *pray for us.*
St. Gabriel, *pray for us.*
St. Raphael, *pray for us.*

All you holy angels and archangels, *pray for us.*

All you holy orders of blessed spirits, *pray for us.*

St. John the Baptist, *pray for us.*

St. Joseph, *pray for us.*

All you holy patriarchs and prophets, *pray for us.*

St. Peter, *pray for us.*

St. Paul, *pray for us.*

St. Andrew, *pray for us.*

St. James, *pray for us.*

St. John, *pray for us.*

St. Thomas, *pray for us.*

St. James, *pray for us.*

St. Philip, *pray for us.*

St. Bartholomew, *pray for us.*

St. Matthew, *pray for us.*

St. Simon, *pray for us.*

St. Thaddeus, *pray for us.*

St. Matthias, *pray for us.*

St. Barnabas, *pray for us.*

St. Luke, *pray for us.*

St. Mark, *pray for us.*

All you holy apostles and evangelists, *pray for us.*

All you holy disciples of the Lord, *pray for us.*

All you holy innocents, *pray for us.*

St. Stephen, *pray for us.*

St. Lawrence, *pray for us.*

St. Vincent, *pray for us.*

Sts. Fabian and Sebastian, *pray for us.*

Sts. John and Paul, *pray for us.*

Sts. Cosmos and Damian, *pray for us.*
Sts. Gervase and Protase, *pray for us.*
All you holy martyrs, *pray for us.*

St. Sylvester, *pray for us.*
St. Gregory, *pray for us.*
St. Ambrose, *pray for us.*
St. Augustine, *pray for us.*
St. Jerome, *pray for us.*
St. Martin, *pray for us.*
St. Nicholas, *pray for us.*
All you holy bishops and confessors, *pray for us.*
All you holy doctors, *pray for us.*

St. Anthony, *pray for us.*
St. Benedict, *pray for us.*
St. Bernard, *pray for us.*
St. Dominic, *pray for us.*
St. Francis, *pray for us.*
All you holy priests and Levites, *pray for us.*
All you holy monks and hermits, *pray for us.*

St. Mary Magdalene, *pray for us.*
St. Agatha, *pray for us.*
St. Lucy, *pray for us.*
St. Agnes, *pray for us.*
St. Cecilia, *pray for us.*
St. Catherine, *pray for us.*
St. Anastasia, *pray for us.*
St. Clare, *pray for us.*
All you holy virgins and widows, *pray for us.*

All you holy saints of God, *pray for us.*

Lord, be merciful, *spare us, O Lord.*

From all evil, *deliver us, O Lord.*

From all sin, *deliver us, O Lord.*

From Your wrath, *deliver us, O Lord.*

From sudden and unprovided death, *deliver us, O Lord.*

From the snares of the devil, *deliver us, O Lord.*

From anger, and hatred, and all ill-will, *deliver us, O Lord.*

From the spirit of fornication, *deliver us, O Lord.*

From the scourge of earthquake, *deliver us, O Lord..*

From plague, famine, and war, *deliver us, O Lord.*

From lightning and tempest, *deliver us, O Lord.*

From everlasting death, *deliver us, O Lord.*

Through the mystery of Your holy Incarnation, *deliver us, O Lord.*

Through Your coming, *deliver us, O Lord.*

Through Your birth, *deliver us, O Lord.*

Through Your baptism and holy fasting, *deliver us, O Lord.*

Through the institution of the Most Blessed Sacrament, *deliver us, O Lord.*

Through Your cross and passion, *deliver us, O Lord.*

Through Your death and burial, *deliver us, O Lord.*

Through Your holy resurrection, *deliver us, O Lord.*

Through Your admirable ascension, *deliver us, O Lord.*

Through the coming of the Holy Ghost the Paraclete, *deliver us, O Lord.*

In the day of judgment, *deliver us, O Lord.*

We sinners, *we beseech You, hear us.*

That You would spare us, *we beseech You, hear us.*

That You would pardon us, *we beseech You, hear us.*

That You would bring us to true penance, *we beseech You, hear us.*

That You would vouchsafe to govern and preserve Your holy Church, *we beseech You, hear us.*

That You would vouchsafe to preserve our Apostolic Prelate and all orders of the Church in holy religion, *we beseech You, hear us.*

That You would vouchsafe to humble the enemies of holy Church, *we beseech You, hear us.*

That You would vouchsafe to give peace and true concord to Christian kings and princes, *we beseech You, hear us.*

That You would vouchsafe to bring back to the unity of the Church all those who have strayed away, and lead to the light of the Gospel all unbelievers, *we beseech You, hear us.*

That You would vouchsafe to confirm and preserve us in Your holy service, *we beseech You, hear us.*

That You would lift up our minds to heavenly desires, *we beseech You, hear us.*

That You would render eternal blessings to all our benefactors, *we beseech You, hear us.*

That You would deliver our souls, and the souls of our brethren, relatives, and benefactors from eternal damnation, *we beseech You, hear us.*

That You would vouchsafe to give and preserve the fruits of the Earth, *we beseech You, hear us.*

That You would vouchsafe to grant eternal rest to all the faithful departed, *we beseech You, hear us.*

That You would vouchsafe graciously to hear us, Son of God, *we beseech You, hear us.*

Lamb of God, Who takes away the sins of the world, *spare us, O Lord.*

Lamb of God, Who takes away the sins of the world, *graciously hear us, O Lord.*

Lamb of God, Who takes away the sins of the world, *have mercy on us.*

Almighty, everlasting God, Who has dominion over both the living and the dead and are merciful to all who, as You foreknow, will be Yours by faith and works; we humbly beseech You that they for whom we intend to pour forth our prayers, whether this present world still detains them in the flesh or the world to come has already received them stripped of their mortal bodies, may, by the grace of Your Fatherly love and through the intercession of all the saints, obtain the remission of all their sins. Through our Lord Jesus Christ, Your Son, Who with You in the unity of the Holy Spirit lives and reigns God, world without end. Amen.

Litany for All

God the Father, *have mercy upon us.*
God the Son, *have mercy upon us.*
God the Holy Spirit, *have mercy upon us.*
Holy, blessed and glorious Trinity, *have mercy upon us.*

From all evil and mischief, *good Lord, deliver us.*
From pride, vanity and hypocrisy, *good Lord, deliver us.*
From envy, hatred and malice, *good Lord, deliver us.*
From all evil intent, *good Lord, deliver us.*
From sloth, worldliness and love of money, *good Lord, deliver us.*
From hardness of heart, *good Lord, deliver us.*
From all blindness of heart, *good Lord, deliver us.*
From contempt for Your Word and Your laws, *good Lord, deliver us.*
From sins of body and mind, *good Lord, deliver us.*
From the deceits of the world, the flesh and the devil, *good Lord, deliver us.*
From famine and disaster, *good Lord, deliver us.*
From violence, murder and dying unprepared, *good Lord, deliver us.*

In all times of sorrow, *good Lord, deliver us.*
In all times of joy, *good Lord, deliver us.*
In the hour of death, *good Lord, deliver us.*
On the day of judgment, *good Lord, deliver us.*

By the mystery of Your holy incarnation, *good Lord, deliver us.*
By Your birth, childhood and obedience, *good Lord, deliver us.*
By Your baptism, fasting and temptation, *good Lord, deliver us.*
By Your ministry in word and work, *good Lord, deliver us.*
By Your mighty acts of power, *good Lord, deliver us.*
By Your preaching of the kingdom, *good Lord, deliver us.*
By Your agony and trial, *good Lord, deliver us.*
By Your cross and passion, *good Lord, deliver us.*
By Your precious death and burial, *good Lord, deliver us.*
By Your mighty resurrection, *good Lord, deliver us.*
By Your glorious ascension, *good Lord, deliver us.*
By Your sending of the Holy Spirit, *good Lord, deliver us.*

Hear our prayers, O Lord our God, *hear us, good Lord.*
Govern and direct Your holy Church, *hear us, good Lord.*
Fill Your holy Church with love and truth, *hear us, good Lord*
Grant Your holy Church that unity which is Your will, *hear us, good Lord.*
Give us boldness to preach the gospel in all the world, *hear us, good Lord.*
Help us make disciples of all the nations, *hear us, good Lord.*
Enlighten (*name*) our Pope and all who minister with knowledge and understanding, that by their teaching and their lives they may proclaim your Word and truth, *hear us, good Lord.*
Give Your people grace to hear and receive Your Word, *hear us, good Lord.*

Give Your people grace to bring forth the fruit of the Spirit, *hear us, good Lord.*

Bring into the way of truth all who have erred, *hear us, good Lord.*

Bring into the way of truth all who are deceived, *hear us, good Lord.*

Strengthen those who trust in You, *hear us, good Lord.*

Comfort and help the faint-hearted, *hear us, good Lord.*

Raise up the fallen, *hear us, good Lord.*

Beat down Satan under our feet, *hear us, good Lord.*

Bless those who administer the law, that they may uphold justice, honesty and truth. *Hear us, good Lord.*

Give us the will to use the resources of the Earth to Your glory, and for the good of all creation. *Hear us, good Lord.*

Bless and keep all Your people. *Hear us, good Lord.*

Bring Your joy into all families. *Hear us, good Lord.*

Watch over children and guide the young. *Hear us, good Lord.*

Watch over the aged, infirm, helpless and handicapped. *Hear us, good Lord.*

Bring reconciliation to those in discord. *Hear us, good Lord.*

Bring peace to those in distress. *Hear us, good Lord.*

Help and comfort the lonely, the bereaved and the oppressed. *Hear us, good Lord.*

Keep in safety those who travel, and all who are in danger. *Hear us, good Lord.*

Heal the sick in body and mind, and provide for the homeless, the hungry and the destitute. *Hear us, good Lord.*

Show your pity on prisoners and refugees, and all who face misfortune. *Hear us, good Lord.*

Forgive our enemies, persecutors and slanderers, and change their hearts. *Hear us, good Lord.*

Hear us as we remember those who have died in the peace of Christ, both those who have confessed the faith and those whose faith is known to You alone, and grant us with them a share in Your eternal kingdom. Give us true repentance; forgive us our sins of negligence and ignorance and our deliberate sins; and grant us the grace of your Holy Spirit to amend our lives and live according to Your holy will.

Holy God, holy and strong, holy and immortal, have mercy upon us.

Litany of Humility
(Rafael Cardinal Merry del Val)

O Jesus, meek and humble of heart, *hear me.*
From the desire of being esteemed, *deliver me, O Jesus.*
From the desire of being loved, *deliver me, O Jesus.*
From the desire of being extolled, *deliver me, O Jesus.*
From the desire of being honored, *deliver me, O Jesus.*
From the desire of being praised, *deliver me, O Jesus.*
From the desire of being preferred to others, *deliver me, O Jesus.*
From the desire of being consulted, *deliver me, O Jesus.*
From the desire of being approved, *deliver me, O Jesus.*
From the fear of being humiliated, *deliver me, O Jesus.*
From the fear of being despised, *deliver me, O Jesus.*
From the fear of suffering rebukes, *deliver me, O Jesus.*
From the fear of being calumniated, *deliver me, O Jesus.*
From the fear of being forgotten, *deliver me, O Jesus.*
From the fear of being ridiculed, *deliver me, O Jesus.*
From the fear of being wronged, *deliver me, O Jesus.*
From the fear of being suspected, *deliver me, O Jesus.*

That others may be loved more than I, *Jesus, grant me the grace to desire it.*

That others may be esteemed more than I, *Jesus, grant me the grace to desire it.*

That, in the opinion of the world, others may increase and I may decrease, *Jesus, grant me the grace to desire it.*

That others may be chosen and I set aside, *Jesus, grant me the grace to desire it.*

That others may be praised and I go unnoticed, *Jesus, grant me the grace to desire it.*

That others may be preferred to me in everything, *Jesus, grant me the grace to desire it.*

That others may become holier than I, provided that I may become as holy as I should, *Jesus, grant me the grace to desire it.*

Guardian Angel Litany

Lord, have mercy on us. *Lord, have mercy on us.*

Christ, have mercy on us. *Christ, have mercy on us.*

Lord, have mercy on us. *Lord, have mercy on us.*

Christ, hear us. *Christ, graciously hear us.*

God the Father of Heaven, *have mercy on us.*

God the Son, Redeemer of the World, *have mercy on us.*

God the Holy Ghost, *have mercy on us.*

Holy Trinity, One God, *have mercy on us.*

Holy Mary, Queen of Angels, *pray for me.*

Angel of Heaven, who is my guardian, *pray for me.*

Angel of Heaven, whom I revere as my superior, *pray for me.*

Angel of Heaven, who gives me charitable counsel, *pray for me.*

Angel of Heaven, who gives me wise direction, *pray for me.*

Angel of Heaven, who takes the place of a tutor, *pray for me.*

Angel of Heaven, who loves me tenderly, *pray for me.*

Angel of Heaven, who is my consoler, *pray for me.*

Angel of Heaven, who is attached to me as a good brother, *pray for me.*

Angel of Heaven, who instructs me in the duties and truth of salvation, *pray for me.*

Angel of Heaven, who is to me a charitable shepherd, *pray for me.*

Angel of Heaven who is witness of all my actions, *pray for me.*

Angel of Heaven, who helps me in all my undertakings, *pray for me.*

Angel of Heaven, who continually watches over me, *pray for me.*

Angel of Heaven, who intercedes for me, *pray for me.*

Angel of Heaven, who carries me in your hand, *pray for me.*

Angel of Heaven, who directs me in all my ways, *pray for me.*

Angel of Heaven, who defends me with zeal, *pray for me.*

Angel of Heaven, who conducts me with wisdom, *pray for me.*

Angel of Heaven, who guards me from all danger, *pray for me.*

Angel of Heaven, who dissipates the darkness and enlightens the mind, *pray for me.*

Lamb of God, Who takes away the sins of the world, *spare us, O Lord.*

Lamb of God, Who takes away the sins of the world, *graciously hear us, O Lord.*

Lamb of God, Who takes away the sins of the world, *have mercy on us, O Lord.*

Pray for us, O Guardian Angel, *that we may be made worthy of the promises of Christ.*

Almighty and eternal God, Who by an effect of Your ineffable bounty has given to each of the faithful an angel to be the guardian of body and soul, grant that I may have for him whom You have given me in Your mercy so much respect and love, that, protected by the gifts of Your graces and by his help, I may merit to go to You in

Heaven, there to contemplate You with him and the other happy spirits in the brightness of Your glory. Amen.

Little Litany of the Angels

Lord, have mercy on us. *Lord, have mercy on us.*
Christ, have mercy on us. *Christ, have mercy on us.*
Lord, have mercy on us. *Lord, have mercy on us.*

Holy angels of God, *be with us always.*

In all our journeys, *holy angels, be with us.*
In all our studies, *holy angels, be with us.*
In all our meditations, *holy angels, be with us.*
In all our labors, *holy angels, be with us.*
In all our pleasures, *holy angels, be with us.*
In all our temptations, *holy angels, be with us.*
In all our troubles, *holy angels, be with us.*
In all our sufferings, *holy angels, be with us.*
In all our good deeds, *holy angels, be with us.*
In the hour of danger, *holy angels, be with us.*
In the hour of trial, *holy angels, be with us.*
In the hour of death, *holy angels, be with us.*

O almighty and eternal God, send Your holy angels to guard and protect us, and grant that we may see them in Heaven. Amen.

Litany for Life

Good St. Joseph, *pray for us.*
Husband of the blessed Virgin Mary, *pray for us.*
Protector of the Mother of God, *pray for us.*
Faithful spouse, *pray for us.*
Good worker, *pray for us.*

Good and gentle man, *pray for us.*
Man of faith and hope, *pray for us.*
Man of kindness and charity, *pray for us.*
Man of love, *pray for us.*
Foster father of our Lord Jesus Christ, *pray for us.*
Guardian of the Christ child, *pray for us.*
Teacher of virtue, *pray for us.*
Model of patience, *pray for us.*
Model of kindness, *pray for us.*
Loving father, *pray for us.*
Kind father, *pray for us.*
Example of holiness, *pray for us.*

For all unmarried fathers, *pray for them.*
For all who are afraid, *pray for them.*
For all tempted to despair, *pray for them.*
For all tempted by evil, *pray for them.*
For refugees and orphans, *pray for them.*
For those condemned to die, *pray for them.*
For those mortally ill, *pray for them.*
For those in the hour of their death, *pray for them.*
For doctors and nurses, *pray for them.*
For those who wait for death, *pray for them.*
For the old and the alone, *pray for them.*
For legislators and judges, *pray for them.*
For our President and Vice-President, *pray for them.*
For our priests, bishops, cardinals, and Holy Father, *pray for them.*
For all who work for life, *pray for them.*

Good St. Joseph, your faithful love protected and nourished the Mother of God and Jesus Christ, her Son. Your fatherly care led to maturity He through Whom all creation began. Through your intercession, may God guide and protect all human life from conception to natural death and lead this nation in the ways of truth and love. Pray for us good St. Joseph, that joined with Christ Jesus, we might give praise to God forever.   Amen.

Litany of Thanksgiving

Father, You bless us with the gift of life. *Father, we give You thanks.*

You give us Your Son as our Savior. *Father, we give You thanks.*

You teach us His Word of Life. *Father, we give You thanks.*

You make us Your holy people. *Father, we give You thanks.*

You cleanse us from our sins. *Father, we give You thanks.*

You give us Mary as our Mother and our model. *Father, we give You thanks.*

You invite us to love You by loving others. *Father, we give You thanks.*

You give us talents and gifts to use for Your glory. *Father, we give You thanks.*

You help us to do good works for You. *Father, we give You thanks.*

You nourish us with the Bread of Life. *Father, we give You thanks.*

You give us the Cup of Salvation. *Father, we give You thanks.*

You have given us Your Spirit. *Father, we give You thanks.*

You promise us the joys of Heaven. *Father, we give You thanks.*

You call us to sing Your praises forever. *Father, we give You thanks.*

Beloved God, You have given us all grace and life through the hands of Christ our Savior. With Jesus, we bless Your Name. With Him we thank You.   Amen

Ann Fitch

ROSARIES & CHAPLETS

Rosaries and chaplets are repetitious prayers said using a string of beads. There are many beautiful and powerful rosaries and chaplets that can be said using different combinations of beads. Most focus on specific devotions and have been taught and utilized by different orders of religious men and women. Chaplets and rosaries can be a nice way to incorporate specific devotions into your prayer life. I have included here rosaries and chaplets that can be prayed using an ordinary rosary. I hope you will find the ones I have included enriching to your prayer life.

"Rejoice in hope, endure in affliction, persevere in prayer."
(Romans 12:12)

The Holy Rosary

1. Make the **Sign of the Cross**.
2. Holding the Crucifix, say the **Apostles' Creed**.
3. On the first bead, say an **Our Father**.
4. Say a **Hail Mary** on each of the next three beads for an increase in faith, hope, and charity.
5. Say the **Glory Be**.
6. For each of the five decades, on the single bead announce the Mystery, then say the **Our Father**.
7. While meditating on the Mystery, say a **Hail Mary** on each of the 10 beads. Then say a **Glory Be** and the **Pardon Prayer**.

8. After saying the five decades, say the **Hail, Holy Queen** and the following prayer.

O God, whose only begotten Son, by His life, death, and resurrection, has purchased for us the rewards of eternal salvation. Grant, we beseech Thee, that while meditating on these mysteries of the most holy Rosary of the Blessed Virgin Mary, that we may imitate what they contain and obtain what they promise, through Christ our Lord. Amen.

The five Joyful Mysteries are traditionally prayed on Mondays and Saturdays and may be said on Sundays during Advent and Christmas.
1. The Annunciation
2. The Visitation
3. The Nativity
4. The Presentation in the Temple
5. The Finding in the Temple

The five Sorrowful Mysteries are traditionally prayed on Tuesdays and Fridays and may be said on Sundays during Lent.
1. The Agony in the Garden
2. The Scourging at the Pillar
3. The Crowning with Thorns
4. The Carrying of the Cross
5. The Crucifixion and Death

The five Glorious Mysteries are traditionally prayed on Wednesdays and Sundays:
1. The Resurrection
2. The Ascension
3. The Descent of the Holy Spirit
4. The Assumption
5. The Coronation of Mary

If praying the five Luminous Mysteries, they are traditionally prayed on Thursdays:

1. The Baptism of Christ in the Jordan
2. The Wedding Feast at Cana
3. Jesus' Proclamation of the Coming of the Kingdom of God
4. The Transfiguration
5. The Institution of the Eucharist

Rosary of St. Joseph

Make the **Sign of the Cross**.

Holding the Crucifix, say the **Apostles' Creed**.

On the first bead, say an **Our Father**.

On the next three beads say a **Hail Mary** for an increase in faith, hope, and charity followed by a **Glory Be**.

On the single beads announce the mystery and pray an **Our Father**.

On the sets of 10 beads say the following prayer:

Joseph, son of David, and husband of Mary; we honor you, guardian of the Redeemer, and we adore the child you named Jesus. St. Joseph, patron of the universal Church, pray for us, that like you we may live totally dedicated to the interests of the Savior.   Amen.

Mysteries of the St. Joseph Rosary:

1. Betrothal to Mary (Mt 1:18).
2. Annunciation to Joseph (Mt 1:19-21).
3. Birth and Naming of Jesus (Mt 1:22-25).
4. Flight into Egypt (Mt 2:13-15).
5. Hidden Life at Nazareth (Mt 2:23; Lk 2:51-52)

Chaplet of Divine Mercy

(St. Faustina Kolwalska)

Pray this chaplet using an ordinary rosary.

Holding the Crucifix make the **Sign of the Cross**. Then on the first bead you can pray either, or both, of these optional opening prayers:

You expired, Jesus, but the source of life gushed forth for souls, and the ocean of mercy opened up for the whole world. O Fount of Life, unfathomable Divine Mercy, envelop the whole world and empty Yourself out upon us.

And/or:

O Blood and Water, which gushed forth from the Heart of Jesus as a fountain of Mercy for us, I trust in You!

On the next three beads say the **Our Father**, the **Hail Mary**, and the **Apostles' Creed**.

You pray the rest of the chaplet as follows.

On the single beads pray:

Eternal Father, I offer you the Body and Blood, Soul and Divinity of Your Dearly Beloved Son, Our Lord, Jesus Christ, in atonement for our sins and those of the whole world.

On the next ten beads pray:

For the sake of His sorrowful Passion, have mercy on us and on the whole world.

After completing the five decades, recite the following, three times:

Holy God, Holy Mighty One, Holy Immortal One, have mercy on us and on the whole world.

Conclude with the following optional closing prayer:

Eternal God, in whom mercy is endless and the treasury of compassion inexhaustible, look kindly upon us and increase Your mercy in us, that in difficult moments we might not despair nor become despondent, but with great confidence submit ourselves to Your holy will, which is love and mercy itself.   Amen.

The Chaplet for the Holy Souls in Purgatory

This chaplet is prayed using an ordinary rosary.

Holding the Crucifix make the **Sign of the Cross**.

On the next five beads pray the **Hail Mary** once, the **Our Father** three times and the **Hail Mary** once more.

On the single beads pray:

O holy souls draw the fire of God's love into my soul, to reveal Jesus Crucified in me here on Earth, rather than hereafter in Purgatory.

On the following 10 beads pray:

Crucified Lord Jesus, have mercy on the souls in Purgatory.

Conclude by praying the **Glory Be** three times.

Chaplet of the Precious Blood for the Souls in Purgatory

This chaplet is prayed using an ordinary rosary.

Holding the Crucifix make the **Sign of the Cross**.

On the next five beads pray the **Hail Mary** once, the **Our Father** three times and the **Hail Mary** once more.

On the single beads pray:

Eternal Father, I offer You the Precious Blood of Your Beloved Son, Our Lord Jesus Christ, the Lamb without blemish or spot for the refreshment and deliverance of the souls in Purgatory. (*You can add here, especially those of my family, of forgotten souls, or any other group of souls.*)

On the following 10 beads pray:

By Your Precious Blood, O Jesus, purify and deliver their souls.

Conclude with:

Eternal rest grant unto them, O Lord. And let perpetual light shine upon them. May they rest in peace. Amen.

Chaplet to the Sacred Heart

This chaplet is prayed on an ordinary rosary.

Holding the Crucifix make the **Sign of the Cross**.

On the next five beads pray the **Hail Mary** once, the **Our Father** three times and the **Hail Mary** once more.

On the single beads pray:

O Sacred Heart of Jesus, burning furnace of Divine Love! Within Your Sacred Heart place my soul, in order that, in that school of charity, I may learn to love You Who have given me such wondrous proofs of Your great love.

On the following 10 beads pray:

Sacred Heart of Jesus, I trust in You!

Conclude by praying:

See where Your boundless love has reached, sweet Jesus! In Your Flesh and Precious Blood You have given Yourself to me. What drove You to this excess of love for me? Your Heart, Your loving Sacred Heart!

Chaplet of the Holy Wounds
(Sr. Mary Martha Chambon)

This chaplet is prayed using an ordinary rosary.

On the crucifix make the **Sign of the Cross**.

On the first single bead pray:

O Jesus, Divine Redeemer, be merciful to us and to the whole world.

On the following three beads pray:

First bead - God powerful, God holy, God immortal, have mercy on us and on the whole world.

Second bead - Grace, mercy, my Jesus during the present dangers; cover us with Your Precious Blood.

Third bead - Eternal Father, grant us mercy through the Blood of Jesus Christ, Your only Son; grant us mercy, we beseech You.

On the single beads pray:

Eternal Father, I offer You the Wounds of Our Lord Jesus Christ to heal those of our souls.

On the sets of ten beads pray:

My Jesus, pardon and mercy through the merits of Your Holy Wounds.

Conclude by praying the following three times:

Eternal Father, I offer You the Wounds of Our Lord Jesus Christ to heal those of our souls.   Amen.

Chaplet for Protection
(Ann Fitch)

This chaplet is prayed on an ordinary rosary.

Holding the crucifix make the **Sign of the Cross**.

Next, on the single bead pray the **Our Father**.

On the following three beads pray the **Hail Mary** for protection from temptation, evil spirits, and harm.

On the single beads pray:

All powerful and triune God, protect me/us please.

On the sets of 10 beads pray:

O holy angels, protect me/us and keep me/us safe from harm.

Upon completion of the final decade, pray the **Glory Be** followed by:

O Holy Trinity, thank You for protecting me/us from all evil and keeping me/us safe from all harm. May You be adored, praised, and glorified forever and ever. Amen.

Chaplet of Divine Providence
(Ann Fitch)

This chaplet is prayed using an ordinary rosary.

With the crucifix make the **Sign of the Cross**.

On the following single bead pray an **Our Father**.

On the following three beads pray:

O Divine Providence, bless us.

On the single beads pray:

O holy, omnipotent and merciful God, I know You will provide all that I need. I believe in You. I trust in You. May Your holy will be done.

On the sets of 10 beads pray:

O Divine Providence, bless us.

At the end of each decade pray:

God provides. God always provides. His mercy will not fail.

At the end of the chaplet pray:

O Divine Providence, bless my family with unity and love.
O Divine Providence, bless my home with peace.
O Divine Providence, bless my loved ones and me with loving friends.

O Divine Providence, bless my loved ones and me with health in body, mind, heart and soul.

O Divine Providence, bless my loved ones and me with faithfulness to the Church and her teachings.

O Divine Providence, bless my loved ones and me with deepened faith.

O Divine Providence, bless my loved ones and me with freedom from all evil.

O Divine Providence, bless my loved ones and me with courage, patience, wisdom and compassion.

O Divine Providence, bless my loved ones and me with all that we need in this life.

O Divine Providence, bless my loved ones and me with eternal peace and happiness.

Conclude by saying a **Glory Be**, an **Our Father**, and the **Apostle's Creed**.

Chaplet of the Immaculate Heart of Mary

This chaplet is said using an ordinary Rosary.

Make the **Sign of the Cross** five times in honor of the Jesus' five holy wounds.

On the single beads pray:

Sorrowful and Immaculate Heart of Mary, pray for those who seek refuge in you.

On the sets of 10 beads pray:

Holy Mother, save us through your Immaculate Heart's flame of love.

When finished recite the **Glory Be** three times.

Chaplet of Reparation Through the Immaculate Heart of Mary

This chaplet is prayed using an ordinary Rosary.

Introductory Prayer:

Mary, my Immaculate Mother, I desire to offer you reparation for the offenses which your Immaculate Heart receives from the horrible blasphemies which are uttered against you. I offer you these praises for so many ungrateful children who do not love you and to console the Sacred Heart of your Divine Son Who is so deeply offended by the insults offered to you.

Receive, my purest Mother, this little act of homage and help me love you more each day. Amen.

For each decade pray the following aspiration, followed by the praises, numbered to correspond to each bead of the decade.

Grant that I may honor you, O Holy Virgin!

1. Blessed be the great Mother of God, Mary Most Holy!
2. Blessed be her Holy and Immaculate Conception!
3. Blessed be her Glorious Assumption!
4. Blessed be the Name of Mary, Virgin and Mother!
5. Blessed be her Immaculate Heart!
6. Blessed be her Virginal Purity!
7. Blessed be her Divine Maternity!
8. Blessed be her Universal Mediation!
9. Blessed be her Sorrows and her Tears!
10. Blessed be the graces with which the Lord crowned her Queen of Heaven and Earth!

After each decade say:

Immaculate Heart of Mary, I love you for those who do not love you; I honor you for those who blaspheme you; I give myself to you for those who do recognize you as their Mother.   Amen.

Ann Fitch

ABOUT THE AUTHOR

Ann Fitch is an active Roman Catholic seeking a more intimate relationship with God, growing in her faith, and learning more each day about what it means and takes to be a faithful Catholic Christian in the world today.

For over 25 years, Ann has been involved in the Catholic Church. From serving as a Eucharistic Minister in her local parish, to a prayer ministry that has taken her to dozens of countries leading retreats for lay people and religious, and praying with individuals for their needs.

Ann has been blessed to be able to speak about prayer and God's love to small groups, as well as large audiences at Marian, Charismatic, and other Catholic conferences around the globe.

Ann currently lives in Arizona with her husband and two daughters. She is also the author of the book, *A Healing Rosary*.

For more information, and to purchase Ann's books, please visit:

www.PracticalPrayers.com and www.AnnFitch.com

Follow Ann's daily blog posts at:

www.catholic-christian.tumblr.com

INDEX

A

Abortion

After an Abortion, **113**

for Aborted Babies, **112**

to End Abortion, **111**

Abused

for Someone Who has Been Assaulted, **49**

for Those Who Have Been Abused, **48**

Prayer for Healing After Abuse, **49**

Victims of Abuse

Prayer to St. Germaine Cousins, **215**

Accident

After an Accident, **150**

Act of Contrition, 14

Act of Faith, Hope, and Love, 13

Addiction

Addicts

Prayer to St. Maximillian Kolbe, **222**

Addict's Prayer, **38**

for a Drug Addict, **40**

for a Gambling Addict, **40**

for a Pornography Addict, **41**

for a Shopping Addict, **42**

for an Addict, **38**

for an Alcoholic, **39**

for Someone to Quit Smoking, **43**

for Someone Who Self-Harms, **109**

to Stop Harming Oneself, **109**

Adoption

for Birthmothers, **87**

Once Chosen to Adopt, **88**

Prayer of Thanksgiving for an Adoption

Finalization, **90**

Prayer When an Adoption Attempt Fails, **89**

While Waiting to be Chosen to Adopt, **88**

Adoration

Act of Adoration, **247**

Act of Faith, **242**

Act of Hope, **242**

Act of Love, **242**

Act of Spiritual Communion, **242**

Adoration Prayer, **244**

Aspirations, **252**

Chaplet of the Adorable Sacrament, **257**

Dear Jesus, **256**

Each Time I Look, **253**

Eucharistic Prayer, **244**

Invocations to the Heart of Jesus, **248**

Jesus, Help Me, **254**

Jesus, Our God, **247**

Litany of the Love of God, **258**

Litany of the Most Blessed Sacrament, **260**

Litany of the Precious Blood, **262**

Lord Jesus I Adore You, **245**

O Sacrament I Love, **242**

Opening Prayer to the Blessed Sacrament,
244

Pardon Prayer, **253**

Prayer for 1,000 Souls to be Released from
Purgatory, **257**

Prayer for All, **256**

Prayer for Conversion, **257**

Prayer of Adoration, **243**

Prayer of Thanksgiving, **266**

Prayer to Jesus in the Blessed Sacrament,
243

Prayer to the Heart of Jesus for the Souls in
Purgatory, **257**

Prayer When Burdened, **255**

Thank You Prayer, **175**

The Angel's Prayer, **250**

The Blessing, **254**

Advent

A Christmas Prayer, **45**

Advent Novena, **196**

Blessing of a Crèche, **44**

Blessing of an Advent Wreath, **43**

Christmas Novena, **196**

Christmas Prayer, **45**

G

H

Made in United States
Troutdale, OR
01/29/2024

17258372R10224